PRAISE FOR *LISTEN TO YOUR BREAD*

"In this beautifully written retelling of her own family's journey, Dr. Ann Haut shares the hard-earned wisdom and life lessons of baker Edward 'Icky' Haut. Wisdom does not come from cheap grace but, rather, from a kind of virtuous, but counter-intuitive, obstinacy—a stubbornness anchored in hope and faith in the ultimate goodness of creation and its Creator. It is not a walk of sugar and spice, even when bread and cookies are its manifestations. It's messy, uncomfortable, and hard on loved ones, and fraught with pain and disappointment. It is a test of one's grit, as the author shows, but a test that can be met when we listen to our bread."

—PETER REINHART, AUTHOR OF *THE BREAD BAKERS APPRENTICE* AND EXECUTIVE DIRECTOR OF THE JOHNSON & WALES UNIVERSITY INTERNATIONAL SYMPOSIUM ON BREAD

"Food, culture, and entrepreneurship converge in this chronicle of the European immigrant experience in the US. Yes, it is one family's story in Olean, New York, but it's also a reminder of the struggles during the Great Depression and World War II. Ann Haut's conversational writing style in this novelized family history captures the flavor of time and place. Bread offers more than sustenance here— it represents connections to cultural identity, faith, and family."

—GAIL BELLAMY, RESTAURANT WRITER, FOOD EDITOR, AND AUTHOR OF *CLEVELAND FOOD MEMORIES*

"*Listen to Your Bread* is a story set in the small town of Olean, New York, where a young Icky Haut finds identity and vocation. The story is subtle and empathetic, delving into the community and family ties of love, duty, sympathy, forgiveness, and faith. The grace of plain and ordinary people serves to raise the human spirit for those today who seek to find their center in a more strife-filled and impersonal world."

—MARK R. RAMSETH, PRESIDENT EMERITUS, TRINITY LUTHERAN SEMINARY

Listen to Your Bread

Listen to Your Bread

ANN HAUT

RESOURCE *Publications* · Eugene, Oregon

LISTEN TO YOUR BREAD

New Revised Standard Version Bible, copyright 1989, Division of Christian Education of the National Council of the Churches of Christ in the United States of America. Used by permission. All rights reserved.

Resource Publications
An Imprint of Wipf and Stock Publishers
199 W. 8th Ave., Suite 3
Eugene, OR 97401

www.wipfandstock.com

PAPERBACK ISBN: 978-1-7252-9005-1
HARDCOVER ISBN: 978-1-7252-9004-4
EBOOK ISBN: 978-1-7252-9006-8

02/02/21

For Mark.
Thanks be to God for you.

Contents

Acknowledgments

LISTEN TO YOUR BREAD would not have been written were it not for the help and support of family and friends whose fond and fearless memories initiated this project. I am especially grateful to Mary Lou (Haut) and Bill Bingham, who shared Haut family stories, and then stayed up all night reading the earliest draft. Thanks to both of you, also, for continuing to answer questions so that this book, while fiction, is true to the family's faith story.

Olean friends Paul and Chris Carlson and Mick and Patty Bizzaro remembered Icky and Millie Haut with great affection, and offered insights that shaped the characterization of their personalities in these pages. Thanks for your friendship and support.

The Rev. Dr. Derek Cheek of Immanuel Lutheran Church in Olean, New York, was incredibly generous with historical research, some of which required finding and fitting keys into old file cabinets stored way up near the rafters with the Christmas decorations. Thanks to you and your staff for the gift of your precious time to accomplish what we could not do from our distance ten hours away.

Mike Shane dusted off background details on the founding of the Haut's bakery, and offered suggestions for identifying additional sources. Your role among the community of friends who helped Icky and Millie get their start is never forgotten.

Several people read the manuscript, including Linda Braswell, Gail Bellamy, and Jean Lawrence, each of whom are voracious readers. Linda, thank you for suggestions on deleting sentimentality from the text, and for lifting up your favorite pages. Jean, thank you for your attention to detail; everyone needs a trustworthy friend with the courage to share what no one else catches. And Gail, thank you so much for years of encouragement, for your expertise in the food world, for your guidance with regard to positioning, and for (and everyone should know this) the title of the book.

Chef Angela Webb of Sandhills Community College read selected pages covering commercial bakery operations. Her reflections on food and culture, specifically with regard to religion, also added important content to the book. Thank you so much, dear friend!

The Revs. Phillip and Vicki Garber are constant companions in our Christian journey. Mark and I are always grateful for the many ways your lives reflect God's glory. Who knew that when you two performed our marriage rites on Thanksgiving eve 2015 that it would lead to this. (Indeed: Who.)

This book would not come into being were it not for the offer from Wipf and Stock Publishers. Thanks to all of you for seeing merit in this work, and for your support in bringing it to fruition.

Biblical references are taken from NRSV Bibles, to whom thanks is owed for allowing use of their work. See http://nrsvbibles.org for more information about their contributions to the Christian conversation.

And Mark Haut—grandson of Edward and Mary Huff and Henry and Emma Haut; son of Icky and Millie Haut; brother of Mary Lou; husband, storyteller, reader, editor, dinner maker, caretaker of our cocker spaniel (who likes you better than she likes me now, since you're in charge of treats and I'm stuck with nasty stuff like putting in her eyedrops) when I was too involved with writing and editing, and always thoughtful partner who welcomed me into his family with his help on this book—thanks be to God for you. You are a gentle soul. I pray that this work honors your grandparents and your parents, and that they might have smiled at what we've done.

Prologue

Toast

MACE BOLLES CHARGED FROM his office and thundered down the stairs to the bakery's main floor—again! He'd had enough!

Deep furrows etched his forehead, and his bushy eyebrows arched into a large angry "v" like the horns of a stampeding beast—and aimed at his head baker.

"You stubborn Kraut!" he spat with staccato precision. "I told you it was Bolles Bakery, or else!"

"But . . . this is *good* for the bakery," the baker insisted, holding out a sample for his boss to taste. "It's good for *you*!"

Bolles slammed the tray violently onto the floor.

"*I* know what's good for this bakery, and what's good for *me!*" he poked a stubby finger into the baker's chest. "And if you know what's good for *you*, you'll head out that door before I kick you out myself!

"Now!" he blasted.

His voice was a negative magnetic force repelling any baker within earshot. Immediately, they retreated to work that needed to be done elsewhere.

IT WAS THE STRANGEST feeling: the high-pitched buzzing in his ears, the floor suddenly absent from beneath his feet, the sense that he was moving through a void. He pounded toward the back exit, his fist lifted to punch the heavy metal door all the way open; it banged against the building as he exploded into the outside world. Then, in a single move, he slid into his car, slammed the door, forced the key into the ignition, stomped down on the clutch, jammed on the gas pedal, and spun out. Angry clouds of flourlike dust chased him from the parking lot and onto Route 16.

His jaw was clenched. His neck was stiff. He was speeding . . . and realized he needed to regain control of the road. Cops patrol this stretch, he reminded himself as he eased his foot from the accelerator.

"Okay, okay," the baker said to the windshield. He strained to take a deep breath. His lungs felt like an engine on a cold morning: shallow, hesitating, jagged.

Finally, he released his fists from the steering wheel, and turned the car toward Union Street.

Can't go home, not yet. Got to clear my mind.

He parked down the block from Lincoln Park. He'd walk, let off some steam, straighten his mind.

He grabbed a crumpled pack of Camel cigarettes from the glove box, and lit one as he stepped onto the sidewalk. Inhaling a mouthful of its harsh smoke, he started to pace. Rough fragments of the final few minutes of his employment with Bolles Bakery flickered in his memory like a fluorescent light bulb gone bad. He'd run a batch of a new product through the ovens, offered some to Mr. Bolles, felt him slam the entire tray out of his hands, heard "out!"

The boss didn't say "fired," but he didn't have to. The meaning was clear: you're toast.

He would never have believed that Mr. Bolles would react so aggressively to his idea.

No, it wasn't the idea that was rejected. He rejected *me*. He called me *Kraut*. Spewed the slur from his lips like a foul obscenity. This was personal.

He felt blind-sided: a t-bone termination in the middle of a career intersection. And witnessed by bakers and apprentices he'd worked alongside for years.

He took a long drag from his cigarette.

What else? Back up.

When he left for work at four o'clock that morning, he'd been so enthused over his idea to expand the bakery's product lines that he brought in a bowl of raw dough to bake fresh for the boss to taste. That's all he wanted to do—well, that, and move up in his career at the bakery, of course. He had another mouth at home to feed now.

But, he recalled, the boss wouldn't listen when I offered him a sample from the first batch. He just ordered me to get back to work. One of the other bakers heard him reject the first samples, and said I should back off . . . I almost forgot that.

"You didn't follow that advice, did you?" a small voice in the back of his brain accused. "No, you steamed ahead, so sure you had this great idea."

And it is a great idea, the other side of his brain defended!

He'd spent weeks working out all the details. All Mr. Bolles had to do was taste one and hear me out, so I gave it another try. Slowly, slowly, the aroma from the second tray wafted up to the executive office . . . and that's when all Hell broke loose.

He crushed the fire from his cigarette, and dropped onto a bench, his elbows on his knees as he leaned forward. With his chin on his fists, he forced himself to face the truth that he'd screwed up.

This couldn't come at a worse time: two kids now, ten years apart, and all of us crammed into a second-floor apartment. And a son really complicates life, as boys need a yard, and equipment for sports, and food: lots of food. Maybe college . . .

He jeered himself silently. Forget tomorrow. Without a job, I can't even pay the rent today.

He ran a hand across his scalp. *Stubborn Kraut.*

He'd been sneered at before. He'd allow, though, that sometimes "Kraut" wasn't meant as an insult—like when it was used among friends. But this wasn't that. No, he'd recognized the coarse edges of Mr. Bolles's scorn the moment he heard it.

How am I going to fix this? If I could feel one ounce of shame or remorse for what I did—going against a direct order to desist from running unauthorized product through the ovens—then I might be able to apologize. Maybe I could convince Mr. Bolles that I know how wrong I was.

But I'd be lying. If I'm not always right, I'm never totally wrong either—so, no, I don't regret what I did. My idea had merit, and he should have at least considered it, especially since I've worked for him half my life. Nearly twenty years of dedicated service! That should count for something!

He felt anger rise like the acid bile in his stomach, and stood to walk back to his car. No sense putting off the inevitable: going home and confessing to Millie that I'm no longer the family breadwinner.

Unless . . . unless I humble myself and go see Mr. Bolles first. Of course, that's what he probably expects: public acknowledgment that he's in charge and I'm . . . not.

What am I going to tell Millie?

He scoffed. Roy was right.

1

The Baker's Apprentice

HE-E-EAT!

He yanked the heavy oven door open and immediately stepped back, pausing as its scorching breath panted into the room. It leaned in heavily, threatening to consume anything in its radius.

He refused to rush, even though he had only two minutes to reach into its gaping mouth and switch out the baked loaves with pans of raw dough. He knew well enough: smooth and steady got this job done.

He was an apprentice: a hopeful, wanna-be baker, maybe someday, if he had the right stuff when one of the old timers retired or died so there was an opening—unless one of the other apprentices was promoted instead. For now, he was working his way up, and already assigned to the first shift. That's where a man got noticed.

Replacing baked loaves with the next run was exhausting, especially during the summer, so the men rotated the job. This time it was his turn. He put on thick mitts and reached between the oven's rotating jaws to grab a long metal sheet full of hot bread with his left hand—and immediately, in a long sweeping movement, shoved a tray of raw dough into the empty space with his right. The goal was to empty and refill all twelve racks before the flame burst on again, and the next heat wave whooshed out. He slammed shut the door.

"By the sw-weat of your brow," he said as he stretched out the stickiness of sin, just the way it was preached on Sunday. "The Reverend sure timed that one right."

As he pulled off the mitts, he felt small rivulets of perspiration trickling down his chest beneath his white t-shirt. His face was damp, too, so he skimmed his chin over his shoulder, and then swung his right arm up to swipe his forehead before reaching into his pants pocket for a small towel. He dried his hands as he strode toward the mixer, and, just before lifting a hundred-pound bag of flour over his shoulder, turned to look up at the clock: just two minutes until the end of his shift.

Nine hours of toting and measuring and pouring and mixing and moving dough in and out of the oven took its toll, even on him. All he could think of now was cooling off with a good swim. He'd head to the community pool and do a few laps, and maybe check out the action on the deck.

He dumped in the last bag of flour just as the bell ending his shift clanged. As the last few grains drifted into the bowl, he stepped aside to keep the powder from settling into the hairs on his arms; otherwise, the gummy mess would cake, harden, and crack in the sunlight when he got outdoors. While he punched out his time card, another apprentice, one with less experience, would take over on the second shift. He headed to the parking lot.

"Great looking car!" called out one of the other first-shift apprentices.

"Thanks!" he shouted back.

"Hey, Kraut! You finally got some wheels!" another yelled. They attended the same church, and their families shared similar backgrounds.

"No more cycling home, Fritz," he returned the friendly taunt, his whole face smiling. The distance was only two miles—not too far—but from now on, he'd motor it. And not in some heap, either. No, he was getting behind the wheel of a new two-door Marquette Sport Roadster!

Well, it wasn't exactly new—four years old—but it was new to him, and a real prize. This one had a retractable windshield, herringbone grille, wire wheels, a spare tire behind the rumble seat, running boards: all the extras. The original owner must have paid over a thousand dollars for it. He got it for just over half.

Pa always said a man has to know where he's going. He thought that was probably true, and about time for him to figure out what his destination was supposed to be. He'd been working at Bolles Bakery for eight years: four years after school from age thirteen to sixteen, then two years of half-days while he finished eleventh and twelfth grades. And always on Saturdays.

He'd started as a part-time laborer: a low-level job title designating not particular skills, but rather, the lack of them; a worker whose only value to the bakery was loading and unloading inventory, scrubbing and steaming baking equipment in the sanitary kitchen, sweeping up flour dust, and whatever else needed to be done. Back then, he counted on those tasks to give him the "in" he needed to move up. He'd hoped to be hired on full-time as an apprentice—and he was.

A recommendation from the day-shift foreman had helped that along, as identifying a conscientious employee was a good way to earn points with the owner. Bolles Bakery didn't hire just anybody full-time—not when jobs were so tight. Still, room might be made for a strong, muscular young man who wasn't afraid of hard work. And if he was a genuine churchgoing man of good character, so much the better.

Even if he was of German ancestry.

Squiggly heat waves rose from the pavement in front of the car as he pulled onto Route 16, and he felt the Marquette's engine pulse with power. Fifteen minutes later, he pulled up to his parents' house on Fourteenth Street, and ran upstairs to the small bedroom he shared with his brother. Before anyone could ask him to help with a chore, he tore off his sweaty white baker's pants and t-shirt, and grabbed his dark blue swimming trunks and tank from a hook inside the closet. He pulled them on quickly, and dashed out the back door.

When he arrived at the pool, someone was already doing laps. The guy seemed to be taking his time, one extended, even stroke after the other, barely interrupting the water's glassy surface. The usual throng of girls was congregated on lounge chairs or perched next to one another on the sunning deck. He thought he knew most of them . . . but maybe not the one standing at the end. She had dark, curly hair, and a cute little figure. In case she was a newcomer, he'd join the fellow doing laps, and give her a chance to notice them.

He drew a deep breath and swung both arms low as he bent his knees, and then snapped up and forward, pausing easily in midair to touch his toes in a jackknife dive. When he surfaced, he was only a few strokes behind the other lap swimmer, and after a couple of turns, they ended side-by-side.

"Care to race?" he invited. The fellow seemed to be a similar age, and had the same long arms and broad shoulders: a good match for a contest. Maybe the girls would spot the two of them taking one another on.

"I've been swimming laps twenty minutes already," was the answer; he'd planned to end his workout. "'Twouldn't be fair."

"Oh, yeah? I'd say you're warmed up, and have the advantage!"

They eyed one another speculatively.

"You're on then!" was the acceptance, and with that, the lap-warmed swimmer pushed off, creating a foamy wake for his rival to swallow.

But his contender was unfazed, and they both cut through the water easily. A few seconds later, they arrived shoulder-to-shoulder again at the opposite end of the pool.

"Good one," said the swimmer who'd made the offer. "I'll be more careful the next time I challenge you!"

"I couldn't resist trying to get one over on you," was the retort. "You seemed so abso-damned-lutely sure of yourself."

He cocked an eyebrow in response, and they laughed at one another agreeably.

"Icky Haut," said the baker's apprentice, extending a handshake.

"Gordon Huff," said the fellow who'd been swimming laps. "What kind of name is 'Icky'?"

"Actually, it's 'Idkä', which translates to 'Edward' in English. But no one seemed to pronounce it correctly when I was little, so my Ma said it was 'Icky'—or 'Eddie'," he said. "European origin," he added briefly, and intentionally vague about his family's background. Once the Great War was over, people whose families came from the losing side were slow to share their ancestry, especially since the President at the time had been so vocal in spreading anti-German hysteria. Not that negative attitudes weren't widespread anyway. But Wilson had elevated the disapproving rhetoric, campaigning feverishly for an amorphous, undefined quality he called "One Hundred Percent Americanism," and insisting that the country was "honeycombed with German intrigue, and infested with German spies."

The truth was that the only thing immigrants of any stripe were trying to do was cobble together enough income to support their families, and nobody whom Icky's parents knew, whether German, like themselves, or Swedish or Polish or Hungarian, treated others as if they were second-class. Well, maybe their attitude toward Italians was stand-offish—but that, they argued, was understandable, given Al Capone's connections up the road in Buffalo. Prohibition's underworld opportunities might have dried up with the repeal of the Eighteenth Amendment, but now the guy had his paws in labor unions, and those cash pots could take him anywhere, including their town.

And didn't Capone like to make overnight stopovers when he was on his way to New York City? Olean happened to be halfway between Chicago and the east coast, and served the "best Italian food outside the Windy City": that's what the guy said. He was becoming a regular in a couple of the local hot spots, a circumstance that raised concerns with the town's law enforcement and political bosses, not to mention putting shivers into their wives and mothers!

But other than that, Olean's population was comprised of salt-of-the-earth folks who had come to the United States for factory jobs. The nation was evolving from its timbering, oil, and tannery roots toward an industrial and urban economy, and prosperity was in the air. Anyone with an ounce of ambition and a pound of grit ought to be able to make something of himself: that's what they all believed, and taught it to their children, as well.

"I have a brother called Edward," Gordon chipped in. "But his name comes from English—or maybe Irish—background."

"You're a good swimmer," Icky diverted from the topic of heritage again. "What do you do for a living?"

"Auto mechanic," Gordon answered. "How about you?"

"Baker's apprentice," Icky said.

"Baker?" Gordon said, incredulously. He'd already noticed Icky's fingernails: clean as a whistle instead of lined in black grease, the way his own were. No, he assumed, those were not the hands of a real working man. "You've got some good hams for a guy who spends all day in a kitchen!" He didn't intend to sound insulting. Not really, that is.

"*You* try hauling hundred-pound sacks of flour on your shoulders for nine hours every day," Icky said without rancor. "I'm at Bolles."

Icky thought that said it all. Bolles Bakery turned out the best bread in the county, no doubt about it. The owner grew his business on uncompromising standards, and for that, no apology was offered. In fact, the boss believed that the only way to get the best out of a man was to expect it, which he did, and said so publicly when *The Olean Times Herald* quoted him on how their town was joining a national trend in commercially baked bread.

"Gord, it's time," interrupted the dark-haired girl whom Icky noticed when he arrived. She'd strolled over to the edge of the pool to tell his contender that she was leaving for the day.

"Wait for me a minute. I'll go with you," Gordon answered her.

Rhatz, thought Icky, noticing her shapely legs. She must be dating him.

"Icky," Gordon said, "Meet Millie."

"Oh," she said flatly, feigning surprise as if she hadn't seen Icky in the pool, too. "Hello. Nice to meet you."

"Nice to meet you, too," he said without the exuberance he certainly would have shown if he thought she might be available.

"She's my baby sister," continued Gordon as he easily lifted himself onto the deck, and took the large towel that Millie offered. She wanted to make a face at him for referring to her as the "baby" in the family, but preferring to make a good first impression, wisely restrained herself.

"Oh!" Icky said, recovering his interest. "Ah, *very* nice to meet you then, Millie," he repeated his greeting. She noticed how at ease he seemed to be, his eyes focused on her silhouette against the direct sunlight.

But before Icky could initiate a conversation, Gordon threw his towel around his neck, and said, "You better get in a few more laps. You need practice if you want to keep up next time." Then, as he waved a friendly good-bye, he put a brotherly hand on Millie's shoulder, and guided her out toward the gate.

Icky started to wave goodbye, but too late.

Still, Millie had looked back at him just as she turned.

Hadn't she?

He thought so, even if it was just for an instant.

He continued to watch her walk away, and liked what he saw. He'd do a few more laps. And a few more after that! And he'd be back to the pool, regularly now, until they met up again. He liked this girl.

2

Divine Providence

As GORDON AND MILLIE walked through the parking lot, he paused to admire the Marquette parked a couple of cars up from his old jalopy. "I'd like to afford wheels like this one day," he said.

"Oh?" Millie said, off-handedly.

"Who wouldn't!" he emphasized as he looked it over. "She's a work of art!"

"She? It's a girl?"

"With curves like that?" he noted.

Millie looked at her brother skeptically.

"General Motors stopped pushing the Marquette down the assembly line just one year in," he continued. "Said they were worried that the economy was going haywire. That's another reason this baby is a gem."

"Well, I admit I haven't seen any others like it," Millie acknowledged.

"I think I spotted this one a few times around town, but I thought it belonged to one of the Dusenburys," he said as they moved on. The Dusenburys were "old money," members of the town gentry whose grandparents made their fortunes in oil, timber, and banking. Folks like them wouldn't swim in the community pool, though—not when they could afford private ones in their own back yards.

"Well, that car belongs to the fella who beat you at swimming," Millie said.

Gordon noticed that she gave the better outcome to his opponent, and he instinctively wanted to disagree with her. But her unexpected revelation kept him from saying anything. Sis seems to be giving herself some latitude with regard to fellas, he thought to himself.

And he was right. Millie had noticed the guy who drove the Marquette—even before the race against her brother. In fact, from the moment he stepped out of the car, Icky had captured her gaze and drawn it along wherever he went. She took note of the way he strode confidently across the lot. A couple of minutes later, she saw how he paused at the pool's edge, surveying the place as if he owned it. When he dove in, she saw how he claimed a lane, so she watched him swim: arms circling in great sweeps, slicing into the water. He had an easy manner that she liked.

Then providence intervened. He started swimming with Gordon, so all she needed to do was choose her moment, stroll over, and interrupt their conversation. Nice girls would never make a first move, of course, but she could take advantage of situations that presented themselves.

Thinking that she'd probably look taller standing at poolside, she'd used the ruse of talking to her brother to check the new fella out. If he seemed interesting, she'd give him a few seconds to do the same. After that, . . . well, she hadn't thought beyond that.

Gordon was smart enough not to tell his little sister that in revealing the owner of the Marquette, she'd also disclosed that she'd noticed him.

And this fella—what was his name? Something unusual, Gordon bit his lower lip as he tried to remember: "Icky," that was it—seems nice enough. At least his family is northern European, like we are. Well, that's what they all assumed. Their Ma held to her Irish roots. As for Pa, he only said that his people hailed from Violet, Ontario. Before that, he didn't know, but Canada was good enough for him. "Good fishing up there," was all he'd ever say.

Regardless, Gordon decided, this "Icky" has good taste in cars. Maybe he'll let me check out that Marquette. He'd ask—if the guy dared to show up for another race. He knew he'd won.

"You're back just in time," Gordon and Millie's mother called from her stove as the two of them came up the back porch steps. The screen door's rusty old spring screeched like a blue jay on a bender, an irritating sound if ever there was one. "Hurry yourselves up, you two. Get out of those swim clothes.

"And Girl," she directed her attention to her daughter, "set the table. We're almost ready for dinner."

Gordon vaulted up the stairs. The smell of lovely sizzling sausages whetted his appetite, and nothing got in the way of filling his stomach.

"Where's Pa?" Millie asked as she set out knives, forks, spoons, and bread. Dinner wasn't usually served until her father arrived home from Luther Manufacturing, where he was a machinist foreman. He should have come in a half hour earlier, but his tool box wasn't next to the back door.

"He ate a quick bite, and left again," her mother answered sharply. In truth, she wasn't happy about Pa's willingness to be in cahoots with Jack Hoard. A recollection of their alliance was crossing her mind just that minute, and a sorrowful notion it was to her.

"To where?" Millie persisted.

"Hoard picked 'im up. He needs Pa t' fix somethin'." Hoard ran a speakeasy, and rumor had it that he also operated a still or two up in the mountains.

Well, it wasn't just rumor; Pa told her, so it had to be true. He'd made repairs on the thing a couple of times, and probably was there now.

Millie went into her little bedroom to change out of her swim clothes as Gordon bounded in and heard the end of the conversation. "Wish they'd have waited. I'd have liked t' go along."

Gordon liked anything mechanical, not to mention his curiosity in Hoard's back woods cabin. Even though Prohibition was history, folks continued to sneak out to his place to sip a swig or two in an old familiar spot. Maybe it was the thrill of remembering how they used to do something they weren't supposed to do, and getting away with it—as if going up against the hair of the dog somehow made them as powerful as the rich guys who always seemed to beat the rap for their law-breaking. After all, the area's most prestigious luminaries carved well-worn grooves into the road from Olean to nearby rural Allegany, didn't they? Hoard could count on a parade of them to show up and imbibe his best gin and other under-the-counter eel juices on the weekends. Then, the following Monday, they'd be back at their jobs, arresting, defending, sentencing, and taking confessions from the rest of the folks in town.

"Police officers, lawyers, judges, and priests: they're all hypocrites!" Hoard would snarl behind their backs. "They belly up to my bar and order rounds of Alexanders, Pink Squirrels, or some other pansy cocktail, and before the smell of hooch wears off their own breaths, they turn around and condemn the little guy for doing the same thing!

"Not that there's anything wrong with responsible drinking. That's why they call it 'responsible'!" he'd guffaw.

Hoard thought instituting Prohibition was one of the dumbest things the fools in Congress ever did, never mind the wrong-headed president who signed the legislation. And if that weren't bad enough, they fuddled it up: writing the Eighteenth Amendment so that he could be tossed into prison on a federal rap for selling the stuff, but the folks who bought it and drank it—including the legislators themselves—would be charged with a crime no worse than jaywalking or illegal parking! What a sucker game that law was for honest barkeepers!

So, no, Hoard didn't like the Feds any better than the local officials. Probably liked them less. "They ought to just stay out of our business!" he'd always add, loudly, too, to reinforce the rightness of his opinion.

Pa Huff agreed with him.

"The only reason they passed Prohibition was because some prissy old Mrs. Grundy types—the sort who never let a single drop of hooch pass their own lips—want to control their husbands," Hoard would continue. "And for over ten years they get away with it!

"Then," he'd ratchet his rant to full force, "the Depression hits, and the same disreputable, half-brain, vote-seeking politicians conjure up some new logic to undo it. Suddenly it's okay to sell the drink—except that now, the only way to legally buy booze is through state-run stores, so the government can tax it. It's all just a bunch of malarkey!"

"And they have the guts to call it a sin tax!" Pa Huff would always add.

"Sin? Hah! The miserable way they do their jobs: that's the crime!" Hoard usually ended his harangue with a final condemnation. "The hypocrites think we don't know what they're up to. But we know it. We know it good."

3

The Compromise

PA HUFF SHARED HOARD'S opinions about the government. And he had no problem with applying his mechanical skills to fix Hoard's still, even though he knew that his wife had no use for the whiskey, or any other grain brew that brought the devil out and tempted humankind to raise Cain. But as Hoard always paid Pa with a jug of his best bottled barley, and he took only a nip now and again, she'd say nothing of it.

She still had a voice with regard to her boys, though.

"Don't be botherin' me with foolish ideas," she snapped at Gordon's craving to drive up to Hoard's blind pig, even if it was just to help his father. She shook her head vigorously, three little shakes back and forth, just as she had done when the boys were little, one for each of them. "Ya' can't go up there. I get t' say somethin' about that, even if I can't tell your father what t' do, or how t' get paid!"

He knew she meant it, too, as several years earlier, when he and his brothers were barely teenagers and spiking in height, they spotted Pa's jug hidden in a closet. No one remembered what they were searching for—probably a baseball mitt for a pickup game in the park, or something like that.

"What's this?" Gordon had asked as he stretched an arm up over the top shelf.

"I can't see. You're in the way," his older brother, Edward, answered. "Get it down."

Gordon pulled the jug from the back corner, and set it on the floor. For a moment, they just stared.

"Open it," one of them suggested. "Let's see what it smells like."

Without hesitating, they pulled the cork. Investigating wasn't indulging, after all. What could be wrong in that?

"Whew!" the first one said after a whiff. "You smell it."

"That's strong!" agreed the other.

They looked from the jug to one another.

"What should we do with it?" asked one brother, venturing options, for the forbidden hooch was right in front of them.

Their eyes returned to the jug.

"We better put it back," the other one said. They could pretend like they never knew it was there. That was one option.

"Finding a jug like this could be a once-in-a-lifetime deal, though," the first brother pointed out. If they decided to check it out later, it could be gone when they came back. Then they'd never know what they missed.

Their eyes returned to the jug again. The only question in this verbal shoving match was which one of them was going to make the first move.

"Maybe we could take one little taste *before* we put it back," one of them finally suggested a compromise.

"Just to see what it's like," agreed his brother.

The jug was heavier than they expected, so more than they intended ended up in each glass. But that was no one's fault; it just happened. Anyone could see that.

As they lifted their drinks, they looked one another squarely in the eyes to confirm that they were in this exploit together. One of them gave his portion a single, stiff nod—as it happened, the same nod their mother made when emphasizing what she expected of them. Suddenly, they halted, revealing that in the dark corners of their half-Irish consciences—despite their attempts at ignoring small voices coming from somewhere deep inside, echoing in their very bones—they knew that this taste might have the power to doom them forever.

They'd do it anyway.

Some sort of ceremony was called for in a momentous occasion of sinfulness and law breaking such as this, the first offense because the concoction wasn't theirs, so in fact they were stealing it; the second because for most of their young lives, the Eighteenth Amendment regarding Prohibition had made it against the official Constitution of the United States of America to drink liquor. If they were going to tempt perdition and maybe end up in prison, too, they had to do it right.

Recalling movies showing privileged adults toasting one another or cowboys throwing back their heads to gulp a shot, they clinked their glasses, and said, "Down the hatch!"

Immediately, they tossed swallows to the backs of their throats.

And immediately they choked, roughly.

Not wanting to expose an obvious lack of experience, one brother admitted, "Probably takes some getting used to."

The other agreed without a hint of sophistication, "Like limburger cheese." That was what their father always said about foods they didn't like.

They poured second tastes to practice, and prepared to clink and knock them back, just one more time. After all, they hadn't gotten this right yet, and they weren't quitters.

Again, they felt a burn in the backs of their throats, but this time they suppressed the inclination to cough. One brother had enough swagger to run his shirt sleeve and the back of his hand across his mouth, just like the hombres in the movies.

Recognizing the move, the other did the same, adding a long "ahhhh."

With third shots, and fourth—larger swallows each time—they felt they'd begun to champion the customs associated with imbibing hooch. Instead of stifling their reactions, they started to enjoy the camaraderie of being one with the jug.

But then one belched, loudly and unexpectedly. Long, too. The other one burbled helplessly, and 'though he tried to repress it, he could not, and spewed "Pf-f-f-f" through pursed lips. Almost immediately they echoed one another: "Ha! Ha! Ha! Hee-e-ooh."

They sagged to the floor. One of them finally tilted his head back to look up at the jug at the edge of the table. Before returning it, he thought they'd try one more taste. But as he prepared to right himself, he saw horizontal orange grease pencil stripes on the side of the jug.

"Oh, no!" he said, flinching unexpectedly. "Oh, no! Oh, no! Oh, no-o-o!"

"What?" said the other, cocking his head and feeling the room spin a bit.

"Look!" said the first.

His brother squinted.

Then he saw it, too. Pa had marked the amount left in the jug.

"He'll kill us!" his brother said.

"Crap!" said the other.

"Crap nothing!" argued his partner in crime, adding a blast of cuss words.

Looking at the dregs in his glass, the first one suggested, "Okay, I got it. It almost looks like tea. We'll add some tea to the jug to bring the level back up."

Without hesitating, they struggled up from the floor, heads spinning, and went to the stove. Red embers were breathing in the ashes, so they threw in a small log to start up a fire. While they waited for the water to boil, they placed tea leaves into the little metal ball, preparing to dunk it. Before they could finish their coverup, though, their youngest brother, Richard, came in.

"What's that?" he pointed to the jug.

"None of your beeswax," one answered.

"You're going to get in trouble!" Richard sang, relishing the possibility that the older two might be on the line with their parents for a change.

"Worth it!" the other brother shot back.

Then, realizing the need to co-opt the little snot before he blabbed, he added, "I don't know about you, though." He looked the kid up and down, hesitating, as if to show he was evaluating him.

Richard's face wrinkled.

"Not fair!" he protested.

"Okay," the other brother said after an affected sigh, and poured a small taste for the pintsized tattler. "I guess you can try some."

Delighted to be included, and expecting something wonderful—for who would risk the wrath of their parents without good reason—he tossed his head back (he had been to cowboy movies, too), and downed the golden sin in one swallow. Of course, he choked at the burning sensation in his throat.

"Augh! That's awful!" he croaked.

"You're just too little," they chided, concealing the maneuver of dragging him into their wrongdoing. "But now that you tried it, you can't tell, or you'll be in trouble, too."

"Yeah," said the other brother. "You can't just un-swallow it."

The implicated brat considered the possibility of puking to restore his innocence, just so he could frame his brothers, but he couldn't force himself to endure a second pass of the horrid stuff.

They finished adding tea, and shoved the cork back into the jug before returning it to the closet shelf. Then the three of them grabbed hands, and swore a solemn pact to never, ever, no matter what, or roll over and die a terrible death, never tell what they'd done.

They didn't realize that their telltale liquored breath would give them away, though. Pa noticed it as soon as he came in. Without saying anything, he checked his stash. Looks normal, he thought, and put it back. If not his jug, where did they get it?

"Come here," he called. He was still in the hallway, next to the closet where evidence of their evil-doing was stored. They approached him slowly, and stood together silently, their promise binding them together, lest they die.

"Got anything you want to tell me?"

They looked at one another, lips sealed. Then they automatically looked to the floor, refusing to make any further eye contact.

He paused, waiting, prepared to sniff out the truth, even though they didn't quite appear to be sloshed.

Heads still down, one by one, they glanced up furtively as they heard Pa inhale a deep breath, and within seconds, they felt their very lives being sucked out of them. Their only option in the heavy thickness of his commanding presence was to remain very, very still.

Until Richard squealed.

"It's their fault!" he slobbered. "They made me do it. I didn't even like it!"

So! The brat was going to give them up, was he?

At least he hadn't said exactly what they did.

Pa didn't move. Featherweight claims of being guiltless, even from his youngest son, who no doubt was not a ring leader in this bird-brained caper, would not mollify him.

They felt Pa's piercing glare fixing on them as they tried to steel themselves for the storm that was surely coming—but they were not made of such sturdy mettle, not yet. They prayed that he would remember they were mere aluminum, pliable as impending puberty, and sure to crinkle as his judgment was laid upon them.

For his part, though, Pa wasn't sure what his next move should be. This transgression with hooch could be a first-time offense; otherwise, they would have known to rinse its smell off their breaths. And since they didn't usually get into mischief, he didn't have the experience of a parent who was practiced in exacting punishments. That's what really riled him. Either way, he had to adjust their moral rudders. But how?

"Aaauuugh," Richard wailed louder, probably equating his father's continuing mute reproach with death. On some level, the little snot was right, thought the older two. They were in grave danger of inciting their father's fury.

Their first sin was bad enough; they were guilty of stealing, even if all they did was take some of Pa's hooch. But co-opting their brother probably amplified that transgression.

Their second sin—which they knew they had committed even if Pa didn't (yet)—was that they tried to cover it up. Hiding the truth essentially meant that they had lied, as in "Thou shall not bear false witness." So, they were guilty of not one, but two, of the Big Ten.

Pa opened the closet door, lifted the jug from the top shelf, and took it to the kitchen. From the hallway, they heard three glasses being poured.

"You want more of this?" he bellowed in their direction.

So, he did know what they did, after all. How did he figure it out?

It didn't matter. They were caught. The only remaining question was how bad the consequences were going to be.

"Come and get it!" he shouted. The challenge, Pa had decided, was getting them to refuse to take any more.

But they were frozen in place, locked together, unable to detach even if they wanted to, which they didn't, for he couldn't kill all three of them at once. Probably. Maybe.

"Now!" Pa demanded in his loudest, sharpest voice.

They jolted. And then, quavering together, they slinked down the hall, one tight tangle, filling the kitchen doorway.

"You seem so interested in drinking what's not yours. Let's finish it!"

Their eyes grew large, like blue marbles protruding from sockets in their skulls.

"One for each of you!" he said, holding up the first glass.

"No-o-o," they said in synchronous small voices.

"No?" he challenged, loudly. "You don't want more? Not ready to guzzle big mouthfuls of the stuff?"

Pa extended the drink as if he was going to hand it to one of them. But instead, he put it to his own lips, and took a swallow himself . . . and then quickly and unexpectedly turned around, and spat it into the sink. "What the Hell?" he said in disgust as he stared suspiciously at the glass.

"What the Hell!" he spewed again, angrily this time.

The crime was worse than he thought. Not only had they sneaked his hooch; they'd also tampered with his jug!

He turned on them, grimly then, and, bending down to put his face into theirs, with instinct for their jugulars, said in his lowest voice, "What. Did. You. Do."

Each word was mouthed separately. His lower jaw was jutted out.

Was it a question or a threat? They didn't know. They'd never seen him like this.

"What-did-you-do?" he demanded, wagging a rough finger so close that they all blinked.

They froze into a mass of boy statues, afraid to move.

"What? What? Tell me!" he poked the shoulder of one of them.

Okay, they realized: They should come up with an answer.

"We tried to fix it," Edward offered. He was the eldest, and in terms of sibling pecking order, the other two expected him to devise excuses for any trouble they got themselves into together.

"*Fix* it?" repeated their father, exaggerating the excuse.

He put a big hand on his son's shoulder, and the boy felt condemnation's weight pressing powerfully down on him. "You thought something was *wrong* with it?"

"Um, we, ah, we saw the lines on the side of the jug," Edward picked his way through the nettles of an explanation, inching toward a plausible justification. He wanted to skip past the part about how they'd removed some of the hooch first.

But Pa was tiring of their attempts at thwarting him.

"So, *since* you three drank my hooch, and you didn't want me to know that you'd *s-t-o-l-e-n* it," he dragged out the word pointing to their first sin, "you did what?"

He wanted the whole story, and he wanted it now.

"We, ah, we made some fresh tea," Edward admitted, his voice breaking in pubertal tension as he offered the defense that the tea was not the old bitter stuff that had been sitting in the pot all day.

"Tea?" their father said in exasperated disbelief.

"It's almost the same color, so we poured it into the jug until the level was back up to the line." There! He'd said it, all in one mouthful.

"Tea?" his father repeated, dumbfounded. "You ruined an entire jug of the finest hooch in the county to avoid getting caught taking . . . *some*? How much did you drink?"

Edward looked at Gordon; it was his brother's turn this time. Gordon reached out gingerly, and tapped the side of the jug to suggest almost how much they'd probably taken.

Pa looked at the lower line, relieved that they hadn't drunk more, and made themselves really, really sick. Nonetheless, they had ruined it.

"You added tea," he confirmed, "so you knew you had done wrong. Right?"

They all nodded. Small little nods. Not too many, not too willing to accept too much responsibility for their huge, sinful, godless behavior. Illegal, too: they couldn't forget that, 'though they'd like to. They wouldn't have to go to jail, though. No, according to the law, they were still just kids. And their father wouldn't turn them in.

Would he? He was really, really upset. Angry, even.

"I don't know what is going to happen to you three," he said, his temper rising again. He wouldn't let them think they could steal his hooch. No! "But you can count on one thing: it's going to be horrible! Horrible!

"Get out of here!" he finished his tirade.

"Out?"

They hesitated. Out where?

Everyone knew Pa Huff always meant what he said. Why, they didn't call him the "Bull in the Woods" for nothing! But the boys weren't accustomed to being on the receiving end of his fury—and this time, they definitely were!

"To your room!" he stormed.

They scurried upstairs in unison.

Behind their backs, Pa nodded in satisfaction. They looked like green-to-the-gills minnows, darting their way out of danger.

4

Whoppers

A FEW MINUTES LATER, Ma Huff arrived home with Millie. The boys heard low talking between their parents, and then smelled dinner cooking. Seems normal down there, they thought, imagining the table full of mouthwatering meatloaf, and mashed potatoes under dark gravy, and fresh peas with butter. They were conflicted between the urge to go down to eat and the inevitable consequence of facing their mother. She hadn't had a crack at yelling at them yet.

They'd wait for her to call.

But no one did. After a while, they heard the dishes being washed and put away.

Next, the radio played, and they knew their father was reading the evening newspaper, just as he always did. And then their little sister, Millie, was put to sleep, and their parents also finally went to bed.

When morning came, they awakened to the familiar smell of home-baked rye toast with butter, followed by the scent of freshly brewed coffee wafting up through the floor vents. But again, no one called them. And since they were ignored the night before, they had qualms about bounding down to the breakfast table as if they were welcome. No, they'd better stay upstairs for a little while longer.

Besides, two of them were suffering with unfamiliar hangover headaches. Even the smallest rays of light penetrating their attic bedroom windows were almost too much to bear.

They heard their father leave for work. Then their mother and sister went out. They guessed she probably was going to help with some volunteer project for the women's group associated with the Loyal Order of Moose. Ma was never idle, that was for sure.

Assuming they were in the midst of the peaceful eye of a hurricane that was sure to swirl back around, they dared to take advantage of the empty house to creep down the stairs and use the toilet. One kept watch out the front window as the other two sneaked in and out of the bathroom, and then slithered back up the stairs.

"Put the toilet seat down, or she'll know!" they admonished the last one as he made a mad dash for the staircase. He doubled back, and dropped it. They were still engaged in sinful coverups.

Before too long, they heard their mother return and make lunch for their sister. Then she cleaned the house, washing dishes, sweeping the kitchen floor, and shaking rugs off the back porch.

They looked longingly out the window. The day was getting hot, perfect for playing ball, or swimming, or fishing. Not them, though. They were trapped. Upstairs. Where their father had banished them.

Almost no air moved between the two tiny windows, one on each side of the small attic room. It felt stuffy, stale, and rank from the hooch sweat of three boys confined to a room together. They spent the afternoon hurling insults and whispering nasty arguments about who was more at fault and who deserved the greatest portion of whatever punishment lay ahead. The older two decided that the only reason they got into trouble at all was because the youngest brother fessed up when all he had to do was keep his mouth shut.

"He'll have to go first."

"Right," his brother agreed.

"Why me?" Richard complained. "It's your fault! You two started it!"

"But you swore an oath with us!" his brother accused, "and then broke your word!"

Now they had him. There was no denying his larger crime.

"But . . . ," he wanted to defend himself, but all he could do was open and shut his mouth over and over again, like a gulping fish that can't get enough air.

"It'll come from Ma, too," said one of the older brothers. "And you know what that means."

"Yeah. Like the last time," said the other one.

"What?" Richard got out a one-word challenge.

His brothers shared a private glance meant to show the brat that he was being left out. The question was how to play his ignorance, for payback was due.

"You don't know what you're talking about," Richard finally chose insult as his best weapon.

"Oh, no? Remember how she . . . " one of his brothers began a story.

"No! He *doesn't* remember," interrupted the other one with the precision of a snare drum: ratta-tat. "And you can't tell."

"Oh. . . . Right," the would-be storyteller agreed. He held his fire, letting the little sucker suffer. Finally, he suggested, "But he needs to know."

Making a disgusted face, his collaborator conceded. "But it's on you this time, if he blabs again."

Richard hadn't moved, waiting for them to execute their judgment. Was he going to be let in on the Big Secret about Ma? Or not?

"All right," the storyteller glared at him, "but if you tell again . . . "

"I won't!" Richard promised. "Cross my heart and hope to die," he proved with an "x" on his chest. It was the first rule of boys' code, which, admittedly, he'd already broken, but his brothers would let that slide since they had him where they wanted him.

One of them inhaled a deep, heavy lungful of air intending double effect: to suggest the same sort of danger that Pa threatened, and to give himself time to formulate some sort of grand tale, as they were making this story up on the fly.

"It happened before you could walk," he hesitated to build drama. . . . "No, I don't think I should . . . "

"Now that you started, you gotta' keep going," Richard quickly insisted; it was the second rule of boys' code: Once you're in, you're in, start to finish—no quitters allowed.

His brother inhaled again then, and sucked in his cheeks to suggest the weightiness of the dilemma of whether or not to include him.

"Okay, but I will do you in myself if you tell."

"I won't! I crossed myself, so I'll be dead!"

"All right, then. . . . You're not gonna' believe this, but there used to be four of us brothers," he finally came up with the whopper.

The blathering little monster had to be made to suffer. This would do it.

"A little crier, he was," the second brother endorsed, for didn't babies always cry? They did.

"Cutting a tooth, and wailing, so much he kept Pa up at night."

"So, Pa soothed his gums with drops of whiskey," the second one poisoned the tale. And wasn't a small sip how the three of them got into trouble? Again: believable.

"Ma wouldn't tolerate that, though," said the first. "Not liquor."

"But the whiskey worked like a tonic, and Pa himself had done it."

"So the next night, when Jimmy started up crying again . . . ," said his brother.

"Jimmy?" Richard repeated.

"His name was James," he confirmed.

"But they called him Jimmy," continued the first.

"Or 'Shamus,'" exaggerated the other, looking down, a guilty look added for effect.

"Yes, there is that," agreed his brother.

"'Shamus,'" Richard repeated again. He thought that maybe Ma once mentioned that name. "What was that about again?"

"Irish for 'James,'" his brother reminded him. "Ma said she'd never burden a child with such as that, so he was christened with the English version."

Richard dropped his jaw.

The two older boys held their countenance, then, realizing they'd mined gold.

"So, Jimmy cried a lot," the older brother returned.

"Very willful he was," interrupted his co-conspirator.

" . . . for he was wanting more of the whiskey," the first continued, "and Ma could see that the taste of it was in him, so . . . " He glanced at his brother, just as he had before starting the tale.

The look on Richard's face revealed that they had the traitor where they wanted him: teetering at the precipice. They'd leave him there.

"Where did he go?" Richard asked immediately.

"That's enough," warned the other one. "He might snitch to neighbors."

"He said he wouldn't tell," his brother disagreed.

"He said that before, and look what happened: We're stuck up here."

"You said!" Richard griped.

His brothers looked at one another. Finally, one of them ended the torment—but only for themselves, as they didn't have a believable conclusion for the tale.

"You know how Ma feels about liquor?" he leaned in and asked in a conspiratorial whisper.

Richard nodded.

"She's . . . not . . . Pa," he paced the words slowly as he stared into the brat's eyes.

"So?" Richard asked quietly, mirroring his brother's serious attitude.

"All we can say is . . . he isn't with us anymore," his brother said quietly. Then he settled back against the headboard, crossed his arms, and nodded to signal The End.

Richard blinked, denying the tale of the missing brother. Still, it was plausible. And wasn't there evidence? Some of the hand-me-downs he got were too large; that seemed to suggest another boy. And there was the old baseball mitt that no one wanted, so he got stuck with it. Also, there were eight plates in the cupboard when there were only six in the family. Even if one of the extra plates was for Pa's mother when she joined them, there was still one more.

Maybe his brothers were telling the truth.

Or not.

After all, weren't they the ones who poured him that taste? They could be like Pa, trying to keep him from whining . . . like . . . Jimmy.

Satisfied they'd given the kid enough worries for a nightmare or two, the older brothers relaxed. Maybe they'd add more later, but for now, leveling the score delighted them well enough.

Besides, whether or not Richard fell for the tale, told as it was due, he was stuck in the attic with nothing to distract his suffering imagination.

Their father finally arrived home from work, and he sounded jovial.

The three brothers were suddenly alert! Now what?

They dropped to the floor, each of them as light as falling autumn leaves, and put their ears over the register vent. Was it safe to go downstairs?

They shared looks with one another, and shook their heads: no, not yet.

Next, Pa was washing up. Then, he was telling Ma to hurry up.

A couple of minutes later, the back door was shut, and they heard somebody going down the steps. They collided into one another as they slid to the attic window, and saw their parents and their sister walking down the sidewalk together.

Where were they all going? It didn't matter; they were out of the house.

How long would they be gone? Wasn't it Friday? Everyone was dressed nice, and their mother had marcelled her hair.

Okay, the evidence suggested their parents would be gone long enough for the three of them to skulk down to the kitchen, grab something to eat, go to the bathroom, and dash back to safety.

The boys made peanut butter sandwiches, and downed them with glasses of milk. Food! Belly-filling food!

Then, thinking they ought not leave any trace of their paltry thievery (even more sin piling up against their souls for Saint Peter to use against them on Judgment Day, but they'd argue that if they hadn't made sandwiches that they'd have starved to death, and wasn't it for the love of God that their parents left them alone for a while, so they could fend for themselves?), they rinsed off the glasses and knives, and put away the bread and can of peanut butter. One of them ran an arm across the table to brush the crumbs onto the floor, for they weren't much for housekeeping.

Before slipping back upstairs, though, they realized they might need sustenance for the next morning, so they got out the knife again, and made more sandwiches. They were almost finished when they spotted their parents and sister coming up the street.

They tossed the peanut butter knife under the sink, and scurried to the attic with a dish towel wrapped around the scavenged sandwiches. One of them dropped the towel on the stairs; another one stepped on it, but they kept going without stopping for their contraband. They needed to be lodged in place before the back door opened so their parents wouldn't hear their feet stumbling clumsily up the creaking wooden stairs.

The radio played downstairs for a while, and their parents and Millie seemed to be having such a nice time, while they had only the smell of the tromped-on peanut butter sandwiches tempting them from the steps just a few feet below. They fell for that devil's trick once before when they thought they could get away with exploring the contents of Pa's jug; they wouldn't give in to his wicked ploy again.

Dusk fell. Their bedroom prison got dark, and they heard their sister being put to sleep. Then their parents' bedroom door shut.

They waited for snoring to begin, but they didn't hear anything. They'd drunk a lot of milk during their escape, though. Without saying anything, they got up and tiptoed stealthily down the stairs to the toilet again.

No light shone through the slot beneath the door at the bottom of the steps, so they turned the knob and slipped out.

Their parents were waiting in the living room, the lights off.

"'Bout time you three decided you'd had enough," their father called out from the darkness.

They froze, fear pounding blood into their aching consciences.

"Come here," he commanded.

It was an order, but now the tone of his voice sounded reasonable. They dared to do as they were told, but they stopped in the doorway as if they were stuck between the frame, huddled together.

Their mother turned on the light.

"Do I need to say anything to you three?" their father challenged.

They shook their heads.

"I can't hear you," he said with raised volume.

"No, we're sorry," and "We won't do it again," and "We promise" poured out of them in a chorus.

"Good," he said. "That's what I need to hear."

The relief in the room was palpable. Some of it was theirs. Some of it was their parents'. Some of it was the odor of three pubescent boys who'd sequestered themselves in the Purgatory lock-up of a hot attic bedroom.

"Go get showers," Pa ordered. They reeked even across the room. "You three stink."

The water washing off the hooch sweat felt like a renewal of their baptisms. In no time, they emerged and went into the kitchen, where the most delightful smell of sausages and eggs invited them back into full communion with their parents. They were free to start over, and get it right this time.

That's how Gordon remembered it, and he knew his brothers shared pretty much the same memory, 'though they wouldn't speak of it when their mother was in the room. No, a mere mention of their evil deed would be neither a comfort nor a pleasure to her, gnawing at her heart as it would be.

But as the boys grew, the shenanigans they got into together not only taught them important lessons; they also bound the three of them together. That jug and its tale remained hidden on the closet shelf, and for a long, long time both of their parents regularly checked the grease pencil line on its side; they probably did so even now, despite the boys being grown up enough to be out on their own.

So, when Gordon suggested that he might like to follow Pa up to Hoard's cabin to help fix the still, his mother wasn't likely to acquiesce, not in her lifetime. No, as long as he slept under her roof, he'd have to focus all of his mechanical skills on cars.

5

Doing as You're Told

Icky smiled as the crisp pre-dawn breeze rushed past his face on his drive to work. Four in the morning was an unholy start time, but the cooler temperature made first shift the best time to work next to the blasting heat of the ovens.

Besides, lots of jobs started before sunrise. He and his father left at the same time, 'though Pa still rode his homemade bicycle the two miles to the other side of town.

Pa Haut was a fireman at Socony-Vacuum: a dirty job with long shifts, often up to twelve hours when a blaze got a mind of its own. And around oil, that sort of danger was always lurking. He said that sometimes a fire caught because of a lightning strike; at other times, it could be an equipment failure or a gas leak, either of which also could lead to an explosion.

"And sometimes, it's just plain human error," he admitted. "Men working the oil fields out west say the smoke runs like water; they call it 'Hell fighting.'"

"Because it's hot as Hell?" Icky discerned.

"Smells like it, too," Pa added. "Oil just stinks."

"Why do you like it then?" asked Henry; he was Icky's brother, and the youngest of the five children.

"Who said I like it?" Pa corrected. "Got to pay the bills."

"Couldn't you do something else?" he persisted.

"Fireman was the only job available when we got here," Pa told them, "and we were grateful for it."

"Got here from where?"

And there it was: the question Pa always ignored. Both he and Ma had avoided answering it, as they kept most things close to themselves. It was their way. And also, in this country, it was no longer wise for a person to admit their German heritage.

"We came here to change our circumstances," he admitted to Ma. "But not to turn our backs on our families; those bonds are not broken. Neither do we abandon who we are."

"But that is not what they know, and you got to tell them something," Ma finally realized. Their children ached to know some connection to their family's story, and if their parents didn't provide it, racist rhetoric about people like them would be all they'd ever have. The question was how to link to their roots without treading into the hard realities of unchosen history.

"See that they honor their birthplace here in the U.S.," she insisted. "Say what is important about Olean first. Then say they are descended from good people, and that the kind of American they are meant to be is German-American. That's how to tell it."

Pa agreed. He could offer a wider history that respected both the country of their birth, and the one of their forebears.

"So, you want to know how we got here?" he started the next time one of them asked. "First, you got to know something about this place, and that means you got to know what was happening when it was settled.

"Years ago, most of the oil used in the U.S. came through Olean," he began. "Owners of the wells needed muscle to do heavy labor, so they ran advertisements in east coast newspapers to lure young men out here—because back then, this was the edge of the mapped country.

"Instead of good jobs, the men found themselves stranded far from civilization as they knew it, with the cost of a return railroad ticket beyond their means. And as many came from Europe—as Ma and I did in later years—they had no relatives to bail them out.

"The refinery had them then," Pa continued, "The mercy of the employer: that was their only hope of survival."

Icky remembered Pa pausing then to let them absorb how those circumstances must have felt: to be forsaken in a wilderness town with no one they could turn to.

"The oil men who owned the wells and the refineries of those early days cared about only one thing: manipulating the market so they could fill their pockets. Striving for quality they did not need to do if they could form trusts and destroy competition."

He paused again, this time to prepare them for a condemnation.

"The German way it is not," Pa asserted, looking straight into their eyes, penetrating their souls. "Where we come from, what is good for the community: that is what you do."

He was defining them now, telling them the kind of people he expected them to be. He would continue if he saw acceptance on their young faces.

He did.

"By the time Ma and I arrived here, Olean was a small town with tanneries, shops, and banks," Pa continued as he shifted to their family's story. "But jobs for foreign-born men—especially those of us hailing from Germany—were still hard to come by."

Their native homeland had been at the losing end of the Great War—and a dirty war it was, too, fought with mustard gas that destroyed American soldiers' bodies. German immigrants weren't simply looked down on; they were reviled.

Pa made a point to say that he had no part in fighting against the U.S. Ma and he arrived many years before that war, but they brought with them their German accents, and a contingent of the American populace felt their kind should be made to pay somehow for coming from the wrong place. Unscrupulous employers who spotted an advantage in enforcing that sort of discrimination gave *der Deutchmen* the worst jobs and most despicable hours. "But we would persevere," Pa pointed out, "because at that time, with two of you children—Herta, and you, Icky—it was all we could do.

"We came to Olean because we were escaping a flood in Austin, Pennsylvania, where we first settled. That storm destroyed our home," Pa continued. "The rains were heavy through the mountains, and our savings were modest, so we stayed overnight in barns where the horses could rest. I remember how Ma always noticed the morning steam rising off their backs as we continued on our way, and we prayed for any help the Lord might send.

"We finally arrived in Olean, and relieved we were to find work here," Pa continued, "no matter how meager or how difficult."

"Or stinky," Henry finally understood.

Pa said he wouldn't complain about it; he didn't dare if he wanted to keep his job.

"But this limitation is not true for you," he asserted. "You were born in the United States. Do something with your American citizenship, but know that you're German, too, so whatever the Lord calls you to do, do it better."

And with that directive, Pa demanded that Icky finish public high school—all twelve grades, not just eight like lots of other boys. Henry would finish one day, too.

Pa also expected them to find work as soon as they were able: beginning at age thirteen, just like in the Old Country. "You're old enough to help with expenses," he told each of them when the time came, and with five children, the family needed the extra money. After the boys made their weekly payments to the budget, they should save whatever remained. Their father had his rules, and they followed them.

After growing up under Pa's tutelage, a job with Socony—which was Rockefeller's acronym for Standard Oil Company of New York—wasn't the life Icky had in mind for himself. The problem wasn't that he was afraid of hard work—or heat. Commercial ovens were just as hot as refinery boilers. But if he could avoid toiling in the filth and stench of that inferno-burning crude, the way his father labored, so much the better.

Bread smells good, too, Icky noted as he pulled into the Bolles Bakery parking lot. He sniffed the ovens' breath hiccupping out of the stack on the roof, and anticipated working in the dough in the same way that he hungered to know his future. He ought to have one, that much he knew. What he didn't know was the direction his life would take. Still, he could almost taste it.

He set the Marquette's hand brake, and removed his key from the ignition. Would he leave the top down? He would. As he turned to sprint across the gravel lot toward the employee entrance, he noticed how the eastern sky was salted with starlight above the silhouette of mountains. The honest cold of the Alleghenies put an extra spring into his step.

Or maybe the reason was that girl: the one he met all too briefly at the pool on Friday. He smiled, and let wonderings about her float around in his head, just as they had taken his attention all weekend. He was distracted even now, so much that he didn't notice the bakery's guard dog approaching from pre-dawn's hazy shadows. The beast didn't deserve even stale bread for its lack of effort in protecting the place. It pounced at Icky's hip.

"Hey!" he shouted in annoyance at the large paw prints on his white baker's pants.

Not to be deterred, the dog jumped at him again, playfully it seemed, and slurped Icky's hand the second time.

"Down! Stay down!" Icky ordered as he took refuge inside the building, and closed the door. He scrutinized the paw marks on his pants under the bright lights in the bakery, and decided to change into a spare. Sanitary conditions were required in food handling facilities, so Mr. Bolles always kept extra uniforms in the locker room.

He'd better hurry, though. The boss was particular about men arriving on time and doing as they were told.

"We can't afford to pay men who come in late or don't keep the pace!" Mr. Bolles told Icky when he promoted him. A new apprentice was wet behind the ears, and hardly worth noticing, but it had to be done. Setting the tone for the level of performance he expected as soon as a man came on full-time was part of what it meant to be in charge. And he was.

Mace Bolles thought of himself as a member of the community's upper crust. But as his wealth was new, he would allow that he didn't possess the power of a Rockefeller or the influence of a Dusenbury. Nonetheless, he shared their business sense. That fact alone, he posited, put him in the same league. Each week, he set aside time to listen to interviews on NBC's *America's Town Meeting of the Air*. Leaning back with his second Highball and a pack of Parliament cigarettes, he imagined himself in a smoke-filled room with the nation's thought leaders. The conversations kept him in touch with important issues, and provided insight into how top minds saw the role of business in society. What was their influence in the 20th century? If problems affecting the nation were to occur, what would businessmen be expected to do? Should they step in? How? Radio told him.

Of course, he didn't buy into all the notions promulgated by self-identified high-minded intellectuals. Even Woodrow Wilson, whom he thought made a lot of sense by backing the open-shop movement and giving voice to union busting when he was president of Princeton University, tripped up when Samuel Gompers yanked on the rug he was standing on when he moved into the White House.

But Mace Bolles would have none of that nonsense! No, he was far more pragmatic, focused marrow-deep on number one, and to that end, on the bottom line. For wasn't the doctrine of profitability the sole purpose, goal, and justification of American business? Of course, it was, and that he would defend! He'd have none of that crooked labor union nonsense in his bakery. Why, the next thing that sort of employee would politic for would be controls on minimum wages and maximum hours! Ha!

"Anyone with half a mind can see wrong-headed thinking in letting interlopers meddle with the way upright businessmen run their own companies!" he'd shout at the radio. "I'd shut down before I let union outsiders infiltrate!"

And the next day, he'd be sure that everyone at the bakery knew it, too. Either the men in his employ would meet the demands of the job, or there would be no jobs at all!

The boss's warnings about lackadaisical employees echoed in Icky's ears as he changed his work pants, and dashed to his post on the bakery floor. The clock overhead ticked to twelve at the top of the dial just as he picked up his first bag of flour.

Whew, he lightly whistled through his teeth, just made it!

Good thing, too, he thought, as Roy was approaching. His supervisor had been on the job for a half hour already, inspecting equipment, and turning on the commercial ovens to give them time to heat up. Hot ovens and steam were essential to achieving the right golden-brown crust and chewy center that Bolles rustic breads were known for. A lower temperature was needed for sandwich bread, though, so he'd start the morning shift on filling those orders.

"How's it going?" Icky greeted him. He liked reporting to his older sister's beau.

"You're on soft-and-white today," Roy nodded as he gave Icky his assignment. White bread was fast becoming the bakery's most popular product. Its refined flour suggested purity, and well-to-do folks who could afford to shop in self-serve grocery stores liked its sweeter, softer texture.

Roy continued to review the production sheet for the day's orders, and divided duties among the crew as he moved around from one station to another. His stride was brisk, setting the pace for the first shift.

"Drop in four sacks, and then mix in the salt," he ordered Icky.

Icky climbed the three steps that brought him alongside the top of the huge mixer, and dumped them in, slowly, slowly, very slowly so that clouds of flour dust didn't blow into the air, and coat the machinery. Controlling the weight of each bag of flour as it lightened took considerable strength, and over the preceding two years, the work had helped him build huge muscles in his arms and shoulders. He wondered if Millie had noticed, and he let his mind wander for a few moments while the flour drifted silently into the bowl.

Roy noticed smiles emerging on Icky's face, and decided that he needed to refocus the apprentice's attention, especially since Mr. Bolles made a habit of inspecting the work flow when least expected.

"Check the instructions before you weigh the salt," he interrupted Icky's thoughts.

Icky snapped back to attention, and studied the card on the board next to the mixer. After the correct amount was mixed in, Roy handed over a large pitcher of bubbling brew: water sweetened with sugar and cream yeast.

"You got the salt in already?"

"Just like the card says," Icky confirmed.

"Good," Roy said. "Salt controls the pace of the rise."

"Didn't know that," Icky responded. He was, after all, only an apprentice.

"Yep, yep, yep," Roy confirmed. "Soft-and-white gets only one rise. Too little salt, and the yeast doesn't do what it's supposed to do. But too much retards fermentation. Then we're off schedule."

"And time is money," Icky repeated Mr. Bolles's mantra. "I got it."

"Next thing you got to start paying attention to is how the formula is scaled. We bake as many loaves as Bolles can sell, and the orders change every day with sales."

"So, every day you compute it," Icky nodded.

"Right. And we do that the Old World way—by weight—so no matter how many loaves we're baking, we pour in the right amount of each ingredient," Roy continued.

"Does Bolles have its own formula?" Icky asked.

"Yep, yep, yep, we do," Roy said. "The relative weight of the water is measured against the weight of the flour, okay?"

"Okay," Icky said cautiously. He was adept at math in school, so this concept was familiar.

"It's like this: if flour is one hundred percent, water is sixty percent," Roy continued. "Then you adjust the salt and the yeast, and in this soft-and-white formula, the yeast is four percent."

"I get it," Icky said, "but I'm going to need some practice to work the numbers in my head so it becomes automatic—like you're doing."

"Yep, yep, yep," Roy allowed. "If you want to move up, though, you got to know how to scale these recipes."

Most of the other apprentices didn't seem as curious about managing the production process. They were happy to merely follow the cards posted next to the mixers, haul and measure ingredients, and at the end of the week, collect their pay.

But Roy saw potential in Icky, and suspected he had bigger plans.

"Okay, now pour it all in," he said, nodding at the pitcher, "slow and even."

Icky climbed the steps to the rim of the mixer again, lifted the heavy pitcher, and slowly poured in the sweet liquid. Then he stepped to the controls, and adjusted the speed to the knead setting.

Roy was right. Icky did hope to advance his career past apprentice to baker. In fact, he'd like to move up as far as his hard work and brains would take him. He wasn't sure what that meant yet, but with the onset of commercial food production, the bakery business seemed to be expanding, and he wanted to be part of wherever it could take him.

6

Distinctions

Over lunch Icky asked Roy to differentiate the various flours Bolles used.

"Some are softer than the others," he said. "When you rub them between your fingers, you can feel how different the textures are."

"That's protein. Some wheat has more than others," Roy told him. "And more protein means more binding."

He held up his sandwich, and said, "This is made from unbleached whole wheat flour: full of protein, full of flavor.

"But the soft-and-white sandwich bread you made this morning?" he continued. "That pulls apart with no effort at all; lower protein flour goes into that one. It's processed all to Hell, too. Folks who can afford it are willing to pay more for soft, white and sweet, though."

Icky nodded.

"You didn't ask about this yet, but I may as well tell you. You gotta' know a flour's gluten strength to adjust your yeast," he added. "When you add water to unbleached whole wheat, which is a high gluten flour, the starch granules are going to swell. That's one thing."

"Okay," Icky acknowledged.

"Now, yeast is alive, remember? And you got sugar in the brew, too."

"Right," Icky acknowledged.

"Well, that yeast is gonna' get punch drunk on the sugar water, and burp out carbon dioxide gas bubbles. Now, when you mix it into the unbleached whole wheat flour that we use in rustic breads, all that fermentation stretches the swollen, starchy, gluten-rich wheat, and makes the dough rise.

"But the soft-and-white dough you were on today isn't like that. It's made with processed—or bleached—flour, which has less gluten than whole wheat. How much swelling and rise do you think you're gonna' get out of that stuff?"

Roy looked at the clock to see how much time was left before they had to get back to work, and decided to save his lesson on the controversy regarding flour bleaching for another time, maybe Sunday. Icky's sister, Herta, had invited him to dinner after church again. He'd see Icky there.

"Let's just say the density of the two kinds of bread we bake here—the rustic whole wheat and the refined soft-and-white—comes from gluten formation.

"But that's enough for now," Roy finished, standing to end the conversation. "Lunch break is over. Back to work."

Icky was beginning to realize that baking bread could be more complicated than just dumping ingredients into a mixer. He'd been building muscles in his arms and shoulders ever since he was hired as a laborer in the shipping and inventory departments. Now he was working on the ones between his ears.

As the men returned to their stations, Roy called the apprentices aside. "Each of you is going to work with a line baker today, learning to form raised dough into loaves.

"Icky, you go first and work with Shots, over there. Spend up to an hour, get the hang of it, and then trade off.

"The rest of you," he said to the remaining three senior apprentices, "take turns. And while one guy is out, fill in on the line so we don't miss a rotation. The ovens don't slow down, so neither can you. Got it?"

They all nodded, and Icky moved over to Shots's station.

John Shotinski was a man of few words. In fact, he rarely said anything, believing that a man ought to watch what was going on, and then just do it. Roy got the two of them started.

"If you want to leap to the position of line baker one day," Roy instructed Icky, "you got to be able to form raw dough into uniform loaves—each one weighing one-and-a-half pounds—without using the scale.

"Mr. Bolles is putting pressure on us to get this precise," he continued, "because our new labels say we're selling twenty-four ounce loaves. That's what they got to weigh."

Shots grabbed four multi-loaf pans, and set them up at the front of his station. Then, with the side of one hand he easily scooped a hunk of the risen dough, and cut it with a dough knife. He dropped the knife, dipped the side of that hand into the flour, and curled it under the hunk to form a loaf. Again and again, Icky watched him size up a handful of dough. Finally, when he thought he might have a sense of how to perform the task, he dug into the bowl with the side of his hand. Before he cut off a hunk with the dough knife, Shots stopped him.

"Too much," he said.

Icky moved the knife closer, and cut his hunk. After he folded the dough into a loaf, he compared it to the ones Shots made, and kept going.

"Why lift the dough with the side of your hand?" Icky asked.

"Even pressure," Shots said. "Clawing into it with your fingers rips into the gluten, and makes it lose some of its elasticity."

After a few minutes, he added, "You don't want to lift the dough too high over the side of the bowl either. You'll overstretch it: same thing—lost elasticity."

Icky was glad he hadn't made that mistake. But eventually, he might have if Shots hadn't told him. By the end of the hour, he felt he'd begun to get into the flow of it.

"Okay, you're done," Shots said. "Next guy."

Icky stepped back. He was invigorated by the opportunity to get his hands into the dough instead of just hauling and pouring ingredients.

As he returned to the mixing line, thoughts of making a career in the bakery business percolated in his mind like the fermenting yeast. He tapped one of the other apprentices on the shoulder to signal his turn with Shots.

"How'd it go?" he asked Icky.

Icky gave him a thumbs up. "You know Shots. Just watch him, and do what he does. It's all about consistency."

Icky already knew about the boss's obsession with accuracy. Roy mentioned it the last time he joined the Haut family's Sunday dinner. Mr. Bolles had just returned from Missouri, where he toured the Chillicothe Baking Company, and got a good look at their new bread-slicing machine. He thought he might want to buy one, too.

"It's one of those Otto Rohwedder models," Roy reported.

Rohwedder was a good German-sounding name, so Pa Haut immediately jumped into the conversation.

"Germans make the best machinery!" he said. "Your boss must like quality!"

"Yep, yep, yep. He showed us a magazine ad that says sliced loaves are 'the greatest forward step in the baking industry since bread was wrapped.'"

Wrapped bread was store-bought: special, and saved in the cupboard, where it was out of sight, out of mind until the housewife decided to offer it. Home baked bread, by contrast, was for everyday use, and stored in a bread box on the kitchen counter, next to canisters for flour, sugar, coffee, and tea.

"Mr. Bolles says we need to produce identical bread loaves that can be run through a slicer. That'll be more efficient, and 'efficiency is the name of the game!'" Roy repeated the boss's directive.

"Because 'if it saves time, it saves money,'" Icky added another one of Mr. Bolles's mantras.

"Again," said Pa Haut, "good ideas."

Icky always appreciated Roy's insider dope, as unfiltered insight into the boss's priorities helped him fit in as a "Bolles Bakery man."

"You did good at forming loaves this week," Roy complimented Icky. Since Herta and he seemed to be getting serious, Roy wanted to continue building a good impression with her family. Giving Icky an occasional boost helped with that.

"There's another thing I meant to tell you when you asked about flour this week," he continued. "The soft-and-white bread we bake uses bleached flour."

"Which you said is processed, and has less gluten than whole wheat," Icky repeated.

"Right," Roy confirmed. "But back twenty years ago or so, some sort of dispute was going on in the government over the safety of bleached flour."

"*Ja*," Ma stepped in. "This I remember from the newspaper. Chemicals they used to whiten the grain, right?" She always looked for confirmation, not because she was unsure of herself, but because she sought respect for the accuracy of what she read. She would allow, of course, that she read slowly, but that was because the newspapers were not in her native language; perhaps that also contributed to the strength of her recollection, however.

"Yep, yep, yep," Roy answered, happy to acknowledge her point. "The larger millers in the Midwest use nitrogen peroxide, and at the time, chemical processing was becoming standard practice. Smaller millers, most of them out in the Dakotas, couldn't afford it, though, so they stayed with the old way of bleaching: out in the sunlight, or in ventilated rooms for several days.

"Both of those older methods took extra time and space, which was expensive, so the smaller millers had to charge more for naturally bleached flour."

"So, how did the government get in the middle?" Pa asked.

The question alerted Roy that he might have unintentionally initiated a controversial topic at the Sunday dinner table. Just to be safe, he would keep his answers above the frack and fray of politics.

"Yep, well, the smaller millers supported their higher prices by saying they offered a superior flour. And they got their state food labs to test the bleached product coming out of the big millers in the Midwest. They asked whether or not the chemicals were causing any problems."

"So, is the Midwest flour poisoned with chemicals?" Ma asked, always watchful.

Poisoned was a strong word, Roy realized, and he didn't want appear disagreeable.

"At first, they said so," he ventured, allowing that she asked a good question. "The chemically oxidized flours were tainted with nitrates."

"Tainted!" Ma repeated with alarm. Tainted was just another word for poisonous: that's how she saw it.

Roy winced at his own word choice. He'd intended to say that a small amount of nitrates remained after processing.

"The bleached flour at Bolles: this is 'tainted'?" she pressed.

"Nope, nope, nope," Roy said. "That wasn't what I meant." He'd really gotten himself into trouble now, and it was with his future mother-in-law. He glanced at Herta for help.

"Is the bleached flour that Bolles Bakery uses safe?" Herta asked, moving the question to friendly ground.

"It is," Roy confirmed. Then, turning to Icky, he said, "And that's what I was getting at when I began this . . . this subject. As you move up, you're going to get questions about bleached flour, and you need to know how to explain what Bolles is doing."

"So, what are we doing?" Icky asked. Like Ma, he wanted to get his answer right.

"When we report the ingredients on our soft-and-white bread labels, we show bleached flour so buyers know what they're paying for," Roy answered.

"But a housewife would not want bread made with poisoned flour," Ma started to protest.

"It's . . . it's not poisoned," Roy gently asserted.

"Tainted, then!" Ma insisted on her point. But then, catching Herta's eye, she decided to step back. "Just tell me: How would a housewife know if she wants bread made with this flour with the chemicals?"

The challenge was rhetorical, of course; Ma baked rye bread. But, she justified, if only to herself, not all housewives still baked on Saturdays. And she wanted an answer!

"As I said when I brought this topic up, which I wish I hadn't done," Roy admitted then, "this question goes back twenty years or so, to the time when Wilson was president."

"Wilson," Pa grunted with disgust.

Oh, no, I stepped in it again, Roy stiffened.

"Let's just say," he paused, "that the Administration ruled that the issue was one of mislabeling. The small amount of nitrate that large millers use was deemed unlikely to warrant a restriction against chemical bleaching. But to reach a compromise that showed support for both the large millers in the Midwest and the small ones in the Dakotas, our bread labels must disclose when we use bleached flour."

Roy looked around the table, hoping his answer would be enough. Before anyone added anything, he said carefully, "So, that is what we do. And that's all I can say about it."

Icky felt that he was in the middle then. Roy had been trying to help him advance in his career, Ma was concerned for other housewives, and Herta wanted both Ma and Pa to like Roy. Pa was against Wilson, but Roy brought up his name, so . . . Icky wanted to build a bridge over the troubled waters.

"So, Roy, how serious do you think Mr. Bolles is about buying one of those Rohwedder slicers you mentioned last week?" he shifted the topic.

Roy looked relieved.

"I think he's working on it already," he answered. "You know how he is when it comes to increasing efficiencies."

"I sure do!" Icky responded immediately. The Depression hit hard, and even in a solid town like Olean, a man was grateful to have a job. If the boss could consider mechanizing the bakery with a new piece of equipment, well, that was good news.

Besides, wasn't *The Olean Times Herald* running National Cash Register advertisements that said "a man should not do work a machine can do"? They couldn't put that in writing unless it was true. Slicing bread by machine was no different!

"The more we produce, the more we can sell, and the more we sell, the longer all of us will be employed," Icky repeated Mr. Bolles's daily message.

Of course, sometimes "longer employment" also meant longer days, which Icky was starting to think could be a good thing. The more hours a man could add to his paycheck, the better—even though employees could forget any silly notion of overtime rates; that wasn't going to happen at Bolles Bakery unless Congress made it the law of the land.

Now that Icky had a car, though, he needed extra pay even at his regular rate to put gas into it. And who knows what else might be down the pike.

Maybe I'd want to go out once in a while and have some fun, he allowed himself to consider.

With some special girl.

7

A Special Girl

"WHAT'S GOTTEN INTO YOU, Girl?" Millie's mother gently admonished her. "You're makin' an awful mess out here!"

Millie was leaning against the wringer washer and gazing out into the back yard from the screened porch while she helped with the laundry. Four men in the house, each of them laboring in the summer heat, made a lot of dirty clothes. Even her oldest brother, Edward, who clerked and did sums all day for REI Freight, changed his sweaty shirt into a fresh one when he arrived home from his job. The laundry chore would be reduced in a few weeks when Edward and Edith were wed, and moved into their own place. Then, his new bride could take care of his shirts, and thank goodness for that small decrease in the load, Millie thought to herself. And Gordon was dating Marg, 'though that relationship was too new to predict yet.

"Sorry," she said, wiping up the wood-planked porch floor. She'd been lost in daydreams, and hadn't noticed that she was standing in a puddle of gray water from the shirts she'd been running through the wringer.

"Not to worry," her mother said.

But Millie's mother always worried. It was her way.

"I'll put 'em out on the line," she added, lifting the hefty basket. "You go gather in some vegetables from the garden for dinner: whatever is ripest, that's what we'll have."

Millie tucked her curls under a straw hat, and took a small garden hod from a nail on the porch wall. As she walked lazily to the vegetable patch, she let her mind go wandering and wondering, winding in and out of the details of her chance encounter with that fella at the pool. Gordon had provided just the right situation to surreptitiously check him out. He seemed to be a good swimmer, powerful enough to keep up with her brother, anyway. Yes, she recalled, strong, muscular shoulders. . . .

And sandy hair . . . or maybe a bit darker; she couldn't tell the color since it was wet from the pool. . . .

And an angular jawline; she saw that, too.

And he smiled, at least she thought so.

"Very nice to meet you," he said. "*Very* nice . . . " He emphasized it. She lingered on that memory, letting the words echo in her thoughts.

And . . . was that it? He'd been waist high in water, so she could only guess, but he must be about as tall as Gordon.

Then too quickly, Gordon lifted himself out of the pool, grabbed the towel she brought over, spun her around, and scooted her away. Her brothers were always herding and corralling her. When she was younger, and the boys could get away with it, they'd huddle around her, and shove her back and forth among them as if she were a football, just for the fun of irritating her.

"The FA-vorite," one would emphasize as he pushed her to his brother.

"Finally! A girl! So special!" another would say. They must have heard it plenty of times when she was born.

"Watch out for the little one. Keep an eye out for her," they'd continue.

And then, all together, they'd say the word she hated the most: "Baby!"

Oh! How she detested that! She despised the notion that just because she was petite that she was some insignificant twig, too little to be taken seriously. She clenched her teeth to bear their childish intimidations when what she really wanted to do was to give them a taste of their nastiness. She swore that if she ever had a daughter, she'd make sure the little girl knew how to defend herself from that sort of so-called affection.

But that was only the negative side of having older brothers. In recent months, she'd learned to appreciate a few advantages, too. Like how they could be useful when she wanted to go to the community pool.

Of course, no self-respecting girl could stroll the deck in her swimming suit without a group of girlfriends or a family member nearby to protect her reputation. But this time, Gordon's unexpected, probably unintended, introduction to an attractive fella—and he was attractive, she'd admit that— also meant she needed to hold herself in reserve, or suffer the consequences of a brother snooping into the musings of her heart. She would not invite that sort of intrusion, not at all!

Now that she was in the garden by herself, though, she could return her thoughts to the preceding Friday. Would she see the fella again? She would, somehow. She'd find a way.

She brought the little hod filled with cucumbers and tomatoes into the kitchen, set it on the table, and looked at it dumbly. Her vacant eyes exposed the truth that her heart was beating in another world, daydreaming as she was.

"You keep up that heavy sighin' over nothin', and folks 'll be thinkin' you're daft," her mother pointed out.

I wish she'd quit correcting me, Millie defended silently as she snapped back to her work. And while it wasn't polite to speak of a person's intelligence, or lack of it, she understood what her mother meant; she hadn't been paying attention.

She took up a knife to begin slicing the vegetables.

"Watch your hand with that sharp blade," her mother warned.

Ma knew what the blank look on her daughter's face meant: the girl was thinking about some fella. Up to this point, she'd been grateful that Millie had never been one of those giddy girls with too many schoolhouse crushes or silly puppy-dog eyes begging the boys to notice. Neither had her daughter been daring or bold, trying to see what she could get away with. No, her girl had been more sensible. In fact, it wasn't until her late teens that Millie had been smitten at all, 'though now it seemed that her dates with that Milano boy were more about learning to stretch her wings than any deep feelings.

This time, the girl's longing gazes and heavy exhaling in the middle of the afternoon were laying bare a new story, even if Millie didn't say a word. Ma would keep an eye on her.

"I'm being careful," Millie insisted as she drew the knife through the crunchy skin of the cucumber. "Why don't we put garlic in the salad?"

Garlic was added to cucumbers and tomatoes served at St. Ann's Lodge, where Franco took her one Friday, and she liked how it made everything taste richer, as if she were able to breathe in the flavors more deeply.

"Garlic!" her mother repeated, disapprovingly. "Augh, no! That's for Italians."

"Ma, . . ."

"Aye, ya' can smell it comin' down the street—and better that ya' do, too, with all their gamblin' and drinkin' ways," she started up her rant. Ma would rather be struck by white lightning than let it pass her lips. She had no patience for liquor. Keep your distance from their odd food choices, too, she'd say. Why, one might lead to the other! "No, no, we'll not be puttin' garlic in our salad!"

Millie sighed again, this time out of exasperation—as if an ingredient bubbled up and led to a person's "ways," she thought. Too many rules, too many constraints, too much protection. What else would her mother banish from her world? Carnations? Wearing yellow? Polka dots? Ma wasn't fond of any of those things either.

I bet she'd decree a law against them, too, she allowed herself to rebel as the knife chop-chop-chopped the vegetables.

"Splash in a wee bit o' cider vinegar and a spoonful o' white sugar to pickle 'em," her mother insisted. "It'll all be ready when the boys get home."

Millie did as her mother asked, even as she allowed herself to dream of slitting a tiny opening to freedom from the apprehensive cocoon her family surrounded her in. She knew their multiple layers of protective silk were meant only to keep her safe, and she knew they loved her. But she was equally determined that the undertone of anxiety in her mother's Irish household would not lay claim to her life. No, she might be just over five feet two inches tall, but she was fierce, and she'd have her own way. Eventually.

And if she could do anything about it, "eventually" wasn't going to be too far off.

As THE WEEK WORE on, the hours of each day seemed to expand in the afternoon, spreading out like a stick of oleo margarine, all soft, and threatening to lose its shape. Millie felt her energy melt, too, as she struggled to help with the chores. What she really wanted was for Friday to come: Friday, when the work week would end, when her brothers would take a break, when one of them would suggest going to the pool. She couldn't initiate the idea herself. Gordon would see right through that. No, she'd wait for the boys, and just follow them along.

Besides, if she wanted to make herself available for a second encounter with that new fella, she ought to repeat the same routine as last time. She was fussing with her hair, pulling up its abundance of curls, when her mother came into her bedroom.

"Goin' somewhere?" she inquired.

"What?" Millie tried to sound uninterested, even listless. "No, it's just too hot. I want all this hair off my neck."

"You been goin' out on Fridays. Where d' ya' think ya'll be headed this time?" her mother ignored the weak attempt at a diversion.

"Oh, I don't know," Millie answered breezily. "Wherever the boys go, probably."

"Probably," her mother repeated. "Certainly's more like it. You stay with 'em, hear?"

"Of course," Millie agreed. That was exactly what she had in mind.

Pa was the first to arrive home from work. But instead of coming into the house, he dropped his metal lunch pail on the top step of the porch, and stomped off in a fury to the back side of the shed.

He was gone only a few seconds, but when he reappeared, he was digging his heels into the lawn with each step. He seemed irritated.

"Gordon home yet?" he called out.

"No," Ma answered. "What is it?"

"Somebody's stealing our wood. I wasn't sure at first, but I been counting logs the last three days. Now, I'm certain."

Ma's kitchen stove was stoked with wood, and if there was one thing she did not abide, running short was it. She could switch to coal, or even ask for an electric stove. But no, her old stove worked just fine, so she saw no need to change.

"Who do ya' think it is?" she asked. Should she be alarmed that a thief might be living in their midst? Such a problem would need to be pondered.

"Don't know, not for sure," Pa said. "But we're about to find out."

For his part, the response wasn't contemplation. On the contrary, it was action!

Gordon came up the back steps and into the kitchen.

"There you are," Pa said. "Get some shotgun shells, and come out back of the shed."

"Pa's not going to aim at someone, is he?" Millie asked as she watched the two of them escape with the shells. She didn't see a gun, though.

"He seems angry enough—an' I don't blame 'im. No one steals from Pa, and gets away with it," said her mother, joining Millie at the window. "But no, I don't think he'd do that. Especially with Gordon involved."

She strained to see what was happening, though.

"Where'd they go?" she asked.

"Back of the shed again," Millie answered.

"Somethin's goin' on," her mother confirmed. "Pa's in a mind t' seek revenge."

They looked at one another, and Ma finally shrugged.

"We'll find out soon enough," she said. She knew that whatever Pa planned, she could count on him to take care of the family, good and proper. "Let's busy ourselves with gettin' dinner on th' table. We'll eat outside tonight."

Millie grabbed a tray to carry out plates and flatware. She knew that once the boys were fed, they'd start making plans for the evening.

In short order, Edward and Richard arrived home from REI Freight. They hurried to wash up before dinner, for they knew better than to come to dinner smelly. Ma would not tolerate unclean men at her table, not if she was expected to spend her time preparing a good meal.

"Where's Pa?" Edward asked. "And Gordon, too, where's he?"

"They're workin' on a project," their mother said. Neither of the other two boys needed to know what was going on unless Pa told them. Especially Richard. That one never could keep his mouth shut, and if she was right, whatever Pa was up to, he wouldn't want it blabbed.

Millie set the table, and then carried the salad and bread outside.

Will they ever hurry up, she thought to herself, annoyed that this scoundrel might now be interfering with her weeklong hope of going to the pool.

Just as she was about to call her father and Gordon to come to dinner, they stomped across the lawn, smug grins suggesting they'd devised some way to identify the wood thief.

"Now we'll see who's stealing from us," Pa said quietly to his wife.

"Ya' laid 'im a trap then," she acknowledged. If someone was pilfering their wood, she believed that Pa was every bit within his rights to lay open who the perpetrator was, and make sure he got the message: thievery won't be tolerated.

"D' ya' think they'll fall for it?" she asked.

"Won't be long," Pa answered. "You just be sure that Gordon or I are the only ones to bring in wood for your stove this weekend."

He took his place at the head of the table, and the boys piled in next. They were famished . . . but then again, when weren't they! Each one ate second helpings, and when their plates were empty again, they eyed the serving bowls and platters for dregs and crumbs.

Why don't they finish and get going? Millie wondered restlessly. She'd been warming up for this evening all day! All week!

"Guess I'll head off," Gordon finally suggested. The trap Pa and he laid wouldn't likely reveal their wood thief until after dark, and maybe, not even until morning. "I want to get some laps in."

"Better wait an hour before ya' jump into that pool," warned their mother. "Ya' don't want t' drown, don't ya' know."

"It'll be 'bout an hour's time before I get in there," he insisted, rising from the table.

"Finally!" Millie thought to herself. But she dared not move to join in. Not yet. Not if she wanted to keep her plan hidden.

"Think I'll go, too," said her oldest brother.

"Me, too," said the third.

Drat, Millie thought. They're all going. I'll have to avoid the lot of them at the pool. Oh, well. I can do it.

"Guess I'll just tag along," she added casually, trying to sound as if she'd go only because she had nothing better to do. She'd also stay hidden in their midst, where they wouldn't notice her seeking a glimpse of that fella. Hopefully, he'd be looking for her, too.

As she slipped into her swimsuit, she wished she owned one of the new backless maillot styles that some of the girls wore, instead of her one-piece from the previous summer. One of the benefits of being petite was that she didn't outgrow her clothes, but that circumstance was a drawback when styles changed. She wanted to look . . . what? Not fashionable, but . . . noticeable. Just a little.

She was too short to view herself in the tiny mirror over her bureau, so she stood on her toes to survey her reflection in the backlight from her bedroom window glass. "This will have to do," she decided, pleased that she had tied up her curls.

"C'mon!" one her brothers shouted though her bedroom door.

"Let's go!" said another one from the front porch.

"I'm coming!" she complained as she grabbed her towel and ran up behind them. "All you have to do is throw on your trunks and tank. I've got to . . . do more."

They ignored her excuses. They didn't want their little sister to tell them what "more" meant. But they did slow down enough to let her walk easily alongside.

The four Huffs arrived at the community pool just as mothers were bundling their children in towels and hustling them toward home. The little tikes had worn themselves out, and now shuddered in the approaching chill of the evening air. A few younger teenagers remained in the water, but not for long. End-of-the-day swimming was left for the adults who worked all day.

Millie staked out a bit of turf at the shallow end of the pool, where she could scan all the goings-on without being obvious. If she decided to make herself available for a conversation with anyone, she could move to the water's edge and dip her feet. For now, she'd look around to see if that fella . . .

She saw him.

He saw her, too, and waved.

Be calm, she told herself. Be casual, be relaxed. The boys would make a big deal of seeing her talk to a fella if they suspected any interest, and that could ruin everything.

She smiled and nodded. She'd act friendly, maybe even interested, but also demure.

Slowly, she stood up, and casually walked into the open. Just like the last time, she thought, but without Gordon hovering at her shoulder.

Her heart was racing.

She sat down, and dipped her feet into the water.

"Millie, isn't it?" he asked as he came up behind her.

She turned her head slightly, and glanced up through her sunglasses.

"Yes?" she answered as if she didn't know who said her name. "Oh, hello, again."

"I was hoping you'd be back," Icky said honestly. "We didn't get a chance to talk last week."

"We didn't," she acknowledged. "But we're back, all four of us this time: all three of my older brothers . . . and me."

Would he catch on? Did he understand that the two of them probably were being watched?

"I didn't know you had *three* brothers," Icky said, amiably. "Mind if I join you?"

"Please do," Millie said. "Yes, Gordon you met. He's in the middle, between Edward and Richard."

"I have one brother: Henry, and three sisters: Herta, Alma, and Erna."

"And where are you in the pecking order?" she asked, making conversation.

"Second born, surrounded by sisters," he answered.

"I know what that's like," Millie said, "to be outnumbered."

"Overwhelming, sometimes," Icky agreed, hoping to make a good impression. "Maybe we could go out sometime, if you like, where we're not so outnumbered."

So, he had understood, she thought. Good!

"Yes, I think I'd like that," Millie said.

Icky's heart soared. He, too, had come to the pool with a plan: to seek out this girl. Thoughts of her pestered him all week, and he was determined to find her again.

"Hey! Loser!" Gordon said in a raised voice as he approached. "Want a re-match?"

"Who are you calling a loser?" Icky answered, getting up. But before he left Millie's side, he turned back and quietly said, "How about if I call you in the morning. If you're available. A movie? Tomorrow night?"

"That would be swell," Millie smiled at him, but since her brother was on the way over, it was just the sort of half smile she'd give one of them when they did something to irk her. Icky seemed to understand; he returned a victory smile before he turned toward Gordon.

She didn't move from the edge of the pool for a couple of minutes. No, it would be more prudent to let her brothers think that Icky had approached her merely to ask where Gordon was, and once found, had moved on.

As Gordon and Icky started to race, Millie retreated to a corner of the deck. She chose a chair off by itself, and breathed in deeply—not a sigh, but a calming of her spirit, for now began the long wait until he called.

And he would call—he said he would! In the morning, he said.

And they would go out, probably to a movie.

She rested her head on the back of the deck chair, and allowed her imagination to take her to Saturday evening: He would come to the house, and pick her up in his car. That would mean meeting Pa. Gordon would be there, and he seemed to like this fella, so she could count on him to be friendly, and signal initial approval. And then they would go out.

Oh, why did time have to drag itself along by the minutes when she was waiting for something good?

MILLIE WAS STILL HALF asleep as dawn streamed into her tiny bedroom. She stretched dreamily and peeked at the day's welcome. Just a few more minutes, she insisted, shutting her eyes again. The house was still quiet.

Time to herself was one of the best things about having her own room. Never mind that it was little more than a closet, just large enough for her small bed and a tiny bureau. It was a sanctuary, a place where she could be alone with her hopes and dreams.

She opened her eyes again and looked out the window through ruffled white cotton curtains. Clouds were floating by, the same clouds overhead wherever Icky lived. He said he would call in the morning, and morning it was.

Oh, no! If the telephone rang and the boys were quicker than she was, they'd pick it up.

She jumped out of bed, and threw on her robe. Before she turned the knob on her bedroom door, though, a loud explosion shook the house. Then another! Then two more!

Gordon flew down the stairs in just two bounds. "Woo-hoo!" he yelled with glee. "We caught 'em!"

"Got 'em!" Pa blasted with equal triumph as he emerged from the front bedroom. Clapping his middle son on the shoulder, he added, "They won't be doing that again!"

"What?" Millie said, meeting them halfway to the front door. "What's going on?"

The two other boys were right behind them. They had no clue what the explosions were about.

"Did you hear that?" one said, alarmed.

"What is it?" said the other.

"Caught a thief!" Pa boasted. "Been stealing our wood, so we set some shells in a couple of our logs, and left 'em on top of the pile behind the shed. I'm guessing they exploded when the dirty crooks lit their stove."

"Wish I could see their faces!" Gordon said as he and his father went outside onto the front lawn. A few neighbors cautiously opened their doors and peered out.

The town fire engine arrived on the street, sirens wailing, and stopped at a little house just half a block away.

"Thought it might be them," Pa said, "but I couldn't be sure, not without proof. Now we got it."

"Well," said Ma as she came up behind them, her robe sashed tight. "They won't be needin' wood for a while, not without a stove."

"No, and they'll think twice about lighting another log from our wood pile," Pa said with a smirk.

"Aren't you afraid they'll call the cops on you?" Richard suggested.

"On *me*? Why me?" Pa eyed him.

"Well . . . it, uh, sounded like you're admitting to blowing up their stove," he said.

"Did it? I don't believe I said anything of the sort," Pa denounced his son's remark in a menacing tone. "I just put gun powder in my own wood logs. If those logs ended up in their stove, that's not my fault. Oh, no, not at all! That's the fault of the criminal who skulked onto our property, and *stole* them."

He didn't think he'd need to remind his son about the evils of stealing.

"You don't suppose they're going to admit to being *thieves*, do you?" Pa glared with intentionally wary eyes at his youngest son.

"Probably not," Richard said slowly. "But . . . ," he paused, his lips still moving, even though no words were coming out, "but you're not worried, then?"

"Not unless some big mouth decides to cause trouble for me," Pa said in the same suspicious tone of voice. "You wouldn't know anyone like that, would you?"

"No!" Richard confirmed, defensively. "Not me!"

"I didn't think so," Pa told him. His words sounded more like an order than acceptance of his son's pledge to family loyalty.

MILLIE STOOD INSIDE THE house, next to the screen door, so she could hear their conversation, and also, so she could block the boys' way to the telephone in case it rang. She wanted to be the one to answer it.

When it did, a couple of hours later, Pa and the boys were out for the day, so she easily picked up the receiver ahead of her mother. Glorious privacy, she thought as she said hello. And yes, she would love to see a movie, and yes, she could be ready by six-thirty that evening for a seven o'clock show, and goodbye for now.

She'd waited all morning for that call, and when it finally came, it was over in just a few seconds. So quick!

And they were going out!

8

First Date

Icky Haut arrived at Millie Huff's house in the third block of Seventh Street at precisely six-thirty in the evening, as he said he would. He carefully parked the Marquette, and climbed the steps to the front door.

Gordon answered his knock.

"Hey, Ick!" he said, eyeing his wheels parked out front. "What are you doing in this neighborhood? Brought the car around for me to check out?"

"I *would* like you to give it a going-over," Icky answered positively, as Gordon would be exactly the right guy to entrust the care of his first vehicle to. He'd also like to learn for himself how to fix it, and thought Millie's brother might teach him a few things. "But maybe another day. This time, I'm here to pick up Millie."

"Oh!" Gordon said, trying not to sound taken aback. Why hadn't she said anything? But, of course, she wouldn't. "C'mon in," he offered gladly. "I'll call her."

Millie met them just inside the door.

"You're right on time," she said, smiling.

"So are you," he answered. Good omen, he told himself. She must be looking forward to this evening, too.

"I'll get Pa," Gordon said. "He'll like meeting you."

That's what Millie hoped for: Gordon's support in creating a bridge between Icky and her parents. But her mother showed up first.

So, this is the reason for all o' the girl's sighin' this week, she thought to herself as she looked Icky up and down.

53

"I'm Millie's mother," she said, hands on her hips as she nodded toward the street. "See ya' got a fancy car out there. Goin' t' take our Millie out in it?"

"Yes," Icky answered, hoping for a positive reaction. "I invited her to see a show."

"An' that thing goes fast, does it?" she asked, beginning a reproving diatribe on the evils of motor vehicles. "Looks like one o' those speedsters. Ya' know, ya' can't take it out t' th' country. Farmers don't like fast cars stirrin' up their dirt roads, and rilin' up their livestock. They'll throw rocks and rotten vegetables at ya'."

Pa and she didn't own a motor car; they didn't need it. Neither did young folks, who, as she'd heard well enough at her women's meetings, were sometimes using them as places of indecency and misconduct. Not their Millie, of course, but it wouldn't be seemly if she were seen riding around the countryside.

"We're just going into town, to the movie theater," Icky assured her. His mind flashed to a conversation he'd had with his father when he brought the Marquette home. Pa said that when combustion engine vehicles were first introduced, rural folk stoned automobilers who raced around and scared their horses.

"I know it'll go sixty-seven miles an hour," Pa said, as he was aware of Icky's penchant for race cars, too, "but don't test it."

"Not to worry," Icky promised. "I worked hard to save up for this car, and I want to drive it for a long time."

Besides, Icky thought to himself, wasn't Gordon a mechanic? . . . And then he grasped the point of Mrs. Huff's warnings: watching out for Millie.

"Don't be putting him off," Millie's father said, taking over as he strode in.

Pa Huff was a tall, strapping man with sharp bones and a firm grip. He offered a handshake to Icky.

"Seems like a nice enough car. I'm Millie's dad," he said, his lips pressed together as he looked Icky over.

"Nice to meet you, Sir," Icky said politely. Millie continued to look on, hoping the conversation would go well. Her father was, hmm, she decided "opinionated" would be an apt word, and he showed no reserve in sharing the wisdom of his perspectives.

"You'll have her home at a decent hour," said her father. Everyone was in the front room then, Millie's two other brothers coming in to see who was at the door. The day had been thrilling, after all, starting with the explosions. And learning Pa's involvement really intensified the level of intrigue!

And now, before the sun set, a stranger appears at the door? Did some-one rat on Pa? Could they be in store for another surprise? That would be great! Er, not great, but exciting for sure.

"Of course," Icky promised. "Right after the show. Maybe a soda after-ward, if she's interested."

"All right, then," her father allowed, one eyebrow raised as he realized that the entire family was scrutinizing the process of authorizing the care of his only daughter into the hands of an unknown young man. "She can go with you."

What? Of course, I can, Millie thought, but she wouldn't embarrass her father by saying so. She'd been out on dates before. Maybe they weren't with someone who had a car, but they were dates, nonetheless. Besides, she was nineteen, not nine!

Icky wasn't accustomed to being inspected by the parents of girls he dated, as most of them were daughters of long-time family friends. Some even attended the same church. This time, though, the girl's parents didn't know how respected his family was: church pillars, after all.

But hadn't his own parents scrutinized Roy before they allowed him to escort Herta? They had. So, he decided, the tables were turned; this inter-rogation ritual with Millie's parents was no different.

"Um, thanks, ah, Mr. Huff." He turned awkwardly to hold the door open for Millie to go through first. As he walked her to the car, where he opened that door, too, and helped her in, he suspected that ten eyes were peering at them from the front room. And he was also willing to bet that her mother would watch to make sure he didn't peel off some rubber as they went down the street.

They'll all probably be waiting when I bring her home, too, and recall-ing his brief conversation with Millie at the pool, he decided that she was right. She was outnumbered.

ICKY THOUGHT THE FIRST date went well, so he telephoned Millie to invite her to see a film again the next week. She'd like that! Maybe he'd take her to dinner first, too, if she thought that sounded okay. She did! Then they could talk a bit more, and get to know one another. They agreed to set the date for the following Saturday.

Even though two-day weekends were becoming standard practice in many companies, no law forbade an employer from demanding extra hours—which meant that if men wanted to keep their jobs, they'd show up as scheduled. As it turned out, Mr. Bolles wanted a couple of able-bodied men to help install the new Otto Rohwedder slicer he purchased, so he assigned Icky and one of the mechanics to work Saturday.

For his part, Icky was glad to have a few extra bucks in his pocket to pay for the dinner date with Millie. By five o'clock, the Rohwedder was in place, and all of its functions were tested. He sped home with barely enough time to wash and shave before he had to dash out the door again.

As he pulled up in the Marquette, he reminded himself that even though he was rushing to be on time, he had to be absolutely—or "abso-damned-lutely," as Gordon would have put it—sure that he didn't race down their street. In no way would he give Mr. Huff a reason for looking sideways at him. Or Mrs. Huff, for that matter. She seemed just as formidable as Millie's dad!

He took Millie to the new Brown Bear Restaurant for dinner, and they talked and talked and talked so much that they almost missed the opening previews at the theater.

"What's playing this week?" she asked as they parked the car, and she removed her babushka. She hadn't wanted the wind to blow her naturally curly hair in every direction.

"It's a Western," Icky said. "Something called *In Old Santa Fe*."

"Oh," Millie acknowledged, trying to sound good-natured. "I don't think I've ever seen a cowboy movie, not from start to finish." If she were to tell the whole truth, however, she'd reveal that once before, she and a couple of her girlfriends left the theater before a Western was half over. It was the only time they wasted good money on one of those rough-talking, tobacco-spitting shoot-'em-ups.

This time, though, she'd have to be a good sport if she wanted to make a good impression. Then, maybe she could suggest something more appealing. Assuming they would see one another again, she reminded herself.

"Well, I hope you like it," Icky said. "The star is Gabby Hayes, and his family lives down the road in Wellsville." Local folks didn't often travel to the west coast, much less end up on the silver screen in Hollywood! That alone ought to make the show worth seeing.

As they settled into their seats, Icky wondered whether or not Millie would think him too forward if he slipped his arm around her shoulder. He could just stretch out, one arm in each direction, and if she moved toward him . . . but maybe he'd wait until the *Newsreel Parade* clips were over. Let her relax first.

The line-up started with news briefs describing a second gold rush in California. Then there was footage of the Columbia University Lions football team and their win in the 1934 Rose Bowl . . . followed by dancers

promoting an upcoming musical production . . . and Elmer the trained lamb
. . . and Joan Blondell . . . recovering . . .

Icky caught his head bouncing up and down as he struggled to pay attention. He was sapped from working all week—and almost eight hours that
day, too. Lifting and hauling and installing and testing Bolles's new slicing
machine had taken more energy out of him than he'd realized.

And then he'd used up all of his adrenaline reserve paying attention to
Millie during supper—which was a pleasure, to be sure, but by the time they
left the diner, he was just so tired. Now, it seemed that the darkened theater
was undermining his effort to stay awake.

Cowboy music finally rose to signal the beginning of the movie. Icky
hoped the show would have a lot of good action to hold his attention. If
not, though, he warned himself, I could begin to drift off. Then, I'd . . . be in
trouble, and . . . he felt a hard pinch on his arm.

"Ouch!" he said out loud. In the theater. In the middle of the movie.

"Shhh!" Millie whispered sharply in his direction. "You're snoring!
Loudly!"

"Sorry," Icky winced.

"And you're leaning on me," she added, gently scooching away.

Oh, this is not going well at all, Icky withered as he straightened
himself.

"Sorry again," he repeated. And blinked a couple of times. Then, more
awake, he realized that she had actually pinched him!

"You pinched me," he said in a loud whisper.

Silence.

"You pinched me!" he repeated with emphasis. He was pretty sure his
last girlfriend, Irene, wouldn't have done such a thing.

"I did, yes," she admitted, quietly. "Twice," she continued with an
equally loud whisper the second time. What was she supposed to say, especially with other theater-goers glaring at them.

"Twice? Twice! Well, . . . " he didn't know what he was going to say
next, but in his somewhat dazed state, he felt that she should apologize.
Or say something more sensitive than merely acknowledging what she had
done.

Twice!

And she had corrected him!

The couple sitting in the row behind them was becoming increasingly
annoyed by their interruptions. "SHHH!" the fellow said, leaning forward.
"If you're not interested in watching the show, why not just leave!"

Icky and Millie glanced back at him, and then looked quickly at one
another.

"Okay?" Icky mouthed quietly.

"Okay!" she nodded.

When they escaped to the sidewalk outside, Icky pulled a pack of Camel cigarettes out of his pocket, and offered Millie a smoke.

"No, thank you," she said, politely. But she was still slightly irked by the way he embarrassed her in the theater.

"Why didn't you just say something?" he asked her then.

He was questioning *her* behavior? She was the one who had a right to be miffed!

"It's kind of hard to 'say something' to a person who's going 'KH-KH-KH' in your ear in the middle a fascinating tale about cattle rustling," she retorted defensively—but with the tiniest smile at her own attempt at imitating his snores. She had older brothers, and she'd grown up hearing their sawing wood chorus echoing down the attic stairs every night. One of them snorted, one wheezed every so often, and the third rattled the shingles. Icky's snoring, by contrast, wavered between shallow and stuttering—and was definitely not the sort of background noise she expected on a movie theater date. Even though the film was horrid.

"Well, I . . . " he started, but she wouldn't let him finish. Not yet.

"Yes, a girl really enjoys a film about a double-crossing cowboy who loses his horse by gambling on a rigged race, and then gets framed for murdering a stagecoach driver."

Catching a glimpse at his wrinkled forehead, she quickly added, "Really! It's quite a thought-provoking story line—and such a lovely selection for impressing a girl."

"Ouch, again," he said. The cool evening air had finally sharpened his senses. And the cigarette was calming his nerves. He was beginning to see her point.

They started walking toward his car.

After a few steps, he said, "Loud?"

"The snoring?" she asked.

"Yes."

They continued walking.

"Really loud," she confirmed, smiling.

He looked straight at her then.

Why was she smiling? He felt an odd mixture of confusion and delight.

"Gabby Hayes heard you all the way out in New Mexico," she added after a short pause.

Okay, now he could tell that she was teasing. He'd play along.

"I suppose this means that it's over between us? You never want to see me again?"

She stopped abruptly, and turned on him.

"Oh, no-o-o. You're not getting off that easy. You're going to have to repeat the second half of this date. Do it again next week. And again, the following week. And again and again, until you get it right."

"Sounds like you think I need a lot of practice," he said, amused by her spunk and sass.

"Uh-huh," she nodded her head.

They started walking again.

"How about another try next Saturday?" he suggested, this time slipping his fingers between hers.

"That'd be swell," she agreed. "But no more cowboy movies. Or boring newsreels."

"None! On my honor, I promise!"

"Well, then," she toyed with him as they arrived at the car, "I suppose it's only fair to give you another chance." He opened the door, and helped her into her seat.

When she was settled, he walked around to the driver's side, and looked up and down the block in both directions. No one was coming.

He got in, and shut his car door. Good thing I left the top up, he thought. I wouldn't want the whole street to see our first kiss.

9

Tensions and Intentions

ICKY PARKED THE MARQUETTE in front of his parents' house, and quietly slipped upstairs to the room he shared with Henry. The kid was snoring, and didn't wake up.

Icky wondered if that was how he sounded in the movie theater. And what was worse, he'd made that noise in front of Millie! She said he'd leaned against her, too.

He hoped he hadn't drooled on her sleeve!

Probably not. She would have told him if he had. She didn't seem to be the sort of girl who held anything back. Millie was so . . . real. Not one of those dainty, lifted-pinky types. No, she was honest. About everything. And she always sounded happy when he called.

Not that she yakked all the time about one useless thing after another, or worse: repeatedly grilled him on what he was thinking. Hell, if a guy ever gave a truthful answer to that question, he'd probably get slapped!

But this girl, this Millie, she didn't do any of that. If she did say something, though, he let his mind wander as he lay back on his pillow with a crooked smile on his face, well, then he'd better pay attention!

Crickets chirping outside the bedroom window sought partners in the warmth of the summer's night. He imagined asking Millie a question the next time they went out. "Tell me . . . ," he'd say with slow deliberation. And she'd parcel out words, each one carefully chosen. She filled all his senses: her sweet smile, the way she listened intently, and looked up to him from her diminutive stature.

There was also that brightness in her eyes when she was teasing him, and narrow darts when he'd crossed her. He rubbed his arm where she pinched him: no bruise. He preferred thinking about that kiss. Just a little wisp of a kiss, soft, if only for an instant. She'd made his heart skip, and then he'd opened his eyes and looked at her.

And in that brief moment, she'd looked down.

She probably thought I was . . . what? Staring at her! I wasn't! My eyes were shut when I kissed you, Millie!

Oh, but hadn't she smiled then, too, after that kiss? She had, and then peeked back up at him. When he kissed her . . . zzz.

MILLIE SLIPPED QUIETLY BETWEEN the muslin sheets on her little bed as her brothers trudged up the stairs. Gordon and Richard had waited up for her to arrive safely home, claiming to be watching the fireflies from the front porch. Their parents had gone in for the night, purportedly needing to get to sleep, as both had early wake-ups the next morning. Besides, they knew the boys would keep an eye out, just like always.

She could hear her oldest brother, Edward, already snoring; he was the one who snorted. Wheezy Gordon and Roof Rattler Richard will join you any minute, she thought to herself. What name would she give to Icky's snoring? She wouldn't. She'd identify him some other way, like by that unexpected kiss.

She hadn't anticipated it—not after the way she'd treated him, pinching him like that, and then teasing him about the movie selection. The film was an awful, though, she defended. He should have spent more time planning their date, and checked out what was playing before dragging her to some cowboy flick.

Maybe he didn't like her well enough, her thoughts suggested. It seemed that she'd spent the entire week getting ready, deciding to add a sweater and a scarf so that her only nice dress looked new. And practicing how to fix her hair, paying attention to her make-up, considering whether or not to wear cologne, thinking about the entire evening, imagining him drive up their street and climb the front steps, recalling the way he opened the car door for her, and the feeling when he took her hand as she stepped in. And . . . and tonight he'd kissed her.

There it was again, that unexpected kiss in the creamy light of a midsummer moon. Even now, she could almost feel his lips gently brushing against hers. Her heart fluttered at the thought of it.

Or maybe it was that soda pop gurgling up. Oh, how she hoped her stomach hadn't made noise, as it was apt to do.

No, she assured herself; she would have felt humiliated, and nothing of that sort interfered.

She smiled in the darkness of her room, and glimpsed out her window at the velvet black of night sprinkled with dazzling stars, the same stars shining into Icky's bedroom window . . . zzz.

ICKY AND MILLIE SPENT almost every weekend together, going on picnics, attending church socials, and getting to know one another's families. Finally, Ma Haut suggested to Pa that they invite her to dinner on Sunday after church.

"You think it's time then?" he said.

"Icky hasn't said, but yes, I do," she told him. "And with Roy joining Herta at the table, the four of them together will make a good time."

Pa nodded. Their church pew would be full indeed, he thought to himself with satisfaction.

Dinner was served as soon as they arrived home from church. When everyone was seated and grace was repeated, Pa passed serving platters of pork and potato pancakes while Ma introduced the news she wanted to be discussed. Family tradition held that the adults gave their views on the topic of the day, and the younger people learned. Wasn't it the German way that "children should be seen and not heard"?

Then, when the subjects Ma and Pa introduced had been fully exhausted, others at the table were invited to suggest new topics. Icky was ready to shift the conversation to work at the bakery. He'd been holding a question all week for Roy to answer.

"Okay, how about this. All we do with the *flour* inventory is count the number of hundred-pound bags, so we don't run out. But with *sugar*, we also track the codes on each bag. What gives?" Icky asked him.

"Recording sugar is a government requirement," Roy explained, setting down his coffee mug. "When Prohibition ended, the Feds started sending around Alcohol, Tobacco, and Firearms accountants to force bakeries to prove that each bag of sugar we buy goes into bread production—and not sold under the counter to illegal moonshine distilleries."

"Moonshine?" Henry asked, interested in any sort of intrigue.

"Yep, yep, yep," Roy confirmed. "Backwoods brewers still make hooch and sell it without collecting taxes—which is a federal crime. Booze is supposed to be controlled by licensed state stores, so the government can collect excise revenue."

"So, *that's* what's going on," Icky said, raising his chin to show he understood. He remembered how, when he was just a newly hired laborer, he'd seen inspectors come by every few weeks to audit inventory against the books. Mr. Bolles had warned him that if the numbers didn't add up, he'd be in big trouble. A single mistake, no matter how small, could cost the company a large fine, and that would mean the end of his job. Now he knew why.

"Yep, yep, yep," Roy confirmed. "Any company that uses a lot of sugar—whether a bakery or a soda pop bottling company or a fruit jam company—has got to keep its records straight."

"A good thing this is!" Ma Haut said, approvingly. Accurate measurements were essential to good controls, and good controls meant ingredients wouldn't be wasted.

"This hooch, as you called it, this is the back woods liquor?" Pa clarified.

Roy nodded.

"Never would hooch pass Germany's strict purity laws," Pa noted. "No, the *Reinheitsgebot* protects the making of the beer, and has been doing so for more than four hundred years. That's why it's the best in the world!"

Ma nodded in agreement. Of course, it was the best beer. And, of course, Pa was right to point it out.

Millie knew that liquor production and beer brewing were taxed. But she had no idea that bakeries were regulated just to be sure they weren't complicit in making illegal hooch. Her father would be fascinated by this topic, and she made a mental note to suggest to Icky that he tell him—and also, to warn him to be sure her mother wasn't around when he did.

"You two are gettin' t' be quite th' item," her mother said to Icky when he brought Millie home after dinner. She then promptly reciprocated the Haut meal by inviting him to dinner the following week.

"Thank you," Icky said. "I'd be happy to join you."

But as Icky left to go home, Millie challenged her mother.

"What if I decided I didn't want to see him again?" she said.

"Nah, any fool could see otherwise," her mother brushed off the remark.

"Well, I could have invited him myself!" Millie continued to take a stand.

"Jus' thought he ought t' know we approve," her mother insisted. "That's how it's done, don't ya' know."

She didn't. How would she? She had three brothers, after all, and none of them ever shared experiences about meeting parents or dating.

THE CONVERSATION AT THE Huff dinner table was all men talk: business and sports and fishing and hunting. But afterward, when Millie and Icky went for a walk, the pace returned to the rambling, easy conversation she preferred.

"What's it like to be a baker?" she asked him.

"I'm not a baker yet," Icky said. "I'm still an apprentice—senior apprentice, that is. But I hope to be promoted to baker one day."

"So, what does being a senior apprentice feel like?"

"Feel?" he repeated. He'd never considered it a feeling.

"I . . . like the smell of the yeast first thing in the morning," he started. "And the variety of textures in the flours is interesting, too. You can feel their differences when you rub them between your fingertips."

"Different how?"

"Some are softer than others. Some are starchy."

"I never looked at flour that way. We use just whole wheat or rye," she told him.

"My Ma does, too," he acknowledged. He didn't want to insult her, or make his job sound all high and mighty. At the same time, he felt a kind of deep respect for baking. When the flour and the yeast were brought together, somehow they came to life.

"So, why do you need to use so many varieties of wheat flour?" Millie asked. She was genuinely interested.

"Different kinds of bread. They all have different recipes. Bolles was known for its crusty breads in the early days. But we're baking more soft-and-white now."

They kept walking, and were quiet for a couple of minutes. He took her hand.

"So you like baking then?" she asked, finally.

"I couldn't see myself doing anything else," he admitted. "I like making something with my hands. And it's different every day, depending on the weather, the amount of humidity: all that detail. It's interesting."

"So, it's worth the extra hours you work—like all of the weekends when you have to go in?"

"You mean like when we installed the new slicer?" he looked at her to be sure she wasn't still upset about that date: the one when he snored. She didn't seem to be making a point of it, though, so he answered her straight. "Yes, at Bolles, you're expected to sacrifice once in a while for the bakery."

It seemed to Millie that the extra hours Icky worked were more than just once in a while. He was forever balancing time he spent with her on Saturdays with the demands of his job.

He sensed her concern then.

"I'm still an apprentice," he noted. "And that's how it is until I earn the right to wear a button-down baker's shirt."

"Then what?"

"Then, well, then I'll have a career. Something we can count on."

He hadn't expected to reveal his intentions by including her in his explanation. It was just so natural, the way that it tumbled gently from his lips.

But Millie noticed, and in that moment, the rising evening moon threw hope across the sky.

"You're easy to talk to," she said as they circled the block, and headed back to her parents' house.

"You're easy to listen to," he smiled at her. He wouldn't be able to kiss her goodnight that evening, not with her family around. He'd save it for the next time. Maybe then, she'd let him give her two.

"How was dinner with the Huffs?" Henry asked his older brother when Icky came in the door.

"Don't be sticking your nose into other people's business," Ma Haut admonished the younger brother. Ten years between the two boys: the eleven-year-old didn't know where he was treading.

"It's okay," Icky said. "Millie has three brothers, so we talked about cars."

"When she was here, you were quieter than usual. And smiling some goofy smile all the time."

"Henry, it's none of your business," Ma Haut intervened.

"Well, he was," Henry insisted.

"You'll be the same way, when your time comes," Icky said, thinking he closed the conversation.

"It's even on your face when you're sleeping," Henry refused to stop.

"That's enough!" Ma Haut insisted. A person had a right to privacy, after all. Especially when they were asleep!

But now she had the answer to the question she would not ask. Icky was getting serious about this girl. A daughter-in-law could be on the way.

10

Starting Out

"I CAN'T FATHOM WHY ya'd need t' show up in a readymade dress," Millie's mother objected.

Millie wanted something special for a wedding that Icky was taking her to, and she thought the best time to broach the topic was when her mother and she were busy preparing the vegetables for canning. "It's not your ceremony, after all."

"No, but the groom, Roy Fisher, is Icky's boss, and the bride is Herta, his older sister. It seems to me that the occasion calls for something more special than . . . oh, I don't know: a cotton hooverette," she exaggerated, indicating the house dress her mother wore.

"This? I'll have ya' know it's very practical," her mother defended the reversible wrap she put on almost every morning. "If something spills on it, I can always retie it in th' other direction. No one ever knows."

"I certainly would know," Millie pressed her point. "And I'm not going to spill anything at a wedding."

The fact was that she did have one special dress. But she'd worn it a dozen times, and Icky had seen it at least half of them. And besides, a wedding ceremony seemed to call for attire that was smarter, and certainly more well turned out than puffed sleeves and a bow that tied in the back.

"Look, Ma. I want to make a good impression with Icky's family."

And then she hesitated. She wanted to continue her argument . . . but was she ready to share the feelings blossoming in her heart? Could she risk it?

Well, she decided, if she wanted her mother's backing, she probably would have to spill the beans.

"Ma, the Hauts . . . they could be my in-laws one day."

Her mother stopped cutting the end-of-season tomatoes, and stood a little straighter.

"So, you'd be gettin' serious over this Icky then," she speculated, looking straight at Millie. Some sort of chemistry must be going on between the two of them, she noted, the way pudding begins to thicken over gentle heat.

Her daughter didn't respond. Millie wasn't positive about whether or not she was getting serious about Icky. But she thought she might be. She'd never felt about anyone the way she cared for him, so how does a girl—a woman—know?

She waited for her mother to finish absorbing what she'd already revealed.

"Well," her mother finally said, "I s'pose we'll just have t' find a way t' afford it, eh?"

"Aw, thanks, Ma!" Millie chirped happily. "And you'll see. Ready-to-wear isn't nearly as expensive as you might think."

"Don't be overdoin' it, Girl," her mother cautioned her. "Ya' made your point. Now let's just get 'er done without any fuss. Ya' don't want Pa gettin' in the middle."

No, she didn't.

WHEN MILLIE FIRST SET eyes on Icky, she had no thoughts of where that encounter would take the two of them. She was simply drawn to the fella who seemed to be besting her brother at a race in the pool. But then he started a little race in her heart when he said, "*very* nice to meet you."

Did she have some sense even in those first moments that he was "the one"? She wondered.

"When does a girl figure that out?" she finally asked her mother. "I mean, how did you know that Pa and you were right for each other?"

"Ya' just know, that's all," her mother answered casually. "Ya' like 'im for a while, and then one day, ya' know that life wouldn't be complete without 'im."

So, that's how it was. Your heart just tells you.

Millie thought of that completeness as she ran her fingers over the brown velvet trim on the neckline and cuffs of the understated bronze satin dress she'd worn to Roy and Herta's wedding. It had a matching brown velvet cloche—Ma had seen to that, praying that her daughter had found the man she'd spend her life with.

She had. Icky proposed, and Millie felt both scared and elated at once. First, scared, since one in four men was out of work because of the Great Depression, so they had to wonder whether or not the two of them could even afford to be married.

And second, elated, because he was twenty-one and she was twenty, and they had their whole futures ahead of them. With more hope than good sense, they decided to throw caution to the wind. Whatever lay ahead, they'd face it together.

She waited for Pa and the boys to leave for their jobs before she told her mother. Monday was laundry day, and the two of them always worked on it together, so she thought she'd just drop it into the conversation, as if she were merely passing the time of day.

"Ya' wouldn't want t' wait a year or two, just 'til Icky can save up a little?" Ma suggested. She wasn't trying to drive a wedge between the two of them. Oh, no, she could see they were made for one another. And he was hard working—which in her book was the most important trait for a man to have.

And interested in doing for himself, too. Wasn't he learning to fix up that car of his? Of course, Gordon was helping him, but Icky was doing most of the work. Ma could see that. The question of Millie and him marrying wasn't one of *if*; it was only *when*.

"A year or two is forever!" Millie said with dismay. Why, even taffy could be pulled faster than it would take to build up a savings account in this economy!

"Fiddlesticks!" her mother countered. "The country . . ."

"We love each other, Ma, we do. Why should we have to wait just because of the government? Things will get better. That's what you're always telling us."

True, Pa and she always tried to keep their children's spirits up. And raise up their expectations, too.

"Where are ya' goin' t' live then?" Ma put out the obvious next question.

That was a problem. Even with a solid job, Icky probably wasn't earning enough to afford a nice apartment. And the idea of sharing a sleeping room at the front of some run-down house was out of the question!

"We'll figure it out," Millie insisted. "Edward and Edith did."

"Edward is ten years older than Icky and you," Ma pointed out. "He's been workin' at REI nearly nine years. And, he didn't propose marriage 'til he got promoted to his Agent position."

Millie stepped off the porch and into the yard with the basket of shirts to hang on the line. "Don't worry so much!" she insisted gaily. "It'll all work out."

And as far as Millie was concerned, that was the end of the conversation.

Not for Ma, though.

"I think those two are goin' t' tie the knot," she told Pa that evening. "An' Millie wants t' do it sooner rather than later."

"Good! Let 'er reel him in!" After all, Pa thought to himself, it was common knowledge that men fished a sea of women until the right girl caught them. And his daughter had done her part, dressing up nice, and fixing her hair. He didn't like the lipstick, but if it was smeared, he'd know she'd been kissing, so he guessed that he'd allow it.

That was history, though, since she'd set the hook! Icky was a mighty fine fish!

"An' what then?" Ma said with exasperation. "I doubt th' two o' them can afford t' pay rent!"

"He'll probably get a little bump in his pay once he's got a wife," Pa said. "And if he's the man I think he is, he'll save it for a place of their own."

"So, 'til they save up th' nest egg, where are they goin' t' live?" Ma pressed. The question needed an answer.

"They can stay right here! Millie's got her own room. Let 'em share it."

"Two people in that little room?" Ma challenged, her face wrinkled. She didn't think Millie would be thrilled with that option.

"Better than setting down in a seedy part of town," Pa pointed out. "Unless she's too proud to live with us."

"Maybe," Ma said as she considered her daughter's propensity to dream big dreams. After all, Millie had pointed out that her oldest brother and his bride moved into their own place.

"Well, I dare say she'd rather be here with Icky than waitin' 'til they can afford t' be on their own," she said as she mulled the option over.

Pa just nodded.

"An' I suppose quite a few newlyweds start out by livin' with family these days," she mused. "She wouldn't be th' first."

"Still," she paused to deliberate the prospect of housing a young married couple under their roof, "we'd be separated from their bedroom by only one wall. That would be another situation t' think about."

Every worry should be considered, she always said. But she supposed they could manage this one.

"We could," Pa agreed.

"All right then," Ma finally concluded. "It's settled, between us anyway. We'll tell 'em when he brings her home."

"We'll tell them after he asks me for her hand!" Pa amended, self-importantly. "He hasn't done that yet!"

"Oh, of course. And he will, he will," Ma assured Pa. "Ya' won't be left out o' th' picture."

"Well, she's the only girl," he pointed out. "I get to say whether or not we approve!"

"And if ya' don't?" Ma asked, turning her face sideways to him, a twinkle in her eye. She knew that Millie was her father's daughter; she had his disposition through and through, so the thought of her wicked temper going up against the guff and gristle of the Bull in the Woods: 'Twouldn't be pretty. "Saints preserve us!" she thought to herself.

Pa looked at Ma quizzically. Not approving Millie's choice hadn't occurred to him.

"Would ya' be willin' t' clash it out with Millie then?" she asked.

"Go up against Millie on whether or not she marries Icky?" Pa said rhetorically. "Not in your life!

"Besides," he continued, lifting his chin to show he'd retain his authority, "I like this one."

THE BRIDE CHOSE YELLOW talisman roses with baby's breath for her wedding bouquet.

"But th' color for weddin' flowers is white," Ma objected. "Ya' know what they say: 'Marry in white, everythin's right. Marry in yellow, ashamed o' your fellow.'"

Even if Millie wouldn't be coming down the aisle of a church in a fancy gown, the flowers ought to say something.

"Pshaw," she countered her mother's counsel. "I couldn't be any happier. And yellow flowers will look nicer with my dress." Besides, she didn't intend to be influenced by silly superstitions.

"I hope Icky appreciates your strong will," Ma said then. She wasn't one to butt into anyone's business, but this was probably the last time she'd be able to offer Millie some motherly advice. Cautiously, of course.

"He knows well enough," Millie said, self-assuredly.

Icky had three days off from his job over Christmas, so the young couple was wed at her parent's home on December 27, with Millie's brother, Richard, as Icky's best man. Nick Carpoletti offered up gentle tunes on his accordion. Carpoletti was often hired to provide background music at parties and picnics. In fact, Icky and he met when Nick entertained employees at the Bolles Bakery summer picnic.

The room quieted as The Reverend Phillip Garber delivered a homily reminding the couple and all the family gathered together that this marriage was blessed by God and holy, just as the Lord's relationship with the creation is holy, and Christ's relationship with the church is holy. Therefore, charging everyone to honor the union in just that way, he asked the couple to repeat their vows.

Icky felt a catch in his throat as he looked into Millie's eyes and repeated his promises. She loved that about him: the contrast between his self-assured exterior, the way he seemed to own the swimming pool on the first day she saw him, and this, the vulnerable side, the one he reserved only for her.

As the minister pronounced their marriage, and the groom and bride kissed, Nick keyed up a few bars of a wedding march to break the tension of the moment. Ma Huff and Ma Haut let their tears roll then, and all the men slapped one another's backs.

"Where's the hooch when you need it?" said one of them.

"Now, don't be bringin' that up at this happy time," Ma Huff reproved.

"No, we need it to toast the newlyweds!" Pa Huff insisted.

"And you know what they say in Germany," Pa Haut interjected: "*Hier steppt der Bär!*"

"Which means?" Pa Huff asked jovially as he poured pony glasses for all the guests.

"Here steps the bear!—or in the English, you throw a great party!"

Ma Huff decided she wouldn't argue, especially since it was but a wee nod to a celebratory ritual. Aye, no, she had a ritual of her own to offer up at the meal.

A wedding supper commenced immediately following the nuptials. Ma's friends from the Moose Lodge volunteered to serve so that she could remain at the table with her family. But before the first course was put down, the ladies placed bowls of hot cereal before Millie and Icky.

"What's this?" Millie said.

"Tradition," said Ma Huff, proudly. If Pa could decide whether or not Icky could marry Millie, and then offer up a little toast in their honor, certainly she could make sure the two of them would be happy, now couldn't she? She thought it wasn't too much to ask.

"The new couple starts their life with wee bowls o' salted porridge," she said. "Eat just a few spoonsful now, before your wedding feast is served. It'll protect ya' from the 'evil eye.'"

"Really," Millie almost protested. But then, thinking better of it, picked up her spoon. "If you say so, Ma."

"We spit in the evil eye," Icky added as he swallowed a large mouthful.

"There ya' go then," said Ma Huff. "It worked for Pa an' me, and it'll do th' same for th' two o' you."

THE FOLLOWING MONDAY, ROY told Mr. Bolles the news of Icky's marriage, just as he would have advised him of any man's change in marital status.

"They know one another well?" Mr. Bolles asked. He had a right, after all, to decide whether or not to provide Icky the benefits generally accorded to a man when his status was changed from single to married.

"Over a year," Roy confirmed. "She's from a good family, and they've moved in with her parents until they can save for their own place."

"Good enough," he said. In due course, he'd increase Icky's pay.

"Men are the family wage-earners," the boss stated with authority, "so they have a right to more take-home pay than single men." It was common knowledge, he noted, that a man on his own was rudderless, and so, without the care of a good woman, reputedly wasted extra money on gambling and bars.

"And I am not interested in contributing to behavior that leads to trouble!" he said, waving an imperious hand. Echoing the vigor of executives he'd heard on radio interviews, he added, "You can be sure that Bolles Bakery is a better member of this business community than that!"

"Right, Sir. And there's one more thing," Roy said before Mr. Bolles walked off, as he always did when, in his estimation, a discussion was over. "We got to replace John Shotinski. He's retiring next month."

"As you know I am aware," Mr. Bolles asserted to indicate that he knew what was going on in his own bakery. "Tell Haut to work with Shotinski starting now. And tell him that the raise he's getting is for both his change in marital status and the promotion to baker. That way we get another year out of him before he expects another pay increase."

Roy nodded, but without meeting his boss's eyes. Mr. Bolles caught the forced restraint, and then remembered that Roy was now Icky's brother-in-law. Family loyalty can be tricky, he hesitated briefly as he considered whether or not this wrinkle would cause a problem.

But no, he decided, it probably wouldn't. A good employee does as he's told, immediately and without question. Roy had done that all along. He was loyal. And if he ever showed he wasn't, letting one of them go would solve it.

Secure in the soundness of his directive, Mr. Bolles returned to his office, taking each step up the stairs deliberately as he mentally listed attributes Haut should be reminded to emulate, now that he was being promoted. He should be reliable, of course. Advance the quality of the product. Set an example for the apprentices. Accept what he is given, for that's what pay is: *given*.

He considered that one, all the while engraving a frown on his face. Pay was not quite the same as a gift; wages were earned, after all.

But as the words "given" and "gift" were generally connected in the same thought, he was disposed to believe that they obviously segregate the man at the top from everyone else. Logic then dictated that the employee ought to be grateful for having been bestowed the great favor of being hired, and thereby, once again, *given* an opportunity to serve the company. That's how he saw it. That's how Icky would need to see it, too, if he wanted to continue to grow in his career with Bolles Bakery.

Roy had been expecting Mr. Bolles to pay Icky the higher rate owed to a baker immediately upon moving up from senior apprentice. But as the boss was always alert to ways he could get more and pay less, the maneuver should have been no surprise.

"Stick around for a few minutes," he instructed Icky as he distributed paychecks to the crew at the end of the week. "We need to talk about your job."

That sounded ominous. What did Roy mean by "your job"?

Icky shoved his pay envelope into his back pocket, and paced the floor, each step ticking off the day's tasks. Had he measured something wrong? Was the mixer turned up too high? Did the boss think he was daydreaming? . . . He admitted that he probably had been smiling a lot, but that was just because everything was going so well. At least, he thought it was going well.

He wanted to light up a cigarette to calm his nerves. Maybe he'd wait for Roy outside.

"Ick! Over here!" Roy called.

"Right!" Icky said, approaching quickly. Don't let this be awful, he prayed silently. I just got married. I moved in with the Huffs only a few days ago. I know there's a Depression, but I can't lose my job, not now. Please, not now, Lord.

"Did you look at your check?" Roy said.

"No," Icky admitted, pulling it out of his pocket. Don't tell me I'm being demoted, not with a new wife. Of course, demoted is better than being fired, but please, God.

"Let me explain," Roy said as Icky tore the envelope open. "Now that Millie and you are married, you're getting a small increase."

Okay, that's good, Icky thought, hesitantly. But what about that comment about "your job"? When was Roy going to get to that?

He'd follow Roy's lead.

"I know it's not much, but . . . "

"Did you get a pay raise when you married Herta last year?" Icky interrupted, unaware that a change in marital status was a reason for a bump in pay.

"Yep," Roy said. "Of course!"

"So, being married makes us better at our jobs, or somehow makes us worth more than being single," Icky tried to make the connection.

"Men work harder once they're married," Roy said.

Icky threw his shoulders back, straightened his head on his neck, and frowned.

"*Most* men work harder once they're married," Roy acquiesced. "Not you, Ick. You always work hard."

Icky didn't say anything. Was this what Roy meant by "your job"?

"You know what I'm saying," Roy insisted. "Some men plod along, just barely moving their feet during the week, and then grab their pay as they bolt out the door on Fridays. You know: good 'today' men.

"But you're the 'tomorrow' sort. You ask questions," he continued.

"Okay," Icky said, relaxing finally. "I get it."

Then, assuming he'd misunderstood the reference to "your job," he prepared to leave and offered a handshake, saying, "Thanks, Roy."

"Not so fast," Roy said, waving the handshake off.

Icky was taken aback.

"One more reason you're getting a pay increase is that Mr. Bolles is promoting you to baker, and he wants you to start working with Shots."

"What?" Icky said, eyes widening. "A promotion?"

"The drawback is that it's third shift, Sunday through Thursday, because demand for white bread is up. We need fresh loaves ready to ship at daybreak on Mondays."

"I'm promoted to baker?" Icky repeated. "I thought, well, you said you wanted to talk about 'your job,' so I was trying to figure out how I screwed up!"

"Nope, nope, nope," Roy said, finally shaking Icky's hand then. "You done good, Ick. Keep it up."

"Wait 'til I tell Millie!"

Icky shoved the paycheck envelope back into his pocket, and dashed out the door.

Roy, meanwhile, sighed with relief. He had been dreading this conversation with Icky all week, imagining that his brother-in-law would be demoralized by such a small pay adjustment given that he was taking on a tremendous increase in responsibilities. And to make matters worse, when Herta found out, he'd have some explaining to do, as she would not like learning about how her husband let the boss be unfair to her brother—which she was sure to hear about, as she was the one to host a wedding shower for Millie and him.

But the situation didn't work out like that at all.

The guy just got married! Roy reminded himself. New wife, new job, new pay . . . admittedly small, but any increase over the fifteen dollars a week he was earning before they were married would be a help. He wouldn't ruin their joy with unnecessary truth, not now anyway.

11

Moving Up

WHILE MILLIE HADN'T DREAMED her married life would begin in the same bedroom she grew up in, both Icky and she were grateful for her parents' offer to take them in.

"At least there's plenty of room for the car!" he told Millie when she apologized for the small quarters they'd be sharing. "I can park along the alley behind the shed, and won't waken anyone when I fire it up to go to work." And because his in-laws didn't own a vehicle, the car wasn't in anyone else's space.

As for Gordon, he was delighted for opportunities to help Icky work on the Marquette. Over the preceding few months, they'd become fast friends, even though neither of them would allow the other to claim being the better swimmer.

"I was trying to impress your sister," Icky said, "so I'm sure I won that race."

"You hadn't even seen her yet!" Gordon asserted. "And I introduced you two, so I'm taking credit!"

"Not a chance! She came over when she saw what a great athlete I am!" Icky retorted.

And so it went, the two of them jibing one another like brothers.

For her part, Millie continued to help Ma around the house, just as always, happily adding Icky's laundry to her chores. Happily at first, anyway.

"Millie!" Icky called out as soon as he slammed the car door.

"Millie!" he shouted again.

She was in the side yard, dropping an armload of dried laundry into a wicker basket, and tossing a handful of wooden clothespins on top. The day was unseasonably warm, so she'd taken a load of clothes outdoors to dry on the line. "I'm out here!" she called back. "The whole neighborhood can hear you!"

"Let 'em hear!" he continued. "I got a raise!"

"What?" Millie exclaimed.

"Yeah!" Icky shouted again, this time running to grab her up in his arms, and spin her around next to him. "A change in status from single to married is the reason for part of the increase."

"So, you got a raise because of me?" she inquired as her toes slid to the ground.

"A little raise, yes," he clarified, kissing her cheek playfully. "You're tiny, the raise is tiny. But together, both are huge."

"So, tiny as it is, this is really *my* raise," she pressed him cheerfully.

"It's our raise, *ours*," Icky insisted. "*We* are going to put it into the bank—*together*."

She cocked her head to the left and narrowed her eyes as she paused to consider whether or not he was really including her. "Okay, as long as *the two of us* are making this decision."

"We are," he said, spinning her around again and again. "We are! We are! We are!

"And I've been promoted to baker," he added. He had been building up to his big news. "Starting Sunday night."

"Oh, Icky!"

"I made it! I'm a real baker!"

"Congratulations!" she said, and then teased gleefully, "Now go bake fresh rolls for dinner. We're all starved."

"I've got a better idea," he said, nodding toward their room in the house.

"Not in the middle of the day!" she shrieked with laughter as her eyes met his twinkle.

It was enough that she understood what he was thinking. Oh, he loved this little woman!

"I MADE AN EXTRA bowl of popcorn for the boys," Millie told her mother. "Some big fight is on the radio tonight."

"A fight again," Ma said, disgruntled.

"Icky said it's between a German fella, Max Schmeling, and some guy out of Detroit, who's calling himself Joe Louis," she reported.

"I don't deny 'em their time together, 'specially when they're right here in front of our own radio," Ma said, "but fightin' is hardly a sport."

"Sometimes, women like to listen to the fights, too," Millie suggested. "I thought I might sit in."

"Augh! Why'd ya' want t' hear such a thing?"

"Icky was an amateur boxer in a club at St. Bonaventure College before we met," she answered. "And he said more goes on outside the ring than inside."

"Aye, that Hitler says Schmeling's victories show superiority o' th' German race. I heard th' nonsense," Ma countered.

"No one here is spouting those lies," Millie defended Icky.

"Augh, no, I'd never expect such a sorry thing out o' Icky—or any o' th' Hauts!" Ma assured her.

"Of course not," Millie agreed.

"Even so, there'll be plenty o' noise an' hittin' an' bleedin' t'night," Ma held firm. "I'll be in th' kitchen with m' darnin'. Ya' can join me when ya've had enough of th' boys an' your dad yellin' at th' radio."

ICKY SHOWED UP FOR his new job an hour early Sunday evening, so he could sort through the supply of baker's uniforms in the locker room to find one that fit. For as long as he'd been employed full-time at Bolles, he had imagined what it would feel like to work in one of the shirts with the two rows of knotted cloth buttons. He yearned to feel the pressed cotton next to his skin instead of just the thin white t-shirt that was the uniform of the laborers and apprentices. Now, though, when everyone saw him, they'd immediately know: he'd made it to the bigtime! He was a baker!

He saw a half dozen sizes of baker's shirts lined up as if they were standing at attention, and pulled out a few. One day he'd rise to senior baker, and then he'd pick out one of the long-sleeved chef coats. It was something to aspire to, he promised himself with a small smile. Today, he was eager to wear one with short sleeves.

A nicely starched boxy shirt seemed to be about his size, so he put it on, and stored his white t-shirt in an empty locker. He stared at himself in the mirror, ostensibly to see that he buttoned the double rows correctly. But in truth, he wanted a moment alone to capture his arrival to this moment, and hold it in his memory.

This is it, he said to the image looking back at him. Yesterday, I was an apprentice. Today . . . he felt his heart racing. He would step through this portal only once in his life. Standing tall, he approached the locker room exit, and placed the palm of his right hand firmly on the door's brass cover plate. He took a deep breath, and thrust it open—not forcibly, but commandingly. Each of the four steps down the short hall represented one of his four years of full-time apprenticeship: taking orders and measuring and hauling and pouring—which he endured.

"Endured" wasn't the right word, he corrected himself. He had persisted, to be sure, but he hadn't suffered. No, he had eagerly soaked up every bit of his work, learning and absorbing what it would take to be promoted to baker.

"Finally," he said out loud, "I'm here." And he turned to the right, and stepped onto the bakery floor he knew so well.

He paused for a moment to hold onto his experience, for although no one else knew what a momentous occasion it was, he did. He had crossed a threshold.

"Aren't you a little ahead of yourself?" asked the shift foreman. He was accustomed to seeing Icky arrive at four o'clock on Monday mornings, not on Sunday just before eight.

"I'm reassigned to work with Shots," Icky told him.

"Okay, yeah." He noticed, then, that Icky was in a baker's shirt instead of the t-shirt of an apprentice. "You're taking over his job in a few."

"Right!" Icky said with energy.

"Shots will be in on the hour," the foreman told him. "You should expect him to move you around multiple stations, learning the scope."

"Makes sense," Icky said.

"You need to pick up the ins-and-outs of this job pretty quick, 'cause on this shift," he jabbed his index finger sharply toward the floor to emphasize the hour, "you got no one else around to help. Got it?"

"Got it."

The foreman looked Icky over speculatively, one side of his mouth puckered into his cheek.

"Don't know what Mr. Bolles sees in such a young guy," he said, seemingly just to himself, but without considering how the remark might erode Icky's self-confidence.

"But the boss must think you got what it takes," he shrugged. "Know what I mean?"

"I expect I do—have what it takes, that is," Icky answered. He'd heard about this supervisor from Roy. The guy wasn't a bad sort to work for, as long as a man didn't need to be watched.

Problems drove the guy nuts though, Roy had warned, "so, don't give him any."

"Okay, that's it. Just go over that way," the foreman gestured, "where Shots works. Like I said, he'll be here in a few."

While Icky waited, he looked over the baker's production area. As an apprentice, he'd operated large equipment, and toted heavy ingredients. He'd hauled and dumped flour into large commercial mixers, slowly, slowly, so as to avoid creating a cloud of dry powder. Breathing in some amount couldn't be helped, of course, and he knew guys with a few years of tenure who wheezed with baker's cough. But he'd avoided it, so far, anyway.

Now, though, he surveyed the baker's tools: dough dividers, multiple-loaf pans, cutting tools, thermometers, thirty-inch bowls, and even the new slicer. He thought of Pa's tool chest and all of its implements. Ma had her tool drawer, too.

"You're on time, and ready to go. Good start," said Shots, startling Icky. "I see you looking over the equipment. Let's get going."

Shots gave him a brief overview. "First thing you got to learn is where everything is," he said. "So, here we got a rack of pans that just came out of the sanitary kitchen. Your first job is to put 'em away, all organized, 'cause later on, when we need to move fast, we can't be taking time to sort out a mess. We need to just grab the ones we want without dropping a stack on the floor.

"'Cause if we did that," he continued, looking Icky straight in the face, "we'd have to send the whole lot of 'em back to sanitary to be washed and steamed again—and in the middle of a production run? Let's just say you wouldn't do that more than once, and still keep your job. We'd lose raised dough in the wait time."

Shots thought he made his point.

Icky remembered working in the sanitary kitchen when he was just a laborer. The pans were hot, so he understood why they were piled up in a mess. Now he was on the other end of the job, and rued not taking a minute back then to stack them more carefully.

"So, go get started at setting up. End of lesson."

Icky spent the first part of his shift organizing pans from the preceding day's work. Then, Shots had him stand back to observe the baking process.

"When we're running soft-and-white, these ovens are set at three hundred fifty to three hundred eighty degrees, and they put out loaves every twenty-eight minutes," he said. "Your next job is to check the bread coming through those rotations, and make sure each row is browning up right."

"What's the check?" Icky asked.

"Just grab up a couple loaves, and tap on 'em while they're still warm. You want to hear if they're done inside.

"You don't have to wait too long with the soft-and-white: they're baked at a lower temperature than the rustic loaves. Anyway, soft-and-whites oughta' sound hollow," he instructed as he motioned for Icky to tap and listen.

"Like that," he showed him. "To check for doneness, listen to your bread."

Icky made a mental note of Shot's instruction: "Listen to your bread."

"And the bottoms," Shots continued as he flipped a loaf over, "oughta' feel smooth. Run your hand over it."

Icky skimmed the loaf lightly with his fingertips.

"Even if the crust is brown, the inside might not be baked," Shots told him. "Brown crust can come from the amount of sugar in the brew—or maybe the humidity in the oven. Color can be deceiving.

"But if these bottoms aren't smooth, the loaves could be under-baked, and that'll make an awful mess when they're run through the slicer. We can't sell 'em like that. They just go to the trash barrel over there, and Mr. Bolles trucks 'em out to Crosby Farm so his niece can feed 'em to her hogs."

"Expensive hog feed!" Icky said with surprise.

"Yeah, we tried to grind the messed-up soft-and-white so we could re-process the crumb as flour, but you don't get good bread product out of it."

"I didn't know bread crumbs could be ground up and re-baked in new loaves," Icky said.

"Works better with the rustic bread. People don't expect each one of those to come out exactly the same.

"The point is that nothing gets wasted," Shots continued. "That's one of the things you got to learn if you're going to be a baker."

Icky continued to make mental notes as Shots and he thunked loaves. His parents would not allow wastefulness either—because of the Depression, of course, but even more because frugality was characteristically German. Squandering a resource was unthinkable.

"When we get to the rustic breads you'll be listening for a cracking sound," Shots continued.

"Cracking?" Icky repeated.

"Rustics are wet doughs, baked at four hundred fifty to five hundred degrees," Shots said. "The point of intense heat is to drive off excess moisture in the dough, and concentrate the flavor from the grain.

"When you take 'em out, let 'em cool for ten or fifteen minutes, and listen for the crusts to crack. Then you know the lot of them was baked through.

"But that's for later, if you're still here at the end of the week. Tonight, keep watching what comes off the soft-and-white rotations," he said. "If they're not right, say something, so we can make adjustments."

"Adjustments to . . .?" Icky said hesitantly. He heard the "if you're still here" comment, and wanted to show he was paying attention.

"Time and temperature: that's all you got to work with—so far, anyway."

"Well, that, and humidity when you're working rustics," Shots corrected himself. "When we're baking those loaves, the oven is set to generate steam during the first half of the bake. Halfway through, though, the loaves need dry heat to develop that crisp crust Bolles is known for."

"How do you know if the oven didn't steam up like it should?" Icky asked. "I mean, what happens to the bread?"

"Without steam, the bottom crust will be thick and hard," Shots explained. "Then the yeast in the dough falls—which means the bottom of the loaf flattens out.

"With steam in the first half of the bake, the loaves firm up in the oven. Then, dry heat finishes 'em."

Shots could see that Icky was trying to memorize details.

"It's not that hard to understand," he insisted. "You know what good rustic looks like: the crusts are thin, crisp and shiny. Just listen for the cracking sound."

Icky prayed for everything to go smoothly with the rotations. All he could think of was Mr. Bolles's insistence that the ovens stay on schedule. "Time is money!" the boss said so often Icky repeated it in his sleep.

As to time and temperature—and also humidity with the rustic breads, Icky wasn't sure which adjustments to make, or how to figure them out. He had so much to learn!

By 5 a.m., he felt that he had earned every penny of his increase. He headed back to the locker room, and grabbed his t-shirt. He could change back into it, but he wanted to drive home in the new baker's shirt so he could show Millie how he looked in it.

Just as he was heading out to the parking lot, though, Roy caught up with him. The early morning shift Icky used to work was rolling along fine, so his brother-in-law could step aside for a minute.

"How'd you do?" Roy asked, trying to sound casual. He was still feeling guilty about not securing the higher pay he thought Icky deserved with his promotion.

"Okay, I think," he said. "Ask Shots."

"*You* ask him," Roy advised. "You're not an apprentice any more. No one expects you to need someone to look over your shoulder."

"Thanks," Icky said. "I wouldn't have thought to do that."

"Nope, nope, nope. No problem, none at all. And remember, if there's anything I can do . . . You know that I can't interfere," he corrected himself, as violating hierarchy, and slipping past proper channels would interrupt the company's order and structure. "But we're family, so I'm here for you."

"I know it," Icky said, gratefully. "G'night . . . or good morning. Whatever it is."

He headed out the door and walked over the crunchy gravel toward his car, shivering in the morning chill. *A week ago, I was just starting my shift at this hour,* he noted. *Now, my shift is ending, and I'm exhausted and full of energy at the same time.*

All the way back to Millie, he imagined telling her about his new skill: listening to bread. *White loaves sound hollow when thunked; rustic crusts crack and snap as they cool,* he repeated to himself.

He could see her smile. *Maybe she'll fry eggs for me for breakfast,* he hoped. After that, he'd have to decide the best time to get some sleep: morning or afternoon. Third shift was a crazy adjustment.

12

A Storm Brewin'

ICKY QUIETLY CLIMBED THE back steps of his in-laws' porch, and slipped into the house. Pa and the boys would be up soon, and he didn't want to rob them of their last few minutes of sleep. But as he hadn't lived with the Huffs long enough to know which floorboards squeaked, he couldn't navigate without making noise.

"Heard you coming in," Millie whispered when he shut the door to their little room. She propped her head up on one elbow. "How'd it go?"

"Swell!" he said. "Well, not super swell yet. I only stacked baking pans, and tested loaves of white bread for doneness. But I'm a baker! A hundred percent!"

"And you look the part, too," she said approvingly. "But you'd better crawl in here, and catch a few winks before the rest of the family is up."

Icky slept until noon, more worn out than he expected from his first day on the new job.

"We made lunch," Millie said as she nudged him awake. "How about coming out to eat."

"You don't have to call me twice," he said, kissing her hello.

As he sat down at the kitchen table, he handed her the white baker's shirt.

"Do you think there's time to launder this before I go back to work this evening?" he asked. "It's the only one my size, so far." He knew he could take another one from the locker room, but he didn't think he saw any that would fit as well. "And my white pants are in a heap at the end of the bed."

"Your other pair," because she knew Icky had two pairs of white baker's pants, "is in the closet. I already found the ones you wore last night, and they're drying on the line outside."

She hadn't realized she'd be the one to launder the baker's shirt since it came from Bolles. Taking it from him, she added, "I'll have to wash this by hand because all the white laundry is done, but that's okay. You just sit down and eat."

After she laundered the shirt, she rolled it in towels to remove most of the rinse water. She was glad it wouldn't dry too fast in the crisp late winter air, as she wanted the cotton to retain a bit of moisture so it would press up nicely.

While Millie finished working on his shirt, Icky tinkered with the car. The engine was hesitating in the cold, especially when he tried to start it up. Gordon said it probably had something to do with the spark plugs.

"You don't look like a baker now," Gordon observed as he came in from work. Icky's head was next to the engine, and dirty splotches of grease marked his face.

"Hey, Gord," he greeted him. "I'm following your advice on those plugs."

"How's it going?"

"I cleaned 'em up, but she still sputters."

"The problem's over here," Gordon pointed.

"What?"

"See that? It needs to be tightened."

"Hand me the wrench," Icky ordered, as if he knew what he was doing.

Gordon did as ordered for the moment. But as he watched Icky carefully turn the wrench, slowly, slowly, he couldn't tolerate his brother-in-law's pedantic pace.

"Just torque it down," he commanded. "Put some elbow grease into it."

"Works just as well this way," Icky contended. "And I won't ruin it."

"You're not going to ruin it. It's metal, not dough. Give it some of that muscle you're always bragging about," Gordon argued.

"Like you could haul your weight in flour every day," Icky tossed back.

"You two are at one another again?" Millie noticed as she approached them. "Dinner's ready."

They washed up quickly, and joined everyone else at the table. Icky ate a small meal, and Millie packed the rest for him to take to work for his midnight break. "Your shirt is ready, too," she said.

"Thanks!" he replied gratefully.

But when he put it on, he was not happy.

"It's all soft," Icky objected. "Like a dress shirt."

"Like what?"

"Like something I'd wear on a date with you."

"So?" she said as she geared up a defense. Didn't I spend a good part of this afternoon heating water, and then washing and rinsing and drying and ironing this special new shirt—because you didn't give it to me before all the rest of the laundry was done? Today is Monday, after all!

But she would not point out to him the inconvenience he had caused, nor give him details about what it meant to launder an item by hand—because, of course, she should not have to!

"So," he continued, rubbing the neck of the shirt between his finger and thumb, and reasoning then that she'd probably never seen a baker's shirt, "it's supposed to be starched. It's supposed to look professional."

Professional, Millie absorbed his instruction. I can give you "professional."

"Fine!" she said, smiling through clenched teeth as a tense, brittle energy formed around her.

"Are we okay?" Icky said as he turned to the mirror to button up.

"How could we not be?" she answered. But his back was turned, so he didn't notice that the tone of her voice did not match the look on her face. "I'll put your lunch by the back door," she ended the conversation, and briskly left their bedroom.

Ma could almost hear them through the door.

"Uh-oh," she said quietly to Pa. "There's a storm brewin' in the newlyweds' room."

"I hear it," he told her. "Keep it to yourself. And pray for Icky. He's going to need it."

A few minutes later, they heard the Marquette cough a little and then fire up as Icky left for work. Millie watched him pull away as she tromped to the cold storage bin next to the back door. She needed two potatoes, preferably the ones that were the least attractive, as they were used for making starch. She washed and grated them into small bits, covered it all with water, and set the bowl at the back of the table for the night.

As she was about to leave the kitchen, she noticed Icky's lunch pail. He'd forgotten it, so she took the food out, and put it into the ice box. He could have it for his noonday meal on Tuesday.

Finally, she joined her parents in the living room, and sat down with a book.

"Icky's off t' work his second day, or rather, second night, as a baker, then," Ma said, trying to sound congenial.

"Mm-hmm," Millie answered, intentionally vague.

Her mother would change the subject. "Did ya' see in th' newspaper that both Hitler and Mussolini are helpin' that dictator Franco in th' Spanish Civil War?"

"Governments are messed up all over the world," said Pa. "They ought to keep out of one another's business."

No one responded to Pa's assertions—not that they disagreed. Or even if they agreed. It was just best to let Pa tell everybody how to think, and leave it at that.

"Looks like spring is on its way," her mother attempted light conversation again.

"Mm-hmm," Millie answered. "Cold at night though." She wouldn't share her husband's displeasure over her wifely skills. No, she'd handle his little demand all by herself.

When Icky arrived home the next morning, he hung his soiled baker's shirt on the back of a chair, just as Millie asked, so she could launder and starch it when she got up. She hadn't slept much, tortured with the memory of his response to her first efforts in making him look professional. She'd get it right this time, though. She'd be sure of that!

He must have been busy last night, she observed as she dipped the soiled shirt and baker's pants into a bucket of hot sudsy water. Up and down, up and down, up and down. She checked the collar and underarms for yellow sweat, just as she had done the afternoon before. Still there. Up and down, up and down, again and again.

She added a little bleach, and dipped the shirt a few more times.

"Finally!" she said after a final inspection. Then she repeated the procedure with his pants.

She'd let them all sit in the bucket for a few minutes while she finished preparing the starch she started brewing the night before. It must be strong enough by now, she noted as she separated the liquid from the top of the bowl. She poured it into a pan, and threw a log into the embers below.

While the potato water was heating up, she took the grated remains to Ma's garden, and added them to the compost pile. When she returned to the kitchen, the pan was just beginning to boil, so she stirred it until it was reduced by half.

Icky wants starch, she said to herself, and Icky's going to get starch.

She poured the hot liquid onto the clean shirt and pants, and twirled them all around to be sure every fiber was coated. Then she squeezed the clothes out, and rolled them in towels to remove most of the liquid. Finally, she hung each of them over hangers. The temperature outside was too cold for the shirt to dry well, especially the collar, so she hooked the clothes hangers over the back of a kitchen chair, and positioned it close to a heat register. Good and stiff, she quietly instructed.

While the shirt and pants dried, she added a tablespoon of cornstarch to two cups of water in a glass bottle, and shook it forcefully until it was fully blended. She thought the water looked like it could absorb a bit more cornstarch, so she added another half spoonful, and shook it again.

That ought to do it, she decided as she inserted a cork sprinkler cap into the top of the bottle.

By mid-afternoon, the clothes were almost dry, so Millie carefully laid the shirt out on the ironing board. First, she pressed the front and back. Icky wants more starch, she reminded herself as she sprinkled on a bit of cornstarch-saturated water. Yes, this shirt will be just what he ordered.

His pants were another matter. They were so stiff that they stood up on their own, like stove pipes. She ironed creases into them, and laid them out on the small bed they shared.

The tasks completed, she decided to take a brisk walk, maybe for an hour or so. Icky could pack his own midnight meal. That way, she told herself, he won't forget to take it with him.

With each step she imagined Icky rethinking how he ought to show appreciation for her contributions to his new role as a professional baker. He could just stew on that one for a while. Yes, she'd made sure he could stew all night in that doubly starched shirt and stiffly pressed pants. Meanwhile, she planned to sleep like a baby.

ICKY'S NEXT NIGHT AS a baker focused on shaping and proofing the soft-and-white dough, as he'd learned during training. This time, though, he prepared several dozen loaf pans for baking. Then he lined them up for the rotating ovens . . . and twenty-eight minutes later, after the apprentices removed them, he inspected and thunked a few.

"Make sure you meet your production goals, and the rest of the week will take care of itself," Shots told him.

Icky wished it were that easy. He watched his predecessor monitor the entire baking process, and tried to understand what was going on as he adjusted measurements in Bolles's standard recipes for the instruction cards posted next to the mixers.

How did he know when a modification was needed?

"Weather plays a role sometimes," Shots said. "When there's a lot of humidity—or lack of it— the yeast acts differently. We talked about that the other night."

As Shots continued to explain, Icky was distracted by the stiffness of his shirt collar; it was rubbing his neck raw. And his trousers were so rigid that he could hear the pantlegs go Whap! Whap! Whap! as he pounded around the production area. Shots didn't say anything about it, 'though he did look over his shoulder at the noise, and give Icky a strange glance.

After their meal break, Shots assigned Icky to running baked loaves through the slicer. It was the first time Icky saw the Rohwedder function in production, and he was thankful that he'd been on the team to install and test it.

Shots said that eventually Icky would have to supervise someone else to run that equipment.

"If soft-and-white orders keep going up, that is," he added. "But the boss wants to see a steady increase in sales before he assigns a man full-time to his Rohwedder."

"What else do you think I'm missing?" Icky asked. He remembered Roy's advice about seeking feedback.

"Just pay attention to what the dough is doing. Amend the formula when you got to."

"Amend?"

"You saw me. Amend it!"

That's all he ever says, Icky complained to himself: "Just do as I do." Or, "Watch and learn." Or, "Get in there and figure it out."

He surmised that Shots felt he'd given all the information that was necessary. The rest was learned by experience.

"But how do I amend it?" Icky persisted during Shots's last night on the job.

"Look," he acquiesced. "You got only four ingredients: flour, salt, and sugar to feed that yeast. Plus water. And heat. And humidity."

He paused, exasperated by the look on Icky's face. He was sure the guy knew all this, but he'd repeat it anyway.

"Yeast is alive, so it's gonna' change on you. Either it'll rise too quick or not quick enough, depending on the amount of sugar. Or maybe the amount of salt, 'cause salt effects the pace of the rise—all of which can mean no holes in the bread when it's baked. You can tell if there's no holes in the soft-and-white when you thunk it."

Icky nodded: listen to your bread, he told himself.

"Then look at the bottoms, like I told you the first night."

Check the bottom crust, Icky remembered that one.

"What else?" he asked.

"If the soft-and-white loaves don't sound hollow or if the bottoms aren't smooth, change the formula on the instruction card, and tell the foreman so he can adjust the brew in the next batch," he concluded his summary.

"Then, the rustic bread cracks when it cools. Remember that?"

"Got it," Icky acknowledged.

"The crust should be thin and crisp, with some pliability to it," Shots reminded him. "Remember to increase the steam in the oven during the first half of the bake if the crust comes out thick and hard."

"Yep, I remember," Icky said, pinching his lips.

"And shiny crumb is a sign of good bread: look for that before even smelling or tasting it. That's it. The rest you learn by doing."

Icky frowned.

"Look, I can't knead your brain anymore," Shots said, comparing Icky's self-doubt to a bowl of dough. "If you overwork this job—if you overthink it instead of just feeling your way through the problems, 'cause you're gonna' have 'em, every shift you're gonna' have 'em—well, then you will screw up.

"But you'll catch on soon enough," Shots assured him. "Your job is to make sure the whole baking process goes right."

He could see Icky wasn't satisfied. Too bad.

"That's all," he ended the conversation. "Shift's over. I'm retired."

"Yeah, that's all," Icky said to himself as he drove home. "Just don't screw up."

"YOU READY TO TAKE over?" the foreman asked Icky when he arrived the following Sunday night.

"Ready to give it my best effort," Icky said with as much confidence as he could muster.

"Here's the production schedule then," he said, handing over the orders for each of the stores that were expecting product in a few hours.

Icky tallied the number of each type of bread they needed to bake, so that all of Bolles's customers received their shipments. Then he double-checked his numbers.

"Okay," he said to himself. "Got it."

All he had to do now was send product orders to the foreman, who would assign third-shift apprentices to start hauling flour and salt. Icky could focus on monitoring the dough as it baked, and then make recommendations to amend the yeast brew.

His heart pounded, but once the first two rotations came through the oven in good shape, he started feeling a bit better.

Still, he thunked more loaves than he probably needed to that night. "I've got to be sure," . . . and for an instant he heard Gordon's voice saying "abso-damned-lutely sure."

He smiled.

He could be sure of family even if he couldn't be sure of his new role as a baker. I've got family to back me, so if I screw up, if I ever have to get another job as a baker—*because I am a baker!*—I could do it. Even in this depressed economy, whatever happens, Millie and I will make it.

13

Negotiations

LIFE HAPPENED SO QUICKLY! A year after Icky and Millie were married, she gave birth to a beautiful baby girl. But as much as they both loved bringing up their daughter among adoring grandparents, Mary Lou was keeping everyone up through the middle of the night. The three of them needed to find a place of their own.

Icky checked rental advertisements in the weekend edition of *The Olean Times Herald*, and located a second-floor apartment on Thirteenth Street that he thought they could afford.

"But second floor?" Millie objected.

"Second floor is less expensive," he explained.

But she didn't think he understood what he was asking. She was the one, after all, who would be hauling heavy, wet laundry down the stairs to the clothesline in the back yard, not to mention carrying it all back up those same stairs a couple of hours later after it dried.

"Every day!" she emphasized. "Babies use a lot of diapers! And I can't leave her up there while I hang it all up on the line, so I'll need to tote her with me.

"And the groceries, too. I'll have to carry those heavy bags up all those the stairs—and again, with our daughter in a basket over my other arm. And..."

"And it's not for long. And I can help you."

"You're sleeping half the day," she disagreed, as Icky was still working the night shift. He had no clue how much work was involved in caring for their baby. While they were living with her parents, everyone—especially her mother—was always stepping in to help. Living on their own was going to be very different. "Besides," Millie continued, "second floor units are hot in the summer. The baby is not going to like it. She'll . . . "

"She'll like it better than sleeping in a box right next to our bed," he interrupted. "And the rest of your family will like a good night's rest, too. I'd bet on it."

He didn't think it would be wise to point out how much privacy they'd lost since Mary Lou was born. Before then, the family respected Icky and Millie's space as their own. It was treated as if it was separate from the rest of the house. Off limits.

But now, . . . well, now, no one hesitated. Why, the room was no longer theirs at all; it was the baby's nursery.

And either the baby was awake: "Good morning, Angel!" Millie's mother would say as she entered without knocking.

Or she whined a bit because her diapers needed to be changed: "Aye, we can take care o' that!" Ma would bustle as she carried the baby off.

Or she was crying: "Granny always knows what our Little Treasure needs," she soothed as she lifted her first-born grandchild into her arms, and walked her around.

Or her cooing attracted her grandmother's attention: "We'll never get too much o' that, will we now!"

Or the baby was so worn out from all the attention she was receiving that she was cranky, and wanted to nap: "Augh, Poor Pet, let's give your mother a wee rest while we rock ya' t' sleep with an Irish lullaby, shall we?"

Of course, there was no arguing, for since she'd reared four children of her own, Millie's mother understood when it was time to feed a baby, change her, or lull her to sleep. And didn't Mary Lou smile every time her grandma appeared? Of course, she did! For wasn't she named for her, both of them going by the name "Mary"? Why, anyone could see how Grandma's spirit was reflected in the child!

But the abundant love given during the day meant Mary Lou wasn't sleepy at night, so Millie was often up late, trying to quiet her. If the baby didn't settle down when she was walked up and down the hallway, Millie would pace around the back porch, and then tread out into the yard. And if the child's little eyes still twinkled wide open at the night stars, Millie would take a little jaunt up the block . . . and then down the block: whatever it took just to get her calmed down for the night.

"You know what it's like," Icky wanted to remind her, but he thought better of it, and instead promised, "As soon as we can afford a first-floor apartment, we'll take it. Until then, this one is all we can do. Okay?"

She knew he was trying to provide as best he could for them, so the next week they moved into the Thirteenth Street second-floor duplex.

WHEN ICKY AND MILLIE lived with her parents, the two of them contributed to the family food budget. Of course, Ma Huff decided what to serve, just as she always had, and true to her Irish roots, most of the meals were planned around boiled potatoes, and boiled cabbage, and boiled turnips, and any other boiled vegetables from her garden, plus a small portion of "mate" as she pronounced the inexpensive cut of beef she prepared, also boiled.

But Icky grew up eating hearty German dishes: Sauerbraten, pork with sauerkraut, buttered spaetzli and dumplings. Baked goods were plentiful, too. Now, the only time he got them was on weekends when Millie and he joined his family for Sunday dinner. Anyone could taste how good his mother's cooking was! So, since they moved into their own apartment, wouldn't his wife want to prepare those dishes?

But, no. Millie boiled meals just as her own mother did.

The question was how he could suggest that she try preparing meals in the German tradition without having a row with her.

"You're lucky," he complained to Roy, "Herta cooks like Ma. But Millie didn't learn that way."

"Women can be very touchy about their cooking skills," Roy cautioned.

"But her cooking is . . . so plain," Icky explained, frowning.

"Well, if you put it to her like that," Roy said, "you're asking for trouble."

"Or worse," Icky said, realizing how his preferences would sound to Millie. He remembered what happened when he asked her to starch his baker's shirt.

But what could he do? At work he just gave instructions to the apprentices, told the foreman about changes needed in the yeast brew, and made out orders for maintenance staff. Couldn't he have a simple, direct conversation with Millie, and just tell her what he wanted?

No, probably not on this topic. He'd have to dance around it. He might talk about good old-fashioned home cooking such as the meals his mother prepared on Sundays. Or suggest one dish. He wasn't sure that would work, but maybe he'd take his chances.

"Ma made great potato pancakes last Sunday," he recalled one evening as he gently picked his way toward the front line of his campaign. "Why don't you ask her to teach you how?"

"What's wrong with my potatoes?" Millie said.

"Nothing's wrong with them. They're just . . . boiled."

Of course, they were boiled, she thought to herself. That was the way potatoes were supposed to be prepared. Everyone knew that.

When he didn't say anything else, she smelled a problem, and dug in with her own questions.

"What would you do with them, other than boil them?"

"I don't know, exactly. But we've had Ma's potato pancakes, and . . . I thought you liked them."

"And you don't like boiled?" she asked again. Now the campaign was turned.

"Yes. Of course. You made them, so of course I like them. But maybe there are other ways to make them, too. . . . Like potato pancakes."

She could see that he was struggling. Part of her wanted to appreciate how hard he was working to be nice; the other part wanted to give him a piece of her mind!

Fortunately, her better side prevailed.

"I could ask her," Millie said. "Maybe next Sunday."

"That would be great," Icky said, trying not to sound too enthusiastic. He really, really wanted her to learn to cook like his mother.

PA AND MA HAUT drove their black Pontiac only twice a week: once to attend church, and the other to buy groceries. Shopping might require stops at more than one purveyor: "the butcher, the baker, the candlestick maker," Pa Haut repeated jovially with a gentle wink toward Ma. They usually finished their chores in time to be home by noon, as neither of them saw any reason to cruise aimlessly around town, or waste valuable time browsing in stores, and making nuisances of themselves.

On Sundays, they drove themselves twelve blocks to church for morning worship services. They left an hour early, and parked near the front door so they could watch other members of the congregation begin to arrive. Then they'd join everyone in the sanctuary, and quietly seat themselves. No one ever dared to sit in their pew, especially since Pa was losing his hearing. He needed to be close enough to hear the sermon, but not so close that he was intruding on the altar. Remembering that Peter and James asked if they could sit at Jesus' right hand, they humbly chose seats further back!

After worship, the family gathered for dinner at their house. Ma Haut always slid a roast into a slow oven before they left for church. Its heavy aroma filled the kitchen with deliciousness that made everyone hungry.

"Pork and plum! Yum!" Icky said as soon as Millie, Mary Lou, and he came in the back door. "I've been thinking about your pork roast all week!"

He knew that the plums came from a gorgeous little tree in the back yard. Ma always said that when the fruit was ripe, it looked like a purple waterfall, and she took great pride in harvesting and canning it.

"Pa asked for it, since the plums are in season," she said. In fact, Pa could eat pork every day. "I make what he likes. After all, he's still a working man, too, you know."

Millie heard their conversation with new ears though: not merely as Icky's appreciation for a dinner invitation, but as genuine yearning for his mother's cooking.

Pa put a leaf in the kitchen table, and extra chairs were dragged in from the sitting room as everyone else took their places. Ma brought the roast in, and set it before Pa at the head of the table as she introduced her concerns from the week's newspaper.

"Did you read *The Olean Times Herald* this week?" she asked as she scooped vegetables onto her plate, and passed the bread basket. World news was at the top of her line-up.

"Which story are you talking about?" Roy asked.

"Several. The ones about that Adolph Hitler." She was chilled by those articles.

"He's already occupying Austria," she continued, "and at a conference in Munich last week, he bullied France and England into letting him take part of Czechoslovakia!"

"He won't stop there," Pa Haut added. "He'll bulldoze the whole thing."

"And then what?" asked Icky, looking for his parents' perspectives on the unrest in Europe. They'd both grown up in the Old Country, and certainly would have a feel for what this Hitler noise was about.

"Depends on who else gets involved," Ma said.

"Won't be this country," Pa asserted. "Americans had enough killing in the last war."

Roy agreed. "Won't be us," he said. "We got enough to worry about on this side of the Atlantic."

"Right you are! The economy can't take it either," Pa said. Like most folks, he believed that since the Great War, no nation would battle and gas the enemy again. Not ever. No, the world had learned its lesson.

"Well, we'll see," said Ma, pursing her lips. She worried that her sons— who were about the age to be drafted—might be victim to this evil dictator's war. Unlike Roy or Pa, she didn't have much faith in the goodness or the wisdom of humankind. Even if she wanted to write a letter telling the President to stay out it, though, she didn't feel she had the right to make him hear her. She probably should have applied for American citizenship when Pa did, but she was busy raising the children. She sighed, for there was nothing to say about it now.

The meal ended, and everyone sat back in their chairs, stupefied over the richness of the meal. But before another topic was introduced, Millie thought she might ask a question of her own. The time seemed right.

"I'd like to know," she directed her eyes toward her mother-in-law, "how you make your potato pancakes. Icky has been asking me for them."

Ma Haut brightened. How nice to hear that her son spoke well of her cooking to his wife. She'd be glad to share her recipe!

"It's easy!" she said. "You just rinse the potato after you grate it, and then squeeze out all the moisture, so it gets good and dry. Then add eggs, milk, flour, and seasonings, and fry little mounds in a hot skillet. That's it!"

What did she mean by "squeeze"? Did she mean to wring the grated potato out with a towel? Or just squeeze it gently in her hands?

Millie hoped for precise instructions, such as the recipes in her *Fannie Farmer Cookbook*. It said that the modern housewife could count on consistent results every time she prepared a meal for her husband, if only she would study the recipes, follow the book's directions, and use measuring cups and measuring spoons.

"How many eggs and how much milk?" she asked, trying to pin down the details.

"Depends on the number of potatoes," said Ma Haut. She thought that was obvious, but didn't want to criticize. Especially not a daughter-in-law, and more: not in front of the whole family. "You know: to make it moist enough."

"Okay," Millie paused. It seemed that Ma Haut was going to be no more precise than her own mother, who would say something like, "Use an amount the size of a chicken egg"—which relied, of course, on the age and type of chicken.

Since Icky asked for these darned potato pancakes, though, Millie was determined to master them.

"How many potatoes?" she asked uncertainly.

"Depends on how many people are coming to dinner." What more could Ma say?

Millie nodded and paused a moment to consider whether or not to pursue this inquiry one more time.

"So, last Sunday, then, how many potatoes?" she ventured. She didn't want to be difficult, but the recipe was just too imprecise.

"About one potato for each person," Ma Haut answered, trying to give more detail then. "As for the rest, you just put in enough until it looks right."

Millie realized that she'd pushed as far as she ought.

"That sounds easy enough," she said pleasantly as she lied through her teeth, all the while feeling guilty; she'd been sitting in a church pew only a couple of hours before. "Maybe I can watch you do it some time."

"That would be fine," said Ma Haut, thankful for the interrogation to be over. "Extra hands in the kitchen we can use!"

Icky was relieved, too. He felt that he had been the instigator of Millie's inquisition, and on some level—he wasn't sure what it was or why it was happening—he felt tension in her little smile. He wouldn't dare intervene.

14

Unexpected Decisions

WHEN ICKY AND MILLIE moved into their apartment, they brought with them one outstanding debt they needed to pay off: the doctor's charges associated with Mary Lou's birth. She came into the world at Pa and Ma Huff's home, so there were no hospital bills. But the doctor had been called in to oversee the delivery, and when he left, he said the baby needed follow-up exams every three months. It was all so expensive! How did their parents, who had nine children among them, ever afford these costs!

"We would never call a doctor back then," said Millie's mother. "Augh, no, never! Childbirth is women's work! Ya'd call your own mother or your sister, but never a man, even if he was a doctor."

"So, we send the men out somewhere," Millie concurred.

"Somewhere. Anywhere!" her mother expanded. "Your Pa always went t' th' pub when you four were born. That's why he took Icky there when Mary Lou was on the way."

But then she paused before continuing with an indulgent smile. "Can't blame 'em. They can't bear t' hear it."

"Cowards," Millie said with disdain as she recalled all the times her brothers had acted so tough around her.

"I dunno," Ma said weakly. "Sometimes th' mother dies in childbirth, an' th' husband knows 'twouldn't have happened if he hadn't given her th' child."

"But with sulfa drugs and such, most of us get through it now."

"Thanks be to God," Ma agreed. "All these medical costs so the mother and baby survive th' birthin': certainly th' help is worth it."

The new parents had whittled the doctor bills down to a manageable sum while they lived with Millie's parents. But now that they had rent to pay, too, the balance wasn't dropping as quickly, and the weight of the debt felt heavy around Icky's neck. He worried that if they didn't eliminate it—and soon—that somehow, bit by bit, the interest would mount, and they'd never be able to pay it off.

"And I don't want to tap our house savings account," he told Millie, "so I've taken a Friday and Saturday night gig, dealing cards."

"What?" Millie said, alarmed at his pronouncement. "With whom?"

"We need the money to get rid of that doctor bill," he explained, avoiding her question about who hired him.

"But you got an increase in pay when Mary Lou was born. Doesn't that cover it?"

"It doesn't," Icky said, "and if anything else were to happen, we'd be in trouble."

"But we haven't even discussed this!"

Why would he need to discuss it? To his way of thinking, the best way to solve a problem was to just handle it. Millie's way, he was finding out, required talking things through first. It was so exasperating!

"Where is this job?" she asked next, and then quickly added, "Not at Hoards!"

"No, of course not. Your mother would have a fit." He knew that if he ever agreed to deal for Jack Hoard that the gossip would somehow get back to Millie's parents. Pa Huff simply had too many connections in that arena.

"You're right about that!" she retorted. "And you never would have accepted this job if we still lived with them!"

"No, if we still lived with them, we wouldn't have rent to pay, and the doctor bill would still be declining. But we're on our own, and unless you tell them, they probably won't find out."

So, this was something he didn't want to let anyone know about, she realized.

"Who are you dealing for then?"

"It's a private game. A bunch of guys."

Wise guys, actually, and if Millie knew, she'd be right to be concerned. The tables were run out of the back of Empire State Brewery, which was owned by J.V. Wyoming. Rumor had it that Wyoming's family was related to Buffalo loan shark and labor racketeer Stefano Melotti.

Actually, Icky knew it was more than rumor. He checked them out with his pals at Carpoletti Distributing, and they said that getting in too thick with this group could be dicey: much worse trouble than dealing for Hoard, who lived his whole life in Olean. A local guy could at least be trusted.

Not Melotti, though. He didn't run his City Memorial Chapel funeral home up in Buffalo for nothing.

"But when will you sleep?" Millie continued to object. More than Icky realized, she understood that he might be stepping in with the wrong crowd. "Your work hours are so long already . . . "

"Actually, this will help me stay on the same shift as my bakery job," Icky pointed out. "I'm already up all night from Sunday through Thursday. This just fills in the other two nights."

"I don't know," Millie objected, her mind substituting the clicking sound of card decks being shuffled with the rattling of machine-gun fire. "Bad things happen . . . "

"You sound like your mother," he interrupted, growing irritated with the inquiry.

About that, she knew he was right: her mother brooded. In fact, she almost seemed to enjoy stirring up her anxiety.

But now, it occurred to Millie that Icky was similarly predisposed to worrying . . . or, it seemed that way when it came to managing their finances.

"You don't think you're overly critical about our budget?" she challenged.

"I'm realistic about it," he insisted. "Look, I'm earning almost twenty-seven dollars a week now—which would be a good living, if we didn't have this bill over our heads. We just need a few bucks to get us flush again.

"Your dad wouldn't have a problem with me dealing," he added, playing his own trump card, "and I'd think you'd be relieved to get rid of the debt."

"I would, and I understand what you're trying to do. It's just . . . I don't see much of you as it is, and . . . I don't like the whole idea of it."

"Millie, here's all I have to say: I'm going to deal cards on Friday and Saturday nights. I am not gambling. I will be paid for this work, and the money will be used to get rid of the doctor bill. *That's the end of it!*"

She didn't like being cut off. In fact, she wouldn't have it!

"No, one more thing," she corrected with a fierce glare, for he vexed her to the core with his dictum. After all, she had been more than gentle in raising concerns, while he bet his entire wad with his declaration! "If you're determined to deal cards on your only two nights free, fine. But *only* until the doctor bill is paid, and when it is, you will quit that job!

"And *that*," she enunciated with a touch of frost, "is *the end of it!*"

And it was.

Icky and Roy leaned against their shovels, inspecting the huge mounds of snow they'd piled up alongside Pa and Ma Haut's driveway. Despite temperatures in the teens, they both were sweating.

One reason was the wet snow—which was much heavier than dry powder.

The other reason was that they were using Pa's shovels—which were also much heavier than store-bought tools. Pa made them with thick oak handles attached to extra-wide blades "so the work can be done faster," he claimed.

"I'm so sick of this cold," Roy grumbled. "Four weeks of ice and snow, and we still got three more months of winter."

"Ma and Pa appreciate the help," Icky offered. "They've got enough to do preparing a midnight meal for everyone to enjoy after Christmas eve service."

"I'm not complaining," Roy defended. "It's just so frigid out here!"

"Millie can hardly wait to see Mary Lou's reactions to Christmas. Last year she was too little to really understand it. But this year, we bet she'll love it."

"Yep, yep, yep, watching her will be great. But Herta and I have had enough snow. This will be our last Christmas in New York."

"Seriously?" Icky asked. The thought of quitting his job and moving never occurred to him.

"Yep, yep, yep," he said with some pride in his voice for having made the decision to move on.

"But how? Why?"

"Look, a man can go only so far when he's working for someone else," Roy said. "If Herta and I don't try to do something on our own now, we'll be too old to recuperate financially if our bakery goes belly up."

"Your own bakery?"

"And no snow," Roy emphasized. "We're going to open up in Havana."

"What Havana?"

"Cuba," Roy clarified. "Havana, Cuba. No snow, Havana, Cuba!"

"No way!" Icky exclaimed, shocked at the idea.

"Yep, yep, yep, we're on our way for sure!" Roy repeated. "Think about it. Your dad moved here all the way from Europe when he was young. Ma, too. It's not such a stretch to think we'd find our own path."

"But what will you bake in Cuba?" Icky asked.

"Bread, of course!" Roy answered. "Everyone likes the smell and taste of freshly baked, crusty breads, and there isn't one housewife today who isn't grateful to have her Saturdays free to do something else."

He added that he planned to assure Mr. Bolles that he wasn't going to go behind his back to take any of his recipes—and also that he intended to recommend Icky as his replacement. "You're ready to supervise an eight-hour shift," he told his brother-in-law.

"But, Ick, listen to me. Don't get stuck in that job," Roy advised him. "Learn all you can, read the trade magazines, meet the vendors—when the boss finally lets you in, that is. He's more protective of the business side of the bakery than you probably know.

"But then, when the time is right, think about doing something on your own, maybe like what Herta and I are doing. You've got what it takes," he insisted.

"I can't believe Herta and you are moving!" Icky replied. "Does Ma know?"

"Yep, yep, yep. So does Pa. And one day, maybe you'll do it, too," Roy repeated.

"I don't think so. I'm doing okay right here," he said. "Job security."

The memory of those early days—when Millie and he married in the face of the Great Depression, do or die—made him cautious about taking unnecessary chances.

"Job security goes only so far when somebody else is in charge," Roy disagreed, "especially when it's Old Man Bolles."

"Aw, he's just being the boss," Icky tossed off the advice.

"That boss is a stiff-necked businessman who likes the smell of money, not the aroma of freshly baked bread," Roy said firmly. "He's never been in a baker's jacket. And he goes off sometimes."

Strong talk, especially for Roy. But no, Icky thought. After more than a decade at Bolles Bakery, he'd trust his own experience. He knew how to take care of himself.

15

Opportunity Knocks

WHEN ROY SUGGESTED THAT Icky would be the right man to replace him, the boss grunted. "I'll decide who moves up, not you," he said brusquely. "Besides, he's your brother-in-law, so I hardly think your opinion can be trusted."

The way Mr. Bolles saw it, he didn't need an employee with one foot out the door to tell him how to run his business. No, he knew who he'd move up, and as it turned out, it happened to be Icky. He'd groomed him since he was in high school, and knew he was a go-getter. Sometimes the guy charged ahead without checking, but that could be managed.

But he'd wait a couple of weeks until Roy was gone, and do it on his own.

When Icky was moved from third shift to first shift, the day operation continued without even a sneeze in the transition. And just as Roy had predicted, the boss eventually brought him into quarterly meetings with the Pillsbury sales representative. Being included was one of the unspoken perks of being the day man, Icky realized, reveling in the glory of job advancement. He ate up the experience, and took Roy's advice with regard to studying bakery trade publications, too. The best ones covered companies that were creating better product, or discussed improvements such as developing a proprietary flour blend.

"Did you see this article yet?" he asked Mr. Bolles one morning. "The larger bakeries get their suppliers to blend flours for them."

While the boss read publications on business profitability, he didn't bother with baking details. He wouldn't tell Haut that, of course. It was none of an employee's business to know what executives read.

"Right here," Icky continued, pointing to the paragraph. "It says premixed flour can save a whole step in the process of measuring and pouring ingredients. That would make the operation more efficient." He knew that improving efficiencies always piqued his boss's interest.

"And," Icky gave one more reason, "regulating the formula will improve quality control, because eliminating one of the steps, time after time, day after day, means the apprentices will have one less thing to mess up."

Mr. Bolles was known to be slow to take advice, but he liked saving money.

"I'll look at it," he said, "when I've got time." An occasional observation by an employee, here or there, might be allowed.

Still, here or there meant not often. Mr. Bolles believed that people should do what they were hired to do, and not go wandering off with a bunch of half-baked ideas. It was one of those self-evident truths that any employee would be wise to follow.

"Back to work," he ordered, lifting his chin and sucking in a large dose of the superior air of management.

Icky could see that he'd caught the boss's attention, though—and he was right, up to a point. Once Mr. Bolles thought about it, he realized that Icky hadn't developed the idea of a proprietary blend on his own; he'd only read about it in a trade publication, and passed the reference on. A great deal more work was needed before that idea was ready for implementation, however. The Pillsbury representative would need to create and test a blend to Bolles Bakery specifications. He might allow Haut to work on that. Then, if, in his estimation as president, using that blend did achieve the efficiencies and quality controls he desired—without raising costs, of course—he could negotiate a contract. Yes, it was clear that the most important aspects of this proprietary blend option were still to be worked out at the decision-maker's level. He'd give Haut's question his consideration.

Icky told Pa that he knew that his recommendation for a proprietary flour blend scored points with Mr. Bolles.

"I mean, it had to!" he reported, proudly. "Anything that saves money or makes the bakery more productive has to be good for the business."

"Sounds to me like you're helping Bolles Bakery improve earnings," Pa agreed. "Keep it up, Icky. You always want to be known for the good you do."

ONE AFTERNOON, WHILE HE was attending the East Coast Baker's Convention, Mr. Bolles took a break from the event to walk around New York City. As he strode up and down the streets, he saw locals lunching on sausages tucked into small loaves of bread.

"Hotdogs!" the food vendors yelled. "Get your dogs here!"

Construction workers, first in line for the cheap sandwiches, were eager for a hot meal in the middle of the day. They piled on catsup, mustard, and onions, and then walked down the street as they chomped on the food in their hands.

"What's going on here?" Mr. Bolles asked one of the purveyors.

"Hotdogs. One or two? And wadda' ya' want on 'em?"

"One. Where does the bread come from?" Bolles refused to be put off.

"We got a coupla' bakeries sellin' 'em wholesale," the vendor answered quickly as he handed over the roll. "Next!" he yelled, ending the chat, and signaling the out-of-towner to move on.

When he returned to the convention center, Mr. Bolles asked around to see if anyone knew about the street corner sausage carts.

"Vendors expected hot sandwiches to be a winter novelty," one of the local attendees reported. "But then spring arrived, and office workers discovered them. A whole new market opened up."

"Interesting," Mr. Bolles said in the monotonic tone of world-weariness he heard on radio business programs, for he didn't want to draw too much attention to his question. He didn't see any reason why housewives wouldn't buy sliced buns to serve at home. Many had already given up baking every Saturday—and hadn't they become so spoiled that they didn't even want to slice their own bread? Any little convenience that contributed to their posh life would be what they'd buy—and Bolles Bakery could make money selling it to them, he decided, once Haut adjusts my slicer to cut smaller loaves.

"I don't know if the Rohwedder can be made to function that way," Icky told him the following week.

"What do you mean?" Mr. Bolles challenged. "It's a great machine! That's why I bought it!"

"Well, yes," Icky said. "And no. Loaves are run through, end to end, and cut clear through to make slices. But buns would need to be sliced in the opposite direction. We'd also have to set up the blades for a partial cut."

"Look, I expect you to make this work," Mr. Bolles ordered. "That's what I pay you for!"

"Yes, Sir," Icky answered, recognizing that the only prudent response was to comply in the moment, and then do some research to come up with an alternative.

❖ ❖ ❖

"Millie, when you go to the market on Thursday, get some Weiner rolls," Icky said. "See if you can find a couple of different brands, too."

"Weiner rolls?" she repeated. "What are Weiner rolls?"

"Those small loaves that hold frankfurters," he said. "You know: hot-dog buns. The ones Mary Lou likes."

"You mean banger rolls," she interpreted. "Why do you need more than one kind?"

"Mr. Bolles is all fired up about them. He spotted them being sold from street carts when he was at a convention, and now he wants to capture a new market for sliced buns. He's betting that housewives will buy them."

"No one else is slicing buns?"

"I guess not," he answered. "Not around here, anyway."

"I don't see the big deal," she contended.

"If they're sliced part way through the middle, the sausages can just be dropped in. The point is that demand in New York City is so great that one bakery converted its entire night shift to putting out small loaves."

"That's your old shift," Millie said.

"Right!"

"So, now you're going to be back on night shift, so you can be in charge of hotdog buns?"

"Probably not. Mr. Bolles just wants me to adapt our soft-and-white bread recipe to make buns, and then adjust the Rohwedder slicer to accommodate smaller loaves," he said. "I don't think that's possible—converting the Rohwedder, I mean—because the smaller loaves would have to be sliced only part of the way through and in the opposite direction. We'd have to keep re-calibrating the slicer during each shift. One or the other product is going to suffer in a commercial environment.

"But," he continued, "I bet I could design a second slicer that does what he wants. And if that's true, then maybe Bolles can create a demand for buns cut through to a hinge on one side."

"A hinge?" Millie asked. She couldn't imagine a hinge.

"Not with moving parts. The hinge would just be the side of the bun that stays closed so the catsup and mustard and kraut and onions and pickles—whatever people put on their sausages—doesn't drip through."

"I think I'd prefer a plate for my sausages, and colcannon on the side," Millie told him.

"And I like pork Wieners with kraut," Icky said. "But since Bolles specializes in bread—and that's all we bake—finding an innovation that can grow the bread business is a big deal."

WHEN ICKY GOT HOME from work on Thursday, he found the buns he asked for on the kitchen counter.

"Thanks!" he said, grabbing both bags and tearing into them.

"What are you doing?" Millie asked after a couple of minutes. Icky was pressing pieces of each of the two brands between his thumb and index finger, and comparing them.

"I'm studying texture," he said, holding up a small piece. "Soft-and-white bread doesn't have the crumb of rustic breads. It's gummy, and stays flat once it's compressed."

"Because?" Millie asked.

"The recipe has a lot of moisture. But every bakery has its own formula, so the question I want answered is which one of these two buns is going to hold in the condiments without soaking through, because catsup and mustard are wet, too. I'm guessing this one," he indicated one sample. "We'll have to test it."

"Let's test both," Millie suggested. She brought bottles of catsup and mustard to the table, and Icky poured liberal amounts onto each.

"Now we'll time the run through," he said.

After ninety seconds, both buns were still dry along the closed side. But at two minutes, only the variety with the smaller crumb and firmer texture—the one more like Bolles soft-and-white bread—was dry.

"It worked!" he said. "Now we know which of these two types of bun is closer to the recipe I need to develop. Then, I'll design a machine that slices only part way through, leaving about a quarter inch . . . ," he paused to guess at the depth.

"Millie, I need a ruler."

"It's on the table," she indicated, nodding her head. She had anticipated his next request.

"Oh," he said, grabbing it up, and measuring the depth of the cut. "Three-eighths of an inch."

Then he opened and closed his preferred bun several times to see whether or not it would separate with repeated motion.

It didn't.

"But no one is going to do that," Millie pointed out. "Once your sausage is in, you're not going to take it out."

"Right," he admitted to the pointlessness of that test. "Guess I just wanted to see what would happen."

"So, now what?" she asked.

"The Rohwedder is shut down on Saturdays for sharpening, so after maintenance is done, I'll take it apart to see how it's constructed," he said. "Then, I'll figure out how to engineer a second slicer to cut smaller loaves in the opposite direction."

"On Saturday," she said, focused on the news that her husband was going to be gone on the weekend again.

"Several Saturdays," he admitted. "For a while . . . 'til I get this worked out."

"Icky, . . . " She was about to complain. But she stopped. Disagreeing with him when he was determined to do as he saw fit made no sense, and that was that.

ICKY SET UP A space in the machine shop at the back of the bakery to engineer a new bun slicer—with Mr. Bolles's permission, of course, since another department's workspace was being borrowed. From the boss's perspective, leeway was being granted to get this job done, never mind that it was on weekends, and without overtime pay. It wasn't long, though, before he expected a progress report.

"Get to the point!" Mr. Bolles said impatiently. "How long is it going to take you to get this up and running?"

"The prototype bun slicer functions, but it's made from inexpensive components that won't last. The next step is to source better quality parts, and build the machine that you want. When we've got that right, we can begin to formulate a recipe . . . "

"Less detail! More results!" Mr. Bolles commanded in chopped fragments to push Icky along.

"Well, I suppose the project could be rushed by pulling used parts from old . . . "

"I don't want rushed," Mr. Bolles corrected. "And not 'used' either. This machine is supposed to be a custom design, not some haphazard jerry-rigged piece of junk made from misfit pieces.

"And let me tell you—in case you haven't figured it out already, Haut: I gave you my permission to handle this assignment because of your family connections. Make it happen."

Icky hadn't realized that Mr. Bolles expected him to tap . . . whom? Probably his father-in-law, since he was a machinist foreman. The boss probably didn't expect to pay for those consultations, either.

He sighed as Mr. Bolles inspected the slicer's back side. To him, it was going to be a money-making machine, a way to increase the price of each small loaf, or bun, without adding to the cost of ingredients.

"Every day that we don't have sliced buns on store shelves is potential money lost to all of the non-sliced bun guys," he pointed out.

"Yes, Sir, and your new bun slicer will be installed as soon as it's ready," he promised, relying on the reputation he believed he'd earned for getting things done.

"Which is?" Mr. Bolles demanded.

"When it works right," Icky answered in a firm, but respectful tone.

Mr. Bolles lifted an imperious eyebrow. He didn't like Haut's answer, but since progress was being made, he decided to allow it.

"ARE YOUR MOTHER AND you going to make popcorn for us tonight?" Icky asked, hopefully. He wanted to spend the evening with Millie's brothers and her dad, listening to the Friday night fights on the radio. It was a rematch between Schmeling and Louis.

"I guess so," she answered. "This is a big one, huh?"

"The reporters say that Yankee Stadium is sold out," he answered. "My Ma thinks the political tension between Nazi Germany and the United States is fueling interest."

"What do you think?"

"I think Ma and Pa know more about politics than I do. And Ma doesn't like Hitler. She insists that we remember that he's Austrian, not German."

"You'd think your parents would have some loyalty to Schmeling, though," Millie posited.

"Some, since Schmeling's German, and also, anti-Nazi," Icky allowed, "but it's not enough to sway them from supporting an American in a sports match."

"So, are we rooting for Louis again?" Millie asked.

"We? You're going to sit in?"

"Of course!" she told him. "I listened to the first fight with you guys. I'm not going to miss this one!"

"Good!" Icky said. "Then we're sure to get popcorn!"

"YOU'VE BEEN WORKING AT the bakery six Saturdays in a row!" Millie objected as Icky prepared to leave the following morning. By this point in his career she expected him to be able to spend weekends with family, but life wasn't working out that way. No, the bakery was continuing to grab her husband's days off.

"The bakery really ought to pay you extra," she complained, and would have threatened, at least on principle, to take her criticism right to Mr. Bolles himself if Icky hadn't seemed so full of energy over this new invention.

"I've almost got it working right," he ignored her comment. "The slicing mechanism is functioning now, but whether or not it cuts to the correct depth or is calibrated at the right speed is still a guess. Today, I'm going to bake a few small loaves to see what adjustments are needed."

"Well, if you're determined to go, hop to it then," she said, changing her attitude as she tried to sound supportive. After all, what choice did she have? Marriage wasn't a bed of roses.

"Thanks," he said. "This is going to be a long day. I might even stop by your parents' house to ask your father a couple of tool-and-die questions."

"Too bad you couldn't catch his attention last night, especially since the fight was over so quickly!" she noted.

"Louis sure did his homework," Icky said. "He had Schmeling down three times, and it took only two minutes and four seconds: that's what the newspaper said this morning."

"Schmeling didn't have a chance," she concurred.

"And now Hitler will have to stop using Schmeling as a front man for his Arian rhetoric," Icky added.

"I thought the announcer said that Schmeling has been resisting Hitler's use of his championship record to promote the Nazi political agenda," Millie suggested.

"I think you're right," Icky agreed. "And I read that Schmeling's fight manager is Jewish."

"Hiring him took guts," Millie allowed, pausing to survey the weather outside.

The apartment was getting stuffy, and the hour wasn't even noon. Icky had been working so many weekends that he hadn't replaced the apartment's storm windows with screens yet, so the sun was going to beat into the living room, and cook the place.

"It's going to be awful hot up here later," she changed the subject, "so if you're going to my folks' house again, I think I'll ride with you, and visit my mother. She wasn't feeling well last night, and I want to check in on her. Maybe having Mary Lou toddle around will cheer her up, too."

16

Sweet Face

"There's the Sweet Face we've been missin," Ma Huff said in the singsong lilt she reserved for her granddaughter. She leaned down and held out her arms, preparing to cuddle Mary Lou.

The little girl toddled quickly to her grandmother, blonde ringlets bouncing across her head with each clumsy step.

"Ma! Ma! Ma!" she squealed.

"Augh, she's all curve and color," Ma Huff admired, "like ya' poured her into that lovely little dress."

Millie saw her mother struggle to pick up the precious child.

"What's going on, Ma?" she asked, noticing her strain.

"Why, th' child is gaining a few pounds, aren't ya', now?" she answered, intentionally vague, as she snuggled Mary Lou next to her in her favorite old rocker. The chair squeaked as Ma pitched it gently back and forth, her toes barely touching the floor.

"Seems to me you're not feeling your best," Millie pushed.

"Augh! Jus' overdoin' it at the Moose Lodge this week," Ma insisted. "Lots o' work over there, don't ya' know, an' th' furnace isn't on now since spring has sprung. Th' chill can be hard on old bones."

"Didn't bother you over the winter," Millie countered, noting that her mother's forehead was a bit damp with sweat. Something was wrong; she could see it. And Ma was an enigma: fretting when she didn't need to, and denying problems when she ought to be dealing with them.

"Now don't be botherin' yourself over nothin'," Ma persisted. She could worry herself to death with this . . . thing, whatever it was, but she wouldn't let anyone else tell her what to do. She'd change the subject.

"How's Icky doin' with that new invention o' his?" she asked. "Has he got it workin' yet?"

"He thinks so. After he talks with Pa, he's going in to Bolles to bake hotdog rolls, so he can run them through."

"How'd they ever come up with that name: hotdogs! No one I know would want t' eat a sandwich if they thought it had dog in it!"

"Hotdogs!" little Mary Lou repeated, expectantly.

"Not now, Sweetness," her grandma said. She didn't have any sausages in her ice box.

Mary Lou wriggled off the rocker as she practiced saying "hotdog" over and over again. Ma Huff shifted her weight uneasily into the corner of the cushion. She refused to wince, 'though she felt she wanted to.

But Millie noticed that she was restraining . . . something.

"Ma, . . . "

"Now don't ya' go worryin' yourself," Ma demanded. "It's just a stitch in m' side."

"But Ma, . . . "

"Ma! Ma! Ma!" Mary Lou repeated.

"I'll tell ya' when there's somethin' t' worry about," Ma continued. "An' there's no sense gettin' worked up before then."

"Ma! Ma!" Mary Lou continued.

"There's fresh cookies in th' jar," Ma directed. "She can have one o' those for now."

"It'll spoil her dinner," Millie cautioned.

"Doesn't seem th' child has any problem with her appetite 't all. G'won now, an' tend t' her."

WHEN BOLLES BAKERY FIRST opened, it was known for hearty rustic breads made with whole wheat flour. But as the quality and cost of refined flour made white bread affordable, buyers' tastes shifted to the sweet doughy product. Mr. Bolles couldn't afford not to divert to that market. The question his bakers faced was one of texture: how much softness could be formulated into this sissy bread without letting it become too cake-like. Each bakery came up with its own recipe.

The original Bolles soft-and-white formula called for flour with a higher gluten percentage than competing sandwich bread brands—which was probably why, Icky realized then, the Bolles soft-and-white held up well when run through the Rohwedder. He'd begin with that formula as the basis for developing the new hotdog bun.

As Icky mixed each batch, adding more or less water, he wrote his changes on a small spiral-bound notepad he kept in the chest pocket of his baker's shirt. The first batch didn't cut well, even at room temperature. The knives yanked at and shredded the interior of the small loaves. The crust was firm, though.

The crumb was better on the second batch, but again, the blades still tore roughly through the soft center. He needed a break to think through his next steps, so he left at noon to drop in at his parents' house for lunch. He knew Ma would make him a sandwich, and she was always a good one to help talk through a recipe.

"Your dinner rolls for Thanksgiving are soft, but also firm," he said. "How do you do that?"

"Just use more milk than water," she said.

"Milk?" he repeated, surprised.

"What do you think?" she held to her first answer. He'd been eating them his whole life, after all.

"Okay," he allowed. "That's it, then?"

"*Ja*," she assured him. "You change the bread recipe at Bolles?"

"Maybe a new product," he said. He knew his mother wouldn't say anything. And even if she told Pa, he could be counted on to keep his thoughts close to his vest.

On his way back to the bakery, Icky stopped at Richardson's Grocery to buy a quart of milk. But as he walked in the door, he wondered whether or not dry milk might work as well. That, he thought to himself, would be much easier to work with, and would probably cost less.

He found the baking aisle, and looked for instant dry milk powder.

"Carnation," he said out loud when he found it. The box said it was "made from contented cows."

He wondered wryly whether or not Mr. Bolles would be more contented if the new bun recipe used dry milk. Probably not, but he'd try it anyway. And the fresh milk, too.

While the next batch of test buns baked, Icky switched the blades on the slicer, replacing heavy-duty, half-inch serrated knives with quarter-inch pitch scallop sharp cutters. Neither were the best steel, but he couldn't justify increased costs until he had a recipe worked out. Then, maybe he'd ask Mr. Bolles to approve the cost of higher quality blades.

When the loaves cooled sufficiently, Icky lined six in a row. Then, in smooth, even strokes, he passed them, one after the other, one after the other, one after the other, across the blades. The cut was cleaner, but a bit of crumb remained.

He adjusted the calibration slightly, and then ran through another half dozen loaves from the same batch.

"Clean! And a single swipe for the whole lot! That's the way to do it!" he said as he recorded his final modifications in his notebook.

He grabbed up the best six buns, and dropped them into a paper bread bag.

"These are for Millie," he said proudly. He could hardly wait to take them home.

But he wasn't done yet. While he'd proven—to himself anyway—that he could adapt the Bolles bread formula to buns that could be sliced automatically, he hadn't finished engineering the machine to function in a mass production environment. That probably would take another weekend, and require parts. He'd have to decide whether stainless steel or carbon blades would be better. Carbon was harder, and took and held a better edge. But it was also more difficult to sharpen, and more brittle, too. He'd make a couple of calls to research options. The boss would want to know what the maintenance costs were going to be.

In the meantime, he set aside a few bun samples for his next meeting with Mr. Bolles. He knew he was gnawing at the bit for status reports, especially on Mondays.

After he inspects these samples, I'll be in a better position to recommend which blades will be better, he told himself as he cleaned up his work area. And now that we have the new slicer functioning, he might ante up.

"LET ME SEE HOW it works first," Mr. Bolles said when Icky showed him the bun samples, and told him about the budget he needed for the better knives.

"Synchronizing the blades helps achieve a clean cut in the smaller loaves," he pointed out as he demonstrated how the knives' reciprocating motion gave a perfect slice on each bun.

"You couldn't do this with my Rohwedder?" Bolles challenged.

"No, Sir. First, the Rohwedder is running at full capacity," Icky explained, ready to provide every detail, as his father would have done, "so we couldn't add another product to its operating schedule, especially one that requires recalibrating the blades."

"Time is money," Mr. Bolles countered, "so if I'm investing in a second machine, it better not cost me any production delays."

"Precisely," Icky responded, "We wanted to be sure we didn't interfere with the sliced bread production schedule. That concern led to the design of a dedicated slicer for the smaller loaves."

"And this one is specifically for buns," Mr. Bolles challenged.

"Specifically."

"No other machine like it," Mr. Bolles insisted.

"I can't say that," Icky answered, as he didn't have access to that sort of data, "but designing our own machine certainly saved money."

But Mr. Bolles knew very well that another bun slicer might exist. He'd asked about sliced hot dog buns after he bought one of those sandwiches from a street cart vendor in New York City.

"I paid a lot of money for all these nuts and bolts, so this better work!" he insisted.

"The only part that's not the best quality is the knives . . . ," Icky started.

"That doesn't seem very smart for a slicer," Mr. Bolles said in a menacing voice.

"Glad you said that, Sir, because now is the time to decide whether or not to switch to stainless steel blades. It didn't make sense to invest in them until the machine was performing the way you want."

Mr. Bolles didn't say anything. He didn't like Icky turning his argument back on him. He also didn't like spending money to replace blades unless absolutely necessary.

"Once production is ramped up, stainless steel will cut cleaner than carbon steel blades. That will mean we won't lose a lot of product to crumb."

"Loss?" Mr. Bolles barked. He didn't have loss with the Rohwedder.

"Yes, Sir," Icky answered. "Loss can be controlled with better knives."

Mr. Bolles ran his finger over the side of the blade.

"Stainless is more durable than high carbon," Icky continued. "And it doesn't rust, so it's less likely to leach a metallic taste when the humidity is high."

"You're not going to tell me that people can tell whether or not a slice of bread has been cut with a stainless blade or a high carbon blade," he responded, incredulous.

"Not everybody," Icky allowed. "But some can. I can."

"The metallic aftertaste seems to diminish as more rolls are sliced," he added, "probably because carbon blades get a kind of patina after a while. But eventually they'd need to be sharpened again, so we've got to balance all those factors."

Mr. Bolles pursed his mouth and grunted.

"And here are the controls for the cut speed and the cut depth," Icky pointed out. "If we install the better knives, we should be able to slice buns for about a week. Then we'll sharpen them at the same time that we do maintenance on the Rohwedder. And, by the way, stainless steel blades sharpen better than carbon, too. That'll save time . . . "

But Mr. Bolles wasn't listening. He'd begun twisting dials, roughly, giving them a good work out. The machine jerked against his commands, its internal parts convulsing at a businessman's rough handling.

Icky thought he saw Mr. Bolles almost smile.

Almost.

"Get me some drawings," he demanded next, his forehead down, lower lip jutted out, and his right thumb under his chin. "I want them tomorrow."

"Will do," Icky answered. He'd work them up as soon as he got home. "And the blades? Which ones do you want me to write into the notes?"

"Leave it open," he answered. "When I get a look at the paperwork, I'll decide whether or not to fund stainless blades."

He turned away from Icky, and marched heavily toward his office. He'd already decided to use stainless, but he'd tell Icky later. He'd also tell him to make space on the slicer, front and center, for the Bolles Bakery logo.

Icky let out a sigh of relief. Mr. Bolles seemed to be happy with the progress.

Millie wouldn't be pleased, though, when she saw him at his boss's command all evening. Work was work, he'd remind her, and those drawings had to get done. He'd take home a couple of loaves of Bolles's best rustic bread, and suggest that she deliver them to her mother. Ma Huff still wasn't feeling well, so a gift of freshly baked bread might give her a break. Yes, that would be a good solution all around.

Mr. Bolles stepped around his mahogany desk, sat importantly in his overstuffed brown leather chair, and picked up the telephone. He wanted to get a patent filed for the new slicer as soon as he had Icky's drawings in his hand, and he wanted it done ahead of anyone else—especially the bakeries supplying street cart vendors.

Because, he told himself, whomever files first owns the patent and earns the royalties. He thought that was how it worked, anyway.

He congratulated himself for his astute financial prowess as he dialed the attorney's number. After that consultation, he'd contact one of the business-to-business advertising agencies up in Buffalo. He'd hire them to design a trade media campaign.

"Responsibility for making a company great always falls to the man at the helm," he said out loud. He didn't know if he'd heard that on the radio, or if he conjured it up himself; either way, it was true. For while lesser men can build a machine, when it comes to making money, only the man at the top knows how to develop opportunity. Didn't Haut talk about how the slicer works? Yes, but he hadn't said a word about how it could increase profits!

Then, feeling generous, he allowed that no employee could be expected to suggest high-minded business strategies. Even Haut, with all his experience, wasn't up to that task.

"After all, he's not a businessman," Bolles told the walls with calculated, mirthless self-importance. "As President of Bolles Bakery, however, I need to reflect carefully on the long-range impact of each decision.

"For prosperity means power, and power means privilege, and privilege means . . . privilege means everything," he decided. He had begun to conjure up catchy little lines that he might use in a speech, maybe at the annual meeting of the American Society of Baking Engineers in Kansas City. Once he had a patent, they'd probably invite him to be their keynote speaker at a dinner. Yes, he'd be deserving of that acclaim.

Afterward, he'd continue up road for a hunting vacation in Montana or Canada. He was willing to bet that his 30.06 rifle could bring down a bison or an elk.

17

The Bitter and the Sweet

THE FUNERAL FOR MARY Elinor Cahill Huff was a simple thing: a short service at a local church, and then a gathering at home.

"It's what she would have wanted," Pa Huff said.

But he hadn't expected the crowd who filled the tiny house afterward. By mid-afternoon, he was exhausted from edging left-and-right through all the women. They were everywhere, their sensible heels clicking from the living room to the kitchen to the porch. Some were sitting at the dinner table or on the sofa. Others were perching on the steps. Every spot was taken. His own easy chair—the only one that was a tall man's size—was occupied by some petite lady. If Ma were here, he knew that gaff never would have occurred, for wouldn't she have offered up a more suitable place to the woman? Realizing how she always looked out for him felt, as she would have put it, like a dark song repeating in his mind, singing to itself. He could still hear her kind voice blending into the chatter.

The boys had escaped the commotion a couple of hours earlier. Icky suggested the three of them join him at one of their favorite watering holes, away from the mourners' tearful expressions of what a wonderful woman Ma Huff was. All of that heartache was deepening their pain, not diminishing it, and the boys needed a reprieve in the quiet commonality of men soaking up a couple of beers at the local.

They grabbed a table at the back, and Gordon reverently placed the jug of hooch in the middle.

"You can't bring your own liquor into a tavern," Richard objected.

"It's not for drinking," Gordon countered. "It's for remembering."

Icky had already gone up to the bartender to place their order.

"First, I need four waters—in whiskey glasses," he said.

The bartender looked at him quizzically. Icky was a regular enough customer, so he could be counted on for some good business, and a solid tip, too. But this was an unusual order, even for the middle of the afternoon.

"Yes, water," he repeated, responding to the bartender's reaction. "We need to lift a toast to their mother who died a couple of days ago: Mary *Cahill* Huff. She wouldn't be caught with liquor on her tongue, so first we need water to honor her."

"Cahill says it all," agreed the bartender. "Either the Irish drink or they abstain, and there's not much in between."

"Well, her sons over there are only half Irish, so we'll need four beers afterward," Icky added.

"Coming right up," said the bartender. "One after the other."

When the four waters came, the men lifted the glasses respectfully over the jug. Icky looked around the table, and realized none of the boys would be able to mouth the words of a toast, so he made it short and sweet, just like she was: "To Ma."

The boys downed their waters, the three Huffs tossing back their heads, just as they had done when they stole their first swigs of hooch from that jug so many years before. Their throats were as constricted as when they downed the stolen bootleg.

"She never forgot what we did," Richard said, swallowing the tightness in the back of his throat.

"And we'll never forget her," Edward added roughly over a small cough.

"Never, ever," Gordon confirmed.

As THE DOOR SHUT past the last mourners, silence fell on the Huff house with a sudden and lifeless thud. Millie leaned back heavily into the sofa, with Mary Lou curled up on her lap. Grandma's Sweet Face was worn out, too.

"Didn't know she had so many women friends," Pa said, finally able to settle into his easy chair. "They just kept coming and coming."

"Ma was always over at the Moose Lodge," Millie acknowledged her father's observation about the number of women who loved her. "And if she wasn't there, she was probably at the Eagles, or doing something for the Protected Home Circle.

"She did lots of volunteer work," she continued softly.

"Ee-yep, she did," he said wearily. "She helped lots of folks, that's for sure."

"Mm-hmm," Millie agreed.

They sat quietly for a while. Pa was a kind man, Millie mused. Not mild mannered or soft spoken: he'd never be accused of either of those traits! No, he was more like the chilly breezes coming off fishing ponds: the sort of man who never felt the need to impress anybody. That kind of honesty could be trusted.

But now, the hard honesty of death was having its way with him. And the toughened edges he wore on the outside, the ones that were easily brushed away by his wife's gentlest touch, were laid open. Ma's stomach cancer had come as quite a shock.

Millie let out her mother's sigh—the one they all knew so well—and in that moment, Pa felt Ma's presence in his daughter. He didn't need to hold to his coarse protective exterior with her.

Mary Lou shifted to the end of the sofa, and settled down with a blanket. She'd had too much company, and her eyelids were heavy, and ready for a late afternoon nap.

"Get you something to eat, Pa?" Millie offered.

"No," he said. He let out a long, shaky breath. "There's enough food in there for better than a week."

"Everybody on the street brought something over," she noted.

He shrugged.

"I expect they'll keep bringing over casseroles for a few days," she said. "That's what people do, you know."

"No. Didn't know that," he said, his gaze unfixed: glassy-eyed, like a fish out of water. No, it was worse: he was broken-hearted, as if Ma's death had filleted him, too. But he was still here, exposed to the elements. "Your mother always took care of . . . everything."

The room went silent again. Millie knew that the house would be quiet chaos for a while as the men figured out how to get things done for themselves. They had no clue how much work it took Ma to care for three men; Ed was married already, so it was only Pa and Gordon and Richard. Still, it had been a lot for one little woman to tend to. A whole lot.

ABOUT A WEEK LATER, Pa dropped in to see Millie on his way home from work. She was the only female in his life, and he missed the softness of a woman's voice. Takes the edge off a tough day, he realized the first afternoon he pulled open the back door when he got home, and felt the empty rush of silence declaring Ma's absence.

"Guess we just wore her out," he confided in his daughter.

"She loved you, Pa," she comforted him.

"Ee-yep," he said. It was about all he could get out of his mouth of late. The Bull in the Woods was treading lightly over memories of Ma, grateful for each one, to be sure. But lost, too, as to how he would get along without her.

"You'll find your way, Pa," she said after a while, squeezing his shoulder.

"Ee-yep," he said again, lifting himself out of the overstuffed chair. "Got to be going. Picking up the laundry on my way home." He never visited for too long.

"How about a ride?" she offered. "We could put the laundry in the back seat."

"Maybe that would be good," he accepted. "Got mine and the boys'. And my tools."

"Cumbersome," she agreed.

She put a sweater on Mary Lou, and grabbed the keys for the family car. "C'mon, Sweet Face," she said, using the nickname her mother liked best. "We're going to take a ride with Grandpa."

As they pulled out of the driveway, she asked him, "You ever going to learn to drive?"

"No," he said. "Don't need to. Gordon's old jalopy is good enough when we need to tote something."

"You could go places," she suggested. "Visit relatives, maybe see the cousins over the state line in Shingletown?"

"No, they know where we are . . . or where *I* am," he corrected himself obstinately. He didn't think he'd ever get used to referring only to himself. "They can come here if they ever want to see me."

He's still got his old gruff inflexibility, Millie noticed as she heaved a sigh. Let's hope that stubbornness keeps him sturdy, she thought to herself.

"How is your father doing?" Ma Haut asked over Sunday dinner.

"Oh, he seems to be working out how to handle house chores," Millie answered. "My Grandma Permilla is still alive—she's ninety-one this year!—and lives with Pa's brother, Kenneth. They're keeping an eye on Pa, and invited him over for lunch today."

"Good. Are you named for your paternal grandmother?" Ma Haut asked. "Is Millie short for Permilla?"

"No, Millie is from Mildred. Ma said it was a popular girl's name when I was born, but it would be just like her to honor her mother-in-law. I'll have to ask . . . Pa," she hesitated then, realizing in the moment that this was one of those things she'd probably never know, now that Ma was gone.

"Families get close together at these times," Ma Haut said, recognizing Millie's loss.

"Mm-hmm," she said, and returning the focus to her father, added, "but Pa's never had to wash his own shirts or cook. He's hiring out the laundry and such 'til he can get a grip on it."

"It'll take time."

"Yes, it will. But I have to tell you: Icky's been great about going over there, too. He's working on a machine for Bolles, and that's given him reason to ask my father for help."

The attention around the table shifted to Icky.

"I thought you were a baker!" Pa Haut said, surprise in his voice.

"I am, of course I am," Icky said. "But I use equipment—mixers and ovens and slicers—and sometimes I've got to maintain them."

"Didn't know that!"

"Nor did I!" said Ma. "So, how's Millie's father in the middle of this?"

"Bolles asked me to adapt his Rohwedder slicer to accommodate some small buns he wants to put into supermarkets. What he wanted it to do wasn't possible. But with Millie's dad's help, I figured out how to build another slicer that will slice buns."

"He's a machinist," Pa Haut recalled.

"And Icky's request has been a good distraction for my father," Millie added. "It keeps him focused on something new, so he's not feeling so lost."

"Mr. Bolles must be grateful to you for building him a new piece of bakery equipment!" Pa said, proud of his son's accomplishment. "You've always been good helping me out, 'though Henry seems to like it more than you."

"I just come by it naturally," Henry said. "And I had the two of you to watch."

"So, what did Mr. Bolles say when you showed him this new slicer?" Ma asked warily. She'd heard through Herta and Roy that he could be a difficult man to work for.

"He just told Icky to get him some drawings," Millie interjected. "Then he filed a patent on it."

"What's this patent?" Pa Haut asked.

"I'm not sure exactly. I guess any bakery that wants to sell *sliced* hotdog buns will have to pay Bolles Bakery a fee called a royalty," Icky offered an explanation. "They can buy a slicer from us. Mr. Bolles found a shop that will manufacture them if we get any orders. Or, they can buy a copy of our plans. Either way, it seems that they'll have to pay Bolles."

"Pay Bolles? To sell their own product?" Ma said. "Unbelievable!"

"I guess," Icky said. "Anyway, it's not forever. I think there's a time limit on the patent."

"And how much do *you* get from this royalty fee?" Pa asked.

"Me? I don't get any of it. It's not my machine; it's his."

"But you built it!" Ma argued on his behalf.

"For Bolles," Icky explained.

"On weekends," Millie chipped in. "Many, many weekends."

Icky gave Millie a look that suggested he didn't need her to counter him. After all, hadn't he built this machine to advance his career? And hadn't he also spent time with Pa Huff as part of the project?

Ma Haut noticed.

"You know what Roy said about Mr. Bolles. Don't count on him," she pointed out. She agreed with Millie on this one.

"This isn't about whether or not *he* can be counted on," Icky argued. "It's about *me* doing a good job."

"You are. We can see that," Pa said. "But what if Mr. Bolles is threatened by all you can do? He's getting a patent on your back."

"Just . . . just be careful you don't rise so high that he punches down on you like the bread dough," Ma added.

"I think I've got a handle on all that," Icky interrupted.

"*Ja,* but dough that rises too high is weakened," Ma refused to be cut off in making her analogy. "The rise isn't as good the second time."

"I don't think Mr. Bolles is trying to weaken my gluten," Icky responded to her worries. But he could see she didn't buy his assertion.

"All I did was build a bun slicer—my first try at designing bakery equipment—and it worked! I thought you'd be happy, not worried."

"We *are* happy for you, Icky," Ma softened her response. "But we don't trust Mace Bolles, not the way you do—and especially not after Roy's experience under his thumb. That man drove Herta and him all the way to Cuba."

"Snow drove them to Cuba," Icky corrected, relieved that his mother's concern was simply ill informed by his sister and brother-in-law's decision to move south. "And we like living *here*, so you don't have to worry about us leaving, do they, Millie?"

"Not in your life!" she said. Millie hated to travel. And the idea of moving south: that was impossible.

❖ ❖ ❖

"I'm home!" Icky announced as he came up the back stairs and into the kitchen of their apartment.

"I'll be right there," Millie called back. She'd spent the morning baking cookies, and was eager to surprise him.

"What are you doing?" she asked as she came into the kitchen to greet him.

"The bottoms should have smooth sheens to them," he reported authoritatively. He'd discovered the plate of cookies on the counter, and seemed to be rubbing the underside of one with his thumb.

Millie looked at him quizzically. "Hello to you, too."

"What?" he said.

Finally, he looked up.

She didn't seem pleased. Weren't these cookies for him?

"Hi," he said. "How was your day?"

"What do you mean?" she enunciated.

"Mean?"

"Yes," she repeated. "What do you mean by 'a smooth sheen'?"

"Oh! The bottom side of a baked cookie is supposed to look a certain way: smooth and shiny, like the bottom of a loaf of bread. And the tops are supposed to look firm and toasty," he answered. "I read about it in a trade magazine over lunch today."

"So?"

"So, I was thinking about it on the drive home, and here I see that you baked some!"

He was trying to say that he appreciated having cookies to examine, and that her timing was perfect! Now he could test the claims made in the article.

But for Millie, seeing her gift reduced to an inspection, as if her cookies were mere laboratory samples, wasn't the response she hoped for. Not at all.

"You haven't even tasted one yet," she pointed out. "Don't you think you ought to at least taste one before you criticize it?"

"I'm not criticizing," he defended.

"You're evaluating," she pointed out again.

"Yes!" he said enthusiastically. "Just like I do at Bolles!"

Wrong response! He's thinking like a Bolles Bakery man instead of like a grateful husband who is welcomed home by an adoring wife who spent the morning preparing a treat for him.

And he still hadn't even tasted one. Certainly, he can see that I'm not thrilled with all this so-called evaluating. He's gone too far with bringing his work home.

"If all you want to do when I bake is evaluate," she paused as her temper started to flare, " . . . well, this isn't Bolles. It's home. So, if my baking isn't shiny enough or toasty enough—whatever it's supposed to be—I guess this is the last time I need to go to all the effort!"

He blinked, and then narrowed his eyes, caught between being upset over her response to his professionalism, and the sudden and very clear realization that she was telling him that her home baking did not need his expert opinion.

And she was right. He hadn't even tasted one.

Should he?

"Sorry," he said.

"Right," she said, matching a one-word response to his paltry apology as she turned to leave the kitchen. His face took on the expression of a child who fears he's about to hear something he'd rather not.

"You know how sometimes a guy just can't leap out of a hole he's dug himself into?" He paused, but just for an instant. "Really, Millie, I'm sorry. I am."

She stopped, her hand on the door frame as she turned back to him. "Okay."

"Can I have one now?" he asked. It seemed like the right thing to do.

"Just don't critique it."

He wouldn't dare. And if it was awful, he'd do what any husband who didn't want to sleep on the sofa would do: he'd tell her it was the best darned cookie that ever passed his lips.

"Thanks, Millie, for doing this. I appreciate it."

"You better," she admonished him. "And welcome home to you, too."

WITHIN THE YEAR, ICKY and Millie's neighbors in the lower level unit moved out, so a first floor apartment was unexpectedly available.

"We could move downstairs," Millie said.

Icky hesitated. The doctor bill had been paid off, and he'd received a small annual raise at Bolles, which the two of them immediately put to buying a car that was more suitable for a family. It was a used one, of course, but trading in the Marquette helped cover its cost. They finally were meeting all of their expenses, and the pressure was off.

"We could. But wouldn't you prefer to keep saving our money for a down payment on a house?" he asked.

"Rent on that lower unit isn't as high as we thought it would be; I checked. So, we can still save for a house. And another summer up here with this heat is more than we can take," she insisted. "Besides, those stairs are dangerous for a small child!"

He knew she was right.

"Okay," he drew a deep breath. "Let's do it then."

The following weekend, Gordon and his fiancé, Marg, came over to help them move down the back stairs. The chore wasn't too great: just the baby's belongings, kitchen utensils, and a few pieces of hand-me-down furniture.

"Do you know if anyone's taken the upstairs unit yet?" Gordon asked as he set the last box down in the kitchen.

"No, I don't. Why? Are you interested in it?" Icky asked automatically.

"Might be," Gordon answered.

"Really!" he replied, surprised at the response. "Hey, Millie!"

"What?" she answered from the hallway. She was on her way to the bedroom where Marg was helping her store Mary Lou's clothes.

"How would you like your family living nearby?"

"How nearby?" Millie asked, hoisting their daughter onto her right hip, and coming into the kitchen. "You're not moving Pa in upstairs, are you?"

"Hmm, hadn't thought of that possibility," Gordon said. "He's going to have only Richard as a housemate soon."

Millie couldn't tell if her brother was being serious.

"Okay, okay," he rescinded the suggestion. "Actually, I was thinking that Marg and I might want to rent the unit upstairs after our wedding."

The date was only a couple of weeks away.

"What do you think?" he asked as Marg came into the kitchen.

"It's how we got out on our own," Icky said. "Could be a swell start."

Both of them looked at Millie. And she looked at Marg.

"What do you think?" Millie asked her.

"We need to find a place," Marg said. "And it's good to be near family."

"Well, I guess that would be all right then," Millie said, smiling at her brother. She knew Icky would like it. As she readjusted Mary Lou in her arms, one small issue came to mind, though.

"There's just one thing," she hesitated. "Are you sure you want to live over us? We've got Mary Lou. Remember what that was like when she was a newborn?"

"We'd be quiet," Gordon assured her.

"She might not be!" Millie corrected his assumption. "Would you two be okay living over a fussy toddler?"

"Marg is around fussy rich women all day," Gordon interjected before his bride-to-be could answer. "Can't be any worse than that!"

"Gordon!" Marg said.

"Well, that's what you tell me!"

Marg worked in the women's fashion department at Bradner's Department Store, and she'd built a solid book of customers who often asked for her when they needed to assemble a stylish outfit for a special occasion.

"Most of the time they're just so happy to be shopping," she said with a shrug and a tilt of her head.

"But they can also be demanding, and kind of hoity toity," Gordon defended.

"So what? If I want to earn a commission, I ignore all that, and smile." The job required gracious customer service and gentle encouragement regarding product selections.

"And if you don't?" Gordon pursued a defense of his earlier assertion. "I tell her not to cater to them," he said to Icky and Millie. Then turning to Marg, he added, "Let them look at the merchandise on their own. If they find something, you can ring up their dresses, or whatever they're charging to their husbands' store accounts."

"Except that that's not how it works," she corrected. "All of us girls are competing with one another. If I don't make a contact first, the customer could give her sale to someone else."

"How do you know who's just browsing, and who's going to buy?" Millie asked. She didn't often shop in Bradner's, so she didn't know the sales girls assessed who would be worth their time. She was curious.

"Well, to be honest, while I'm serving one customer, I'm also keeping an eye out for anyone wearing expensive Italian shoes and carrying a matching bag. She's the one whose husband has a thick wallet."

"And she decides whom she prefers to have write up her sale—not the other way around," Marg continued her counter to Gordon's recommendation on how she ought to do her job.

"Sounds like a lot of pressure," Millie sympathized.

"Most of it comes from our department manager. He thinks we girls are interested in only temporary work, as if all we want is a little pin money, and once we get some, we'll quit."

"So," Gordon said, "she's taking guff from both sides: from the boss, and from the snooty customers."

"It's fine now that people ask for me. So, to your question about noise, at the end of the day, I'm so tired that I probably won't even notice if Mary Lou is fussy," she said, grateful for Millie's consolation.

"Then it's settled," Gordon decided.

"Great!" Millie concurred, pleased with the prospect of family living upstairs. "Mary Lou will be happy to have her Uncle Gord and soon-to-be Aunt Marg here."

"Couldn't be better!" Icky agreed. "And I've got an idea for a men's shooting club. You can help me put it together."

"As if you don't have enough to do," Millie said.

"At least it's not extra time at the bakery," Icky pointed out.

"Whoopie," Millie said as flatly as she could, but still smiling back at him.

18

Or Threats of War

"Pa, look at this!" Ma Haut said, handing over the newspaper.

"Which story?"

"Front page. Right there!" She tapped the headline repeatedly with her fingertip: "Bakeries Urged to Fortify Bread; Nation Needs Nutrition in Face of War."

"I can't read it if you're going to keep bumping it," he said, finally flattening the page on the table before he read aloud. "The National Research Council's Committee on Food and Nutrition . . . is recommending a new flour enriched in vitamins and minerals. . . . for the nation's defense."

"Don't skip the words," Ma insisted. "At the end—that's important!"

"Okay, okay," he said, repeating the last sentence as written, " . . . a diet fully adequate in vitamins, minerals, and other nutritive essentials is better able to withstand the stresses and strains of war or threats of war."

"See there!" she said. "War!"

"Now, Emma,"—he called her by her first name only when he wanted to grab her attention—"it doesn't say we're at war. It says 'stresses and strains.'"

"Or 'threats'!" she insisted.

"It doesn't mean the U.S. will join the European fight."

"It's more than that," she insisted, for she would remind him that she knew as much history as he did.

"The last war was more than twenty years ago, and folks our age lost brothers and uncles. And men who came back crippled from the mustard gas are a constant reminder."

"And this time our boys are the age . . . " she started.

"You're getting riled up," he interrupted.

"No, Pa! I am not!" she defended herself. "We should watch out! That *Austrian* is dangerous. He's going to force the U.S. into his fight, just as he runs over Czechoslovakia, and . . . "

"Now why would Hitler want to involve the United States?" Pa tried to calm her. "Way over here on the other side of the Atlantic Ocean, we are barely a third-rate military power. Even Portugal has more weapons."

Pa read the newspapers, too.

"*Ja, Pa!*" she said, affirming the facts, but disagreeing with what they meant. "*Und das letzte Mal, als die Amerikaner den Engländern halfen, diesen zu Krieg gewinnen!*" She would speak the German, if she had to, to make him see her point: make him hear all the reasons why she was right.

"It wasn't only Americans who helped Great Britain win the Great War. I think you're irritating yourself without cause," he said, gently patting her arm then.

But his patronizing consolation stiffened her resolve.

"The newspaper says . . . " she refused to be mollified.

"And Roosevelt says," he interrupted, "that the American people don't want war. And the Congress says that the nation is not ready. Sounds to me like we're not going."

"I'm going to ask Icky about this," she resolved. If Pa wouldn't listen, she'd fortify her position by adding people in the family to her side of the argument.

"Ask him what? About Bolles using enriched flour in their bread?"

"*Ja!* If they make a change in the flour, then to war we are going!"

There was no arguing with her when she had her mind made up like this.

BEFORE THE END OF the week, Mr. Bolles called Icky to his office for an unexpected meeting requested by Tom Hubbell, their Pillsbury representative.

"It's mighty brisk out there!" Hubbell said, shaking off the cold. "The roads were clear, though, thank goodness!" He'd taken a direct flight from Minneapolis to Buffalo, hoping the inclement weather wouldn't keep him from driving the remaining seventy miles south to Olean.

"We're used to it," Mr. Bolles said, nodding at his secretary. She took Hubbell's coat and hung it in the executive closet, setting it off to one side where it wouldn't shed its fibers on her boss's fine camel topcoat.

"Up in northern Minnesota, we are, too—but we don't have your mountains. Sliding around on freezing roads is no fun!" he added. "Not today, though, and I'm glad of that!"

Bolles pointed Hubbell to a side chair at a long table that ran the length of his office, and settled himself into a black leather armchair clearly designated for the person in charge. Icky stood across the table from Hubbell until everyone was seated, and then took a chair.

"I noticed you got a few schoolgirls touring the bakery today," Hubbell continued, trying to break the ice with pleasant conversation.

"Some Blue Bird scout group from School 3," Mr. Bolles answered. "Twenty-four little screamers. They're done with their walk around, and are finally headed to the back room to hear some radio show before they go."

"Ah, yes," Hubbell said. "My daughter likes to listen to *Tip-Toe Time* in the afternoon."

"I think they'll like the peanut butter sandwiches made with Bolles bread, too," Icky added.

Mr. Bolles waved a dismissive hand at Haut and Hubbell.

"So, what have you got for me?" he said, superbly uninterested in chit-chat. "Let's not waste time."

Hubbell handed copies of a report issued by the National Research Council to Mr. Bolles and Icky.

"You probably received a copy of this in the mail," he began. "Basically, the Council is urging flour millers like Pillsbury to fortify the nation's supply of flour with nutrients such as thiamine and calcium."

"Saw it," Mr. Bolles said, trivializing the report. "What of it?"

"I know you're already blending your own proprietary flour," Hubbell said, glancing at Icky, "so, unlike smaller bakeries that aren't as advanced as yours, Bolles is accustomed to additives." It was always good to butter up Mr. Bolles. "Here, the NRC is asking millers—such as Pillsbury, and bakers—such as Bolles Bakery, to fight malnutrition by fortifying the products we put on the market. I thought it would be important to discuss how you want to do that."

"Who says I *want* to do that," Mr. Bolles challenged, stubbornly. "My bread is selling just fine. I don't see any reason to change it—that is, no reason that benefits my bottom line."

"Other bakeries of your caliber are preparing to comply with the NRC request," Hubbell said. "And even though your products are arguably better than most, I didn't think you'd want to be viewed as . . . well, something else."

"Bolles bread isn't just better than 'most'. Bolles bread is *the best* that money can buy!" Mr. Bolles argued.

"Of course, Sir, but perception may be another thing," Hubbell said.

"Just you wait a minute!" Mr. Bolles said, preparing to wage an argument. Hubbell showing up with some government report probably meant a price increase. He could smell it coming.

But Hubbell nodded, and held up the palm of his right hand to enjoin Mr. Bolles in listening. "I don't mean to bring up what your competitors are planning, but right here, the report says that one of them is working on a new advertising campaign to urge mothers to buy their new enriched bread because it 'builds strong bodies eight ways.'"

"Eight ways?" Mr. Bolles repeated. "What's this 'eight ways' nonsense?"

"They're referring, I believe, to the eight essential nutrients identified by the NRC. Clinical trials show diminished incidence of diseases such as beriberi and pellagra through improved nutrition. And they learned this through tests involving enriched white bread."

"Listen! I remember back before the Great Depression when housewives spent every Saturday baking whole grain breads. They were good, crusty loaves filled with moral and dietary fiber: that's what they boasted."

"Yes, . . . "

"It was the same rustic bread we baked!" Mr. Bolles chewed on his argument.

"Later, when we offered soft-and-white bread—because that's what supermarkets said their customers wanted—those same housewives said store-bought loaves were just for rich people. They sneered that processed white flour didn't provide roughage, and gave well-to-do members of this great society bodily constipation and clogged thinking!"

"I did hear that . . . " Hubbell tried to comment, but Mr. Bolles still wasn't ready to listen.

"Rubbish!" he snapped at Hubbell. "Bread is the staff of life! When I took over this business, bakeries like mine were baking only a third of all the loaves consumed by American families.

"Today," he continued with authority, "eighty-five percent of the nation's bread is baked by men in commercial bakeries."

"Right you are," Hubbell agreed again. "And now, the nation's leading commercial bakeries are engaging in a war against malnutrition, and businesses like Bolles should be commended for taking on that fight."

"Glad you see it that way," Bolles said, not quite ready to let go of his role as the person in charge of the meeting, but he'd allow Hubbell to agree with him.

"As President of one of the leading commercial bakeries in this part of the state, then, what do you propose as the right way to respond to the NRC recommendation?"

"That depends," Bolles said. "What's this going to cost?"

"Doing the right thing often comes with sacrifice," Hubbell said, leading to his answer.

"I knew you were going to pin this on my bakery!" Mr. Bolles said, irritated again.

Hubbell continued, "The NRC estimates that the cost of enriched flour will be about twenty-five cents per hundred-pound sack, and Pillsbury will hold its prices down to meet that recommendation."

"A quarter a sack!"

"This means that for a highly efficient bakery, the production cost of each twenty-four ounce loaf will increase less than two-tenths of one cent," Hubbell explained. He was prepared for Mr. Bolles's objections, and had already done the math. "In other words, if you choose, you will be able to tell housewives that Bolles Bakery is offering *enriched* white bread to her family at virtually no additional cost."

"Somebody's going to have to cough up that quarter," Mr. Bolles growled, refusing to swallow Hubbell's explanation.

"Yes, Sir," Hubbell replied. "How that expense is managed is an executive decision, and I would not dare to interfere in the wisdom of how you run your business—that is, whether to absorb the cost, or to pass it on to the consumer. My mission is merely to keep you apprised of the data we are receiving from the National Research Council, so that you can tell us how you would like to respond."

"Respond to what?"

"Would you like us to deliver the *enriched* flour in your next order? Or would you prefer to retain the *current* proprietary formulation?"

"How's this going to affect our proprietary blend?" Bolles directed his question to Icky, who had remained on the sidelines throughout the meeting. Now, suddenly, the boss seemed to be dropping the whole mess into his lap.

"I'd have to see the numbers," Icky said. "The bottom of the NRC report shows how much of each nutrient will need to be added if we want to label our bread 'fortified.'"

"Let me see that," Mr. Bolles said, flipping to the last page of the document.

"See here," Icky pointed to the page. "For each pound, the amount of thiamine is 1.1 to 2.2 milligrams; riboflavin will be 0.6 to 1.2 milligrams; nicotinic acid is 10 to 20 milligrams, and iron is 8 to 16 milligrams."

"Looks like calcium, vitamin D, and a couple of others, are optional," Icky noted.

"They are, but we're including them," Hubbell said.

"You still haven't answered my question," Mr. Bolles eyed Icky.

"Right," Icky responded. "I'll work out what these numbers mean as bakers percents in our proprietary blend.

"But if I may, I have another question," he said to Hubbell. "How will these additives affect the taste of Bolles bread?"

"Shouldn't change it at all," Hubbell answered.

"*Shouldn't?* Or *won't?*" Mr. Bolles challenged, seizing on an opportunity to object again.

"Why don't we mix a couple of sacks of your proprietary blend using the enriched flour, and have them delivered to you, free of charge. You can try it out. Let me know what you think."

"Haut's sense of taste is highly developed," Mr. Bolles warned Hubbell. He remembered Icky's comments about an unpleasant taste when bread was sliced with carbon blades. "He will report to me whether or not he thinks this enriched flour gives our bread a metallic edge, or any other off-taste."

"Understood," Hubbell said. He stood, and offered a handshake to Mr. Bolles, and wisely, simply nodded to Icky. Mr. Bolles wouldn't approve of a mere employee receiving the same regard as would be to accorded to the decision-maker. "Thank you for your consideration," he said as he grabbed his coat and exited down the stairs.

Mr. Bolles led the way as Icky returned to the baking floor, too.

"I expect you to fully test this so-called 'enriched' flour," he said. "I don't want it to ruin my product. And I definitely don't want a vendor to get away with any funny business."

"Yes, Sir," Icky said, stuffing the report into his back pocket. "And I'll get you those numbers by the end of the day."

"If not sooner," Mr. Bolles directed. He decided to walk off his irritation by pacing around the bakery floor.

"Roosevelt!" he grumbled. "First, he says workers have fundamental rights to bargain for higher wages and better working conditions. Rights! Hah! They have the right to apply for a job, the right to come to work on time if they're hired, the right to follow orders, and then—and only then— the right to get paid something for it! That's what they have a right to!"

He was talking to no one in particular, but also, to everyone in his way.

"And now this interfering know-it-all in the White House is putting his nose into the bread I produce! *I* say that just because some back woods family can't feed their brood, *my* company should not be forced to eat the cost of fortified flour to solve *their* problem!"

He started up the stairs to the executive offices.

"No one should have the right to tell the employer how to run his own company! No one!"

He finished his tirade as he walked past his secretary's desk.

"Are those little screamers still in my bakery?" he directed his final rant in her direction.

"They just left," she answered, dryly. She had learned to sidestep Mr. Bolles when he spouted off.

"Good," he said, and slammed the door to his office.

19

Running Interference

"I'M HOME!" ICKY ANNOUNCED as he let the back door slam shut with the cold autumn wind. Mary Lou ran to him from the living room.

"There's Daddy's little girl!" he said as he picked her up and gently nuzzled the back of her neck, all the while making her favorite sound, "Pfzzz!"

She squealed, and wriggled in his arms.

"Down!" she demanded, and then ran to find her mommy.

As Millie came in, Icky put out his arms, and said, "Next?"

"Oh, no," she refused. "You've got the outdoor chill on you. And those nuzzles belong to Mary Lou!"

"Just a kiss then," he said, leaning toward her like a Delft pottery figurine. "How was your day? Did you get to the bank?"

"Yes, Marg is working Saturday, so she had today off. We walked downtown together, and we both got our rents paid."

On the way home, the two of them browsed past all the shop windows as shoppers loaded down with packages darted in and out. Traffic was backed up on all four lanes, even blocking the intersection at State and Union Streets. Marg and Millie were glad they didn't need to contend with all that weaving around, and took their time sauntering home.

"On the way back, we passed by a house for sale on Seventh Street. It looks interesting."

"We've been in this apartment only a year," Icky hesitated.

"Over a year—almost two, and we've been in this duplex for nearly three years. We could start looking for a house, and start owning instead of renting." While Icky's ambition was to rise in his career as a baker, Millie dreamed of rearing their daughter in a house on a nice street. She'd like one with a yard and a swing set for the neighborhood children to play on together. She'd have loved that as a child, and she wished it for Mary Lou.

"We'll see," he said. If Millie wanted to look into it, he guessed she probably was right about putting their money into a house.

"How did Mary Lou do on your walk?" he changed the subject.

"She did her best. We wore out her little legs, though, so she napped for almost two hours this afternoon."

"She'll be full of energy this evening," Icky realized.

"Already is," Millie said. "Dinner will be ready in a half hour. You're having meatloaf."

"I can smell it!"

"It's your mother's recipe. How about taking Mary Lou out to the back yard for a few minutes of play time while I finish?" she suggested, reaching for her daughter's jacket, scarf, and hat.

"C'mon, Mary Lou. You can show me what's going on in the back yard," he said as he urged her outdoors. "Maybe you can find some pretty autumn leaves for Mommy!"

OVER DINNER, ICKY TOLD Millie about the tense meeting between Tom Hubbell and his boss.

"Hubbell came in to talk about this new flour that Pillsbury is putting out, and Mr. Bolles balked," he said.

"It's no surprise that he'd resist a price increase," she answered, passing the platter so Icky could help himself to another serving. A boss who expected employees to work weekends without overtime pay was certainly not going to be happy about higher costs on an essential ingredient.

"This is good," Icky said, taking a slice.

"So, what's this new flour?" Millie asked.

"Oh, they're putting vitamins and minerals back into it to help fight malnutrition. Early trials show that it reduces incidences of pellagra and beriberi in families struggling with poverty."

"That's good, isn't it?"

"Yes, of course!" Icky said. "Mr. Bolles just doesn't want to pay for nutrients he didn't order, unless they increase sales."

"But wouldn't the millers just automatically fortify the flour?"

"Probably, eventually," Icky said. "I don't know how long it takes to enact new recommendations across the board. Sooner rather than later, I suppose, though, the way tensions are rising in Europe."

"Europe? What does that have to do with Pillsbury?"

"The report says . . . here. Just look at this." He pulled the paper from his back pocket where he'd shoved it earlier in the day. He pointed at the paragraph, where she read,

> The Council advises American millers to strengthen wheat flour by adding nutrients . . . That way, even if the enemy cuts off farm supplies, for who knew the ravages of war, the food that was available would "build strong bodies eight ways," or so one of the soft white bread makers claims.

"Eight ways? That's Bolles?" Millie asked.

"No, it's Continental Baking out in Indianapolis. It's a new advertising campaign for their Wonder bread product."

"Who's this enemy that's going to cut off farm supplies?"

"It doesn't say," he admitted.

"They make it sound like the NRC knows something we don't. Is war going to break out? Does the government think we're going to face food shortages?"

"More like they're imagining the worst, and readying the nation for it. That's just a guess, though," he said.

"ICKY, ARE WE GOING to war?" Ma Haut asked as the family came together for dinner the following Sunday.

"What? How would I know?" Icky answered. He wasn't sure why his mother was asking him about the nation's foreign policy, but the tone in her voice suggested she was arming herself to make some point.

"Here," Pa passed the platter of pork roast with potatoes on the side, both to share the meal and to interrupt the conversation.

"Ma thinks that if Bolles Bakery starts using enriched flour that the United States will join up with the Allies, and fight Germany," Pa clarified. "I said changing the flour doesn't mean we're entering the war."

"Well," Icky said, preferring not to be in the middle of a disagreement between his parents, "I don't know yet whether or not Bolles Bakery will agree to use enriched flour. And how did you find out about that?"

He looked at Millie. Had she been talking to his mother about the NRC report he showed her?

"It's in *The Olean Times Herald*," Ma said. "Right on the front page in black and white, so it must be true."

Millie returned Icky's look with a small, single nod.

"And the story says that Bolles Bakery is going to switch to enriched flour?" Icky refocused attention on his mother.

"No, no," Ma protested. "It says we need good nutrition to bear the threat of war!" Why wouldn't he just answer her question? She could get the newspaper, and show it to him if he didn't believe her!

"Well, Mr. Bolles hasn't made a decision yet, so I can't answer," Icky repeated.

Ma looked at him with unbelieving eyes, her lower lip protruded just enough to suggest she might be willing to argue.

"You two are just alike," she said slowly, referring to Pa and Icky. "You keep to yourselves things you should be telling the rest of us."

"Okay," Icky said.

"Okay, what?"

"Okay, I'm not going to argue over something I don't know about. And the pork is really good. Thanks for making it."

"Well, I know it's your favorite meal," Ma acknowledged sharply. "I was hoping you'd return the favor by telling me what you know."

She wasn't being pushy. She was simply holding to the German way, expecting unbiased and authoritative proof from the family's professional baker so that Pa would see that on the topic of understanding the story in the newspaper, he was wrong and she was right!

Icky had already laid out his position, though, and he saw no reason to upset her—or anybody else for that matter—with some half-baked speculation about whether or not the United States was going to war.

"Well?" she said.

"I appreciate this great pork, but I don't know anything," Icky answered.

Ma shook her head, and lowered her eyes to her plate. She'd been waiting all weekend to be justified, but Icky wasn't going to bend.

She'd have to find some other way to confirm her suspicions.

"YOU DIDN'T TELL YOUR mother that you worked out the percentages, so Pillsbury can deliver a sample of the enriched flour," Millie said later when Icky and she returned from dinner with his parents. "What was that all about?"

"Pa and Ma are sparring about a newspaper article, and I don't want to referee," Icky said. "That's all."

"But Bolles *is* adding nutrients to its flour," Millie said.

"Bolles is going to run simple taste tests using the fortified flour," he corrected. "More to the point, I am going to run those tests."

"And?"

"And my guess is that adding nutrients to the flour will have no effect on taste."

"Why did you put up that stumbling block when Mr. Hubbell was in town?" she asked.

"Because," he sighed, "because it provided an easy and temporary problem that I was pretty sure was going to be overcome."

"Which then means that Bolles will have no reason for ignoring the NRC recommendation, right?"

"No reason other than cost, which is nominal," he answered. "And then Bolles Bakery will be on board with helping to fight malnutrition."

"Why couldn't you have just said that?"

"Because, Millie," he sighed, "because I don't want to be in the middle when it comes to Pa and Ma!"

"You'd only be in the middle if you wanted to see it that way."

"Okay."

"Okay?"

"Yes, okay."

"So, you'll tell your mother the results of the tests?"

"If she asks," he said, his fingers laced behind his neck.

"But she doesn't know that you're the person who's running the tests, so she's not likely to ask."

Icky looked at Millie with a straight face. "That's right."

"Sometimes, Icky, you can be such a . . . man!"

"Glad you noticed," he said playfully, trying to encourage her good humor.

She flashed fiery eyes at him, and gently shoved his shoulder, the way Ma Haut often responded to Pa Haut's teasing.

"All right then," she said. "Have it your way."

"Exactly what I had in mind."

20

Critical

"Darkness is coming so early," Millie said, piercing her needle through a shirt she was mending. "Sunset was at five o'clock today, so seven-thirty feels much later now."

She and Icky were sitting quietly in the living room, the radio tuned to soft music to soothe Mary Lou to sleep in the next room.

Icky shifted the newspaper uneasily. He'd been waiting for the right moment to talk with Millie about a decision he made.

"Just two weeks to Thanksgiving," she continued. "We're going to your parents' house this year. I'd like to take something, but as usual, your mother wants to do it all on her own."

"I wanted to talk to you," he finally said, folding the newspaper crisply. "I'm thinking about enlisting."

Millie felt time suddenly skid as her world shifted from reality to absurdity.

She put down her needlework.

"I stopped by Ma and Pa's house on the way home. They told me that Henry signed up today, on the one hundred sixty seventh anniversary of the Marines—at least, that's what the recruiter said," he continued. "The kid is taking a stand for what's right, and . . . and I can't let my brother go into battle by himself."

"Battle?" Millie said, struggling to make sense of his pronouncement. "But . . . " she tried to continue. Icky had never been impetuous, so he must have been thinking about this for some time, maybe even before Henry enlisted. And without telling her. When did all this nonsense start? Why was she just hearing about it now? Her questions shot off into several directions.

"But . . . ," she repeated, not sure of how to counter.

"But, Icky!" she finally got her words out, "Henry is single. You've got a wife and a child. Your situations are completely different."

"Not really," he said, redirecting her to the needs of the nation. "Roosevelt is asking every able-bodied man to step up. And I'm able-bodied."

"You're ten years older than Henry."

"My job keeps me in great shape," he countered. "Better than most guys."

"That's not what I'm saying, Icky. Of course, you're in great shape. But with Henry going to war, your mother will have only one son left here. You don't have to go."

"That applies only if Henry is killed in the course of his military service," Icky corrected. "Besides, the country needs me."

"*We* need you!" she made her claim. "Mary Lou and I! We need you more!"

He'd been prepared on some level for her to disagree, but he'd been so focused on what was going on with Henry that he hadn't thought through how he might answer her objections.

"Millie, look . . . "

"No, you look! Mary Lou is almost four years old. If you leave us now, even for just a year, she won't know you when you come back. She'll be afraid of you! You can't do that to her!"

"That's not fair, Millie. Mary Lou isn't a bargaining chip."

"It's not fair of you to leave us! And I'm not trading on her. I'm just saying we need you here, Icky."

"And I need to keep you two safe," he said, tapping the front page of *The Olean Times Herald*. "Read the paper. Germany isn't attacking only servicemen on the ground now. Their submarine attacked an Allied passenger ferry. And they're launching something called V-2 rockets that bomb cities miles away, so . . . "

"I know," Millie interrupted. "I read the papers!" she lunged her counter-offensive. "And those reports are reasons for you to stay out of the fighting!"

"All the more reason to fight!" Icky returned fire. "The only nation left standing between Hitler's takeover of Europe is Great Britain. And last December Japan bombed Hawaii! Next will be the west coast, and . . . "

"Icky!" she interrupted.

"So, then they'll be sending ships toward both coasts: east and west! I don't want Mary Lou and you on those front lines!"

That perspective hadn't crossed her mind, not at all. Where does he get these crazy notions?

"I bet your Pa and Ma aren't happy about Henry enlisting!" she argued.

"Ma's afraid to let him go, but they both support his decision," Icky answered. His father had even served in the Prussian cavalry when he was a young man. Icky couldn't allow himself to be the only one to deny the responsibility to serve!

"Supporting Henry's decision, one already made, isn't the same as encouraging it before it happens," she said.

"No, this isn't a huge leap for them," he insisted. "They're German, Millie! Maybe your parents haven't suffered war, but mine certainly have!"

"You just wait just a minute," she interrupted. "My mother was born in Ireland, so we know war, too!"

"Sorry," he said. "I didn't mean that the way it sounded. It's just that . . . Ma and Pa don't talk about this, but we still have relatives in Germany."

"Do you know them?"

"No. They're my second cousins. But Ma sends clothes and blankets to them every winter."

He paused.

"I remember finding a letter they wrote at the end of the Great War stored in a drawer. It said their farmland was destroyed, and their orchard was burned. Their cows and pigs were killed to feed enemy armies, mostly the French, while the British Naval blockades cut off supplies," he recalled. "They said they were in Hell—that they were the damned, and their punishment wouldn't wait. They had no food, and their final days were being consumed by watching their children starve."

Instinctively, he looked toward Mary Lou's bedroom door. His decision to enlist was deeply personal. And he finally had Millie's attention, too.

"Is that why your mother was so insistent about getting an answer on the enriched flour report a while back?" Millie said.

"I don't really know," Icky allowed. "Maybe she was trying to read into the meaning behind 'threats of war.'"

Millie felt dazed by Icky's decision to enlist. While she didn't want to deny the hard truth of his parents' experiences, she also thought it wasn't right for him to use stories about the last war as grounds to join up, and fight in this one.

"Your parents' experience: that's not what we learned in school," she finally said, hesitantly. She could pose only a weak argument to family history. Besides, she attended school only through the tenth grade, while Icky studied world history in his upper classes.

"School children don't need to learn about other little children suffering and starving to death," he said, calmly.

As they stared at one another, Millie searched him out for some small crack in his argument. The space between them, invisible as it was, was hard.

She stiffened, too. Her eyes threatened to become pools of tears, but she refused to blink, and let them fall. She hated that sort of manipulation. She'd never used crying as a mechanism to deal with her brothers when they teased her, and she certainly wouldn't use it with her husband.

But she would stand her ground. She'd fight Icky here at home if she had to, as if she were the soldier in a battle that needed to be won, to keep her family safe.

"Can't you just see how all this goes?" she took another tactic.

"Millie," he started to defend. He could see refusal tightening the muscles around her eyes. She was biting her lips, too. He knew she wasn't going to understand, and she wasn't going to change her position.

But he couldn't give in either. If he were to be true to himself, if he were to be able to live with himself, if he were to be a man of integrity, he'd have to step up.

"No, I can't. I've got to do this," he finally answered.

She shivered uncontrollably, refusing to acquiesce to the cold air that wrapped itself around her like an unwelcome embrace. What could she say to make him stay out of it?

"Can't you just wait until after the holidays then? Just so that your parents can have both of their boys at the table at Thanksgiving, or around the tree at Christmas. Can't you at least do that?"

He hesitated. He didn't want to let Millie think his decision would change. But he did see kindness in her argument to wait a couple of weeks.

"Yes, I can do that," he said. "But not much longer."

"No time like the present," Icky said when he told Mr. Bolles that he planned to sign up for military service. He'd enlist now, and then be inducted right after Christmas: that was his plan. "And I hope my job will be waiting when I return."

"*You're* not going!" Mr. Bolles barked. "Apprentices and entry-level bakers can enlist, but I filed paperwork to keep you here!"

"Paperwork? What paperwork?" Icky asked, surprised by his boss's revelation.

"With the government," Mr. Bolles answered. "This bakery is giving up enough men, all of them abandoning good jobs right here to fight in a war over there.

"But I've put a decade of training into you," Mr. Bolles continued.

"So, . . . ?"

"So, *you* are not going anywhere. *You* are staying here on an occupational deferment."

"Can you just do that?" Icky asked, shocked that his boss had taken steps to restrain him from enlisting, without even telling—or asking—him.

"Of course, I can do that!" Mr. Bolles accepted the challenge. "The government can't steal all of a company's employees, and put a stranglehold on its business!"

Icky's head fell back suddenly as if he'd been sucker punched. The very freedom that he wanted to defend had been stolen from him by his own boss!

His jaw tightened as he held himself back from telling Mr. Bolles what he thought of his uninvited intervention.

"You don't have to thank me. Just forget all this nonsense about the Army, and get back to work."

Mr. Bolles had spoken. End of discussion. He turned, and headed toward his office.

But Icky wasn't finished. Under his breath, he corrected Mr. Bolles: "It was going to be the Navy."

"So, you can't enlist?" Millie asked when Icky told her about his boss going behind his back, and filing "essential employee" status to keep him at the bakery. "They won't take you?"

"I could challenge it, I think," Icky said, "but not without causing trouble. And when I get back, I couldn't count on the bakery for a job."

"Assuming you come back," she asserted softly.

He ignored her remark. She wasn't the one he wanted to spar with. No, that was Mr. Bolles. He had expected his boss to assure him that his job would be waiting, not to undermine him!

"If it weren't for our start during the Depression," Icky said, "I'd fight him on this!"

Millie didn't say anything.

"But he's got me trapped! What if the country falls apart when the war is over? I couldn't support Mary Lou and you if Bolles refuses to take me back."

"How did he do this?" Millie said. She wanted details. Could she count on this restriction to keep Icky from going to war?

"The word he used is 'critical'," he said. "Mr. Bolles wrote that I fill a 'critical need' that can't be replaced."

He had a disgusted look on his face. "As if I do anything so important that one of the other bakers couldn't step in! I don't!"

"Icky, . . . "

"And since so many of the younger men are gone, he threw staff shortages into the paperwork as reason for holding me back home, too."

He paced around the room.

"I'm not 'critical'," he protested. "I bake bread! What's so important about that?"

"Mr. Bolles always says that bread is the staff of life, and essential to the nation's health," she tried to appease his anger. "Especially now that he's using the enriched flour."

In truth, she felt conflicted. Of course, she didn't want Icky to enlist! But she also didn't want him to feel that Mr. Bolles had pushed him around. Or to feel looked down at for getting some sort of deferment when friends and neighbors were going off to fight. And Henry. Especially Henry.

"I'm sorry this didn't work out the way you wanted," Millie said. "But you are critically important to Mary Lou and me. Maybe that will have to be enough for now."

She admitted that she was prejudiced when it came to Mr. Bolles. His expectation that Icky work extra hours anytime he wanted meant they gave up a lot of family time.

But in this instance, she wanted to shout for joy over his meddling. Icky's role in protecting Mary Lou and her: that was just as sacred as fighting for the nation. She was sure of it.

She wouldn't say it now, though. She'd let this situation settle down.

"Alma is marrying Dick next week," Ma announced at Sunday dinner.

"Next week!" Icky said. He'd wondered why his sister hadn't joined them at the table after church, but guessed that she must be dining with Dick's family. And she was, but the reason wasn't what he'd have guessed.

"It will be Friday evening at the church, and then they'll have the weekend together before he's inducted into the Army."

"Kind of sudden, isn't it?" Icky said.

"She decided she doesn't want him to worry about losing her while he's overseas," Ma said.

"Seems that everybody is enlisting," he complained, making the obvious point that he wasn't among them.

"Nobody thinks any less of you," Pa said. "And you registered for the draft, like the government requires. That's all you can do now."

"It just doesn't feel right."

"The decision is not yours to make," Pa said. "Find your peace with things as they are."

"There's more news about your sister," Ma said. "She's moving to Buffalo."

"What?" Millie exclaimed.

"She's got herself a factory job in a munitions plant," Ma repeated. "She's going up tomorrow to see an apartment she'll be sharing with two other Army wives."

"I can't believe all this!" Icky said, disagreeably. Even his little sister was planning to be involved in serving the nation's defense. And he, the older brother, was going to do what? Bake bread, that's what.

"What's got into Alma that she thinks she needs to work in a munitions factory?" he scowled, more at himself than at her decision.

"She says that once Dick's unit heads overseas, she'll be doing her part by working on the line. Maybe it will make her feel closer to him," Ma offered.

"I know some of the girls are taking men's jobs at Olean Tile, or even working the production line at the oil distillery," Icky acknowledged. "But why does Alma have to go all the way to Buffalo? When the weather's bad, that's a two-hour drive from home."

"Like she said, she'll be living with other Army wives. Maybe she's not coming home that often," Ma guessed.

"She's the youngest girl," Icky said. "It doesn't seem like she could be old enough for all this."

"They grow up before you know it," Pa responded, tousling Mary Lou's curls affectionately. "That's why we love 'em all we can while we got 'em."

"We do, Pa," Icky said, smiling at Mary Lou. "We sure do."

"I have a new friend!" Mary Lou announced, since she seemed to have the adults' attention. "Her name is Wilda, and we're going to be best friends forever!"

"How nice," her grandma said, dishing another small pork sausage and a bit of gravy onto her granddaughter's plate. "Is this enough?"

"Mm-hmm!" Mary Lou said definitely. "And we tell secrets!"

"Do you now?" Ma Haut encouraged. "Well, that's very nice to have someone to share thoughts with!"

"I didn't know you had secrets," Icky said. "Tell me one!"

"I can't, Daddy! Then it's not secret!"

"Aw," he said. "Don't you have just one secret for me to know?"

"You tell me a secret, and I won't tell Mommy," Mary Lou suggested, reversing his request on him.

"Why do I get left out?" Millie asked.

"You're not left out!" Mary Lou explained. "Daddy will tell me a present he's getting you for Christmas!"

"Oh, okay then," Millie said. "I didn't know I was getting a present!"

Mary Lou nodded, and swallowed a spoonful of her dinner. The problem of secret telling was over. She'd worked it all out to everyone's satisfaction.

"Sounds like Mary Lou likes the new house," Ma said.

"Everyone likes it," Icky answered. "Millie did a great job getting us settled. She even put on fresh paint in the living room, so we're ready for the holidays."

"Looks pretty good, if I say so myself," Millie concurred.

"And . . . ," Millie started, but then hesitated, and looked at Icky. "I guess we can tell people. It's been three months."

"I know! I know!" Mary Lou said. "The secret is . . . shhh! A baby!"

"A baby!" Ma Haut exclaimed.

"Gord and Marg are expecting," Icky said quickly.

"Oh, for a minute I thought you . . . "

"Ah, no," Icky said. "Not that I know of, that is."

"No," Millie confirmed solidly. "Mary Lou is getting a cousin!"

"What's a cousin?"

"A baby relative who lives with Uncle Gord and Aunt Marg. You'll see when he or she gets here," Millie said. "You'll be happy."

"Oh, I remember about cousins. I want a girl cousin this time," Mary Lou said. "Then I can share her with Wilda."

"We'll see what Aunt Marg can do about that," Millie said.

"Also, because boy cousins are mean!" Mary Lou added, making a frown.

"You don't want your pretty face to freeze like that, do you?" Millie said. She knew what Mary Lou meant, though. When his parents weren't looking, Mary Lou's cousin liked to pinch, and hard! She'd stopped his antics when he went after her daughter, though, by giving his arm a little pinch, and telling him that he deserved it because "turnaround is fair play."

"I heard you gave the kid some of his own medicine," Icky said.

"He cried worse than the girls, probably because he got caught," Millie answered.

"That one messed with the wrong person," Icky replied, "because as I recall, you pinched me once, too."

"I remember," she smiled at how she woke him when he fell asleep in the theater on their second date. "As for mean little boys, pinching needs to be stopped. Getting tweaked back served the little bugger right."

Pa and Ma Haut blinked at one another. Maybe that one did respond best when his behavior had consequences.

21

The Flood of '42

A FLASH OF LIGHTNING and a loud crack shook the house. Icky and Millie instantly leapt from bed to look out the window; its glass trembled as thunderboomers rumbled down nearby hillsides. Treetops in the front yard were swaying, and their leaves rustled nervously.

Another crack!

They both jumped as lightning bounced off limbs, creating tree x-ray skeletons against low-hanging, dark clouds. A jagged wind swooped in then, ripping smaller leaves from branches and flinging them around. Within seconds, the rain turned into liquid shrapnel, pelleting the ground.

"I thought this storm would have passed through by now," Icky said, switching on a lamp.

"I'll turn on the radio while we still have power," Millie said, delicately moving the tuner dial back and forth to find a sweet spot between the rough static:

> Flooding of the Allegheny River is nearing twelve feet, with no expectation of rain ending soon. Smethport residents are asked to evacuate to emergency shelters at higher elevations. Towns downstream, such as Eldred, Portville, Salamanca, Allegany, and Olean are in imminent danger of flooding. Also rising is the Genesee River, putting Belmont and Wellsville at risk. Many secondary roads in southwestern New York and north-central Pennsylvania are undrivable. In several communities, power lines are down, and additional outages are expected. . . .

The phone on the hall stand rang. Millie turned down the radio volume as Icky answered. He listened for a few seconds, and then finally said into the receiver, "Okay, we'll meet you there. . . . Right. . . . Be careful driving! . . . We will. . . . We love you, too. Bye."

"Millie!"

"Right here," she said. Mary Lou was in her arms. "Who was it?"

"My parents," he answered. "The Allegheny is flooding, so we need to get to higher ground. They said the Eagles Club is the nearest shelter, and they're on their way."

"I'm hungry," Mary Lou said.

"I'll get your cereal," Millie promised, and then to Icky she added, "And I'll get some food packed."

"Good!" he agreed. "I'll throw on clothes, and pack a few things." He went back to their bedroom.

"I'll pack my own things!" she yelled toward him. He'd never know what a woman needs to pack, especially in an emergency.

The two of them scurried around. As Icky set the first box by the front door, he peered out the front window. The street was becoming a river.

"Hurry up! We've got to leave before Seventh Street is too deep to drive through!"

"We're ready!" Millie told him anxiously.

"Did you pack the sleeping bag for Mary Lou?"

"Got it. Also, blankets and pillows, underwear, and light sweaters," Millie confirmed.

Icky double-checked the boxes of food Millie put by the door.

"Canned goods, pasta, rice—anything that can be made into soup or casseroles or a dish to pass," he noted.

"Yes! I said we're ready!"

"Did you grab the bourbon? And spices: all of them," he commanded as he marched to the kitchen.

"I'll get them! Good grief! I didn't know we'd need all of that," she challenged.

"Never mind," he said. Returning with his hands full. "I'll just drop all these little spice tins into the box with the canned goods."

"This storm seems to be getting worse!" Millie said as she put on her raincoat. Icky was at the window again.

"A torrent is gushing down the street. We need to get going! Now!"

"Did you reach Gord and Marg?"

"Their phone must be out. We can swing around to check on them."

"Your parents are probably at the Club already," Millie said. "It's been twenty minutes since they called."

"Yeah, Ma said they were on their way out the door. They know floods," he added, remembering Pa's story about how the family ended up in Olean. "We've got to go."

"Here, put this on," Millie said, handing a jacket to Mary Lou.

"I don't want it," she protested. She'd been sensing tension in her parents' voices, and decided that the best place to be was home.

"Uncle Gord and Aunt Marg and Baby Patty will be there," Millie cajoled. "You don't want to be the only one left out, do you?"

"But I can't take my toys!" Mary Lou whined. She wasn't sure that this little excursion was all the fun her mommy was making it out to be.

"You'll have so many girls and boys to play with," Millie insisted as she guided Mary Lou's arm into her jacket sleeve. "And everything will be right here when we get back, so you'll have something to look forward to."

"But . . . "

"No more complaining," her mother ended the conversation as she buttoned the top button on Mary Lou's jacket.

"Did you reach your father?" Icky asked about Pa Huff.

"No answer. Richard is with him, though. They probably bundled up, and walked in to town."

"The water is rising over the curb, Millie," Icky said. The street sewers were so clogged that instead of emptying, the drains burbled and spurted like angry fountains.

Icky opened the front door, and as the rain stung his face, his thoughts turned to Henry for a brief moment, for under normal circumstances he would have helped Pa and Ma to the shelter, and then come to their house to lend a hand. Icky prayed for his brother's safety, even as he worked to get Millie and Mary Lou out of harm's way.

"I'm taking these boxes to the car," he announced, hunching over the two he'd stacked in his arms. It was time to make a run for it. A horn blared from the street as he stepped out, and he turned his face into the pelting rain.

"It's Gord and Marg," Icky yelled back to Millie.

"Going to the Eagles Club," Marg yelled through the passenger window.

"Right behind you!" Icky yelled as he dashed to his car.

"We'll wait," Marg insisted. "Better to convoy, just in case something happens!"

"Thanks!" he returned, the wind roaring in competition.

"C'mon, Millie! Mary Lou!" Icky ordered as he grabbed the remaining boxes.

The house didn't have eavestroughs, so the rain streamed like a waterfall over the roof's edge in front of the door. Millie tore through it with Mary

Lou in her arms, and by the time she got to the car, they both had soaked heads. She snuggled Mary Lou into the middle of the front bench seat, and Icky backed out. Everyone headed toward State Street.

"Oooh, I hear water sloshing up around the wheels," Millie said.

"Good Lord, help us!" Icky prayed. The current in the street had grown muscular, thrashing and churning and ready to fight; Icky clenched the steering wheel with tight fists, and continued to drive upstream.

Mary Lou clung to Millie.

"It's okay," she calmed her. "Just a lot of water. A big, cold bath for the car."

"I can hardly see through the windshield," Icky said.

"Streetlights on after daybreak seem unnatural," Millie noted.

"I'm scared, Mommy," Mary Lou whimpered.

"Oh, Mary Lou, the clouds just came down, and puffed up their big cheeks, and now they're blowing all over town—like this," she reassured her as she made a face, and blew kisses.

Mary Lou considered the explanation, and finally blew kisses back.

"One more block," Icky said. "We're going uphill; the water isn't as deep."

As they turned the corner and approached the Eagles Club, the sideways rain slammed into the side of the car, swaying it left and right.

"When we get there, I'll pull up to the door to let you two out. You run in," he said. "Tell anybody inside to hold the door open, and I'll hand in all the boxes."

But as they came into the parking lot, a team was already lined up to receive newcomers. They opened the car door, reached in to help Millie, and then grabbed Mary Lou to bring her quickly into the building.

"We've got boxes in the back seat, and more in the trunk," she said loudly enough to be heard over the storm.

"Give us your trunk key," one of them ordered Icky.

He turned off the engine, and handed over his keyring. The car was emptied in seconds, and Icky started it up again to find the highest spot in the parking lot. As he made a mad dash for the Club, he glanced over his shoulder. Even nearby buildings seemed to be huddled together, bracing against the mean wind and threatening rain.

Gord caught up, and strode quickly alongside him.

"Whew!" he said. "This is abso-damned-lutely the worst storm I have ever seen!"

"Even wetter than the day I beat you in our first swimming contest," Icky said.

"Your memory is fading, old man," Gord said. "You lost that race."

"Won the girl," Icky countered. "How's everything on Thirteenth Street? Any trouble getting to us?"

"I wasn't sure we'd make it to you, but once we were going, it wasn't as deep over your way. You must be at a higher elevation."

"Not by much!" Icky said as they entered the building.

"Haut!" someone called out from the kitchen. "Thank God! We need you back here!"

Icky shook the rain off his slicker, and grabbed two boxes of canned goods from the stack by the door.

"How's it going?" he said as he set them on the counter.

"I'll tell you how," one of them answered. "The women are going to watch the kids, and get everyone settled. And we've got you, so the men are taking over the kitchen."

"Great plan," Icky agreed. "Let's see what we've got here."

Everybody brought food, and the guys had already begun unpacking and organizing cans and boxes.

"What's this?" Icky said. "A whole ham? And a roasted chicken?"

"You wouldn't leave 'em behind, would you? We got a few packages of ground beef in the refrigerator, too."

"Okay, first, we make soup!" Icky said. "This storm has everyone on edge, and soup will calm 'em all down. And we need to use up that chicken."

"Who does what?"

"Debone the bird," Icky ordered one of the men. "And keep the carcass; we'll make stock with some of those onions, a carrot or two if you see any, and celery. And I know we have celery because Millie packed it."

"You," he said, pointing to Gord, "chop up the deboned chicken meat, small pieces—child-sized—so we can feed a lot of people, and then refrigerate it 'til the stock is done.

"You," he said to another one of the guys, "start chopping celery leaves and the smallest ribs. Less than a quarter inch thick."

Icky continued giving orders: "Somebody look through the stores to see if anyone brought noodles. If not, we can make some. I saw a couple dozen eggs on the counter over there."

"We'll need salad," one of the men said.

"I'm on it," another volunteered.

"What about the ham?" one of the guys said, eyeing it.

"Tomorrow's lunch, if we're still here!" Icky said, preparing to guard it. "There's enough for sandwiches, and the bone can be used for another pot of soup. And you can start that soup now by soaking some of those dried beans over there. They need to soften overnight."

Everyone found a task to complete, while the women set up a buffet with bowls and spoons.

"Anyone think to make coffee?" one of them asked. "We could use some. A couple of men walked all the way here, and they're soaked to the bone."

"Sounds like it could be Pa," Gordon said.

"He doesn't drive," Icky said as the two of them headed into the community room.

"There's an urn in the pantry," one of the guys responded to the request for coffee. "I'll plug it in."

"I've got Pa," Millie said, turning Icky and Gordon back to the kitchen. She already helped her father pull off his wet coat, and found a blanket to wrap him in.

"Sit here, Pa," she instructed. "Away from the front door drafts."

He did as she ordered, this time.

"No need to fuss," he grumbled through chattering teeth.

"What were you thinking, dressed like that!"

"Couldn't find my rain slicker," he defended himself. "Thought this one would do."

"Well, it didn't, did it!" she admonished, rubbing dry the back of his neck.

"I can do that!" he grabbed the towel from her. "I'm not Mary Lou!"

"You wouldn't know it!" she argued.

"Hot coffee in just a few minutes," announced the woman who asked that the urn be plugged in.

"Thanks," Millie said.

"Glad to do it," she answered. "We all could use some. I'm Eva, by the way."

"I'm Millie Haut, and this is my father, Ed Huff."

"Nice to meet you, Millie. And Ed," she said, smiling intentionally into his eyes.

"I'm going to check on Mary Lou," Millie told her father. "I'll bring coffee, Pa, as soon as it's ready."

"I can do it," Eva offered, her voice as sweet as a wren's syrupy warble. "I'd like a cup, too."

She sat in the metal folding chair next to Pa Huff. "Mind if I wait here 'til the coffee is brewed?"

"Glad to have the company," he said off-handedly. But then, realizing the situation he'd put himself into, he wished he hadn't been so cordial. He didn't know where to start a conversation with a woman, especially not one as pretty as this Eva. Ma had always talked with the gals at the Moose Lodge; he had gravitated to the men. But now he was stuck.

"How far was your walk to get here, Ed? The street where you live must be flooded already," she guessed.

He noticed that she squinted, like she was always ready to smile. And her face was framed in the prettiest silver curls.

"Well, Olean is only about two miles, one side to the other," he answered. "I walk it every day, to and from work."

"Do you?" she said with interest in her voice. He noticed her tone, soft and gentle, and it eased him from the drenching he'd taken.

He looked down at the sopping wet hat he'd been wadding up in his lap, and ran a hand through his thick salt-and-pepper hair. It's matted, stuck flat to my head; I must look like a drowned rat, he realized self-consciously.

They chatted for a few minutes, and found they shared a common history. They liked the same hardware store, shopped at the same butcher, and preferred their coffee hot and black.

"I'll be right back with two cups," Eva said.

"I can walk up there."

"Oh, no! You have to save our seats!" she insisted. She wanted to do this little thing for him: show him she knew how women cater to their men, just in case he might be someone she'd want to get to know better.

She returned quickly with two thick white mugs, expecting to continue their conversation. Before they knew it, two hours had passed, and the smell of homemade noodle soup filled the community room.

Icky marched in from the kitchen authoritatively, taking long strides as he carried the large pot to the end of the buffet table. Everyone cheered and applauded with as much enthusiasm as if he'd delivered a Thanksgiving turkey.

"Dinner's ready!" he shouted, adding, "and the line starts here!" He handed a ladle to Richard.

"Get your bowl, and come on over!" his brother-in-law echoed.

"Would you like to have our meal together?" Pa Huff asked Eva.

"Why, that would be lovely!" she accepted.

"I hope they have crackers. I always like to break crackers into my noodle soup. Makes it good 'n thick."

"I've never tried that!" she said. "I bet it would be tasty!"

"After you," he said, extending his arm for Eva to go before him.

"Thank you, Ed," she said sweetly as she slid in.

As DAY PASSED INTO evening, the children were snuggled into sleeping bags or tucked into blankets, and the radio was turned on in the background for the latest weather reports.

"Thank goodness we still have electricity," Millie whispered to Icky.

"Even if it does go out, the stove and oven are gas," he said. "As long as those lines aren't broken, we can prepare hot meals."

"You did a good job feeding so many people today, and in such a short time, too," she complimented him. "Almost like you work in a kitchen for a living."

"I've had some practice," he said, kissing her forehead, and then yawning. "I could fall asleep right here in this chair."

"Good," Millie said, studying the row of people lying on the floor, "because that's about all that's left."

"Where's Mary Lou?" he asked.

"The little ones are upstairs in the party room," she nodded toward the doorway leading to the steps. "Your mother suggested she invite Patty to share your sleeping bag, so they're having a secret slumber party."

"Sounds like Ma," Icky said, yawning again. "She used to do the same thing with Erna and Alma when they were little."

He crossed his arms over his chest, and closed his eyes. In seconds, he was snoring, loudly, his rumble blending in with the rain pounding the roof.

THE CHILDREN WERE THE first to wake the next morning. One by one, they rubbed their eyes and wrinkled their faces, finally realizing they'd slept in a big room upstairs from lots of people they didn't know. Childhood instinct suggested that some grownup would tell them to get back under their blankets if they stirred, so they stayed put for a while.

Icky was accustomed to being at work before dawn, and had already slipped into the kitchen to mix a few loaves of bread dough. While they were baking, he diced tiny bits of ham to season a skillet; he'd make scrambled eggs as soon as folks were up—which wouldn't be long as the aroma of fresh bread had the men on their feet. One of them waved silently at Icky, and pointed to the coffee urn: he'd take care of that. Another got a bowl, and started beating eggs. A third rustled through the supplies, and found peanut butter and jelly.

"Let these loaves cool as long as possible before breakfast, and then slice half of them," Icky told one of the men. He'd have preferred to cool them completely, to intensify the flavor of the wheat, but this morning the priority was hungry mouths.

"And use a serrated knife," he added. "The rest can be cut later for lunch sandwiches."

The morning din was subdued, as adults stretched limbs gone sore from sleeping on a hard floor. A second urn of coffee was prepared, and Icky delivered bread to the buffet table. Gord and Richard were right behind him with huge skillets of scrambled eggs.

The smell of food tempted a herd of children down the stairs.

"Get some now, while it's hot!" Icky announced to the waking crowd.

People lined up slowly, the children running ahead to see what was being offered before deciding whether or not to take a plate.

"This is all we got," Icky said to one of the little grumblers. "No picky eaters allowed, so take some or starve until lunch!"

They got plates.

Ma Haut smiled, thinking that that was just how she used to speak to Icky and his sisters and brother.

"Just a tiny spoonful of eggs, Daddy," Mary Lou said. "I'm having bread with peanut butter!"

"You got it!" he said, agreeably.

"Look out those windows! The parking lot is a lake," one person observed as they stood in line to fill plates.

"Hope our car doesn't get damaged," said another.

"We're all safe and sound, and here together," said a third, nodding at the children. "Let's just focus on that."

Someone turned on the radio, and tuned it to the news:

> And in southwestern New York and northeast Pennsylvania, there's no end in sight to the biggest summer rainstorm this part of the nation has ever seen. The Allegheny River flooded to over sixteen feet overnight. Governor Herbert Lehman has called in the Coast Guard, Red Cross, and American Legion to rescue New York residents who may be trapped in their homes, this on the heels of similar actions of Pennsylvania Governor Arthur James, who declared a state of emergency yesterday. In international news, fighting overseas continues as the United States Army Air Forces flew their first mission in Europe a few days ago. Elsewhere, just northwest of Cairo, Egypt, the German forces are said to be stalemated, as Rommel's men are running out of ammunition.

"Where is Henry?" Millie asked her mother-in-law. "Any news from him?"

"We're not sure," Ma Haut said. "He thinks he'll be sent somewhere in the Pacific when he finishes his training, probably in a year or so."

"I read that Japan invaded the Aleutian Islands off of the Alaska Territory," Millie said.

"They say it's an important spot strategically."

"I guess we better hold on to it then," Millie said.

"Seems so," Ma Haut agreed. She paused. "But whether he's there or someplace else in the Pacific Ocean, it seems he'll be fighting the Japanese. And you know what that means."

She wouldn't finish her thought, not out loud, not in front of the children.

Millie nodded. She understood.

22

Perfect Misfortune

As soon as breakfast was over, a crew of men washed the dishes, while the women tended to the children. Pa Huff had a second cup of coffee with Icky's parents, and caught up on their family news. His eyes eventually wandered over to Eva, who was sitting just a couple of tables away. She smiled, and gave him a small wave, so he nodded back, and held up his coffee cup. Taking his gesture as an invitation held over from the day before, she walked over.

"Good morning!" she greeted everyone. "How are you this fine day?"

"Kind of cheery at this early hour, aren't you?" Pa Huff said with a smile on his face.

"Well, I've enjoyed a most lovely rest on this nice solid floor, and dreamed the sweetest dreams. And the food in this establishment is yummy, too! Just smell!" she added, whiffing the air.

They all laughed.

"That's my son-in-law baking the bread," Pa Huff bragged. "These are his parents, Heinrich and Emma Haut."

"I'm so happy to meet you!" Eva said genuinely.

"Eva's the one who got the coffee perking yesterday," Pa Huff said. Including a woman in a conversation was as unusual for him as fish swimming upstream, but he didn't seem to notice.

"We thank you for that," Ma Haut said.

"Your son bakes bread?" Eva repeated. "How impressive!"

"He does it for a living at Bolles Bakery," Ma Haut nodded.

"Been there for over a decade," Pa Haut said, proudly.

"We're lucky he's stranded with all of us then," Eva responded. "I'm going to get another cup of coffee. Can I warm anyone else's cup?"

"I'll go with you," Pa Huff offered. "I could use a drop or two more myself."

Ma Haut watched the two of them mosey off to the other side of the room.

"Seems like a nice person," she said when they were out of earshot.

"She does," Pa Haut agreed. "This flood could be the best thing that's happened to Ed in a long while."

"Yes," Ma Haut agreed. "And it's unlikely he would have met her otherwise."

"Well, we'll wait to see if anything comes of it," Pa said. He wasn't one to speculate on how folks spent their time. That was private.

ICKY CONTINUED TO COMMANDEER the kitchen crew until finally, on the fifth day of the storm, the rain subsided.

"The sun is taking its own sweet time melting the morning fog, though," Icky said, "and we're running low on stores."

"How much is left?" Ma Haut asked.

"Enough for a day or two longer, but all of the flour and sugar are gone. I used up all of Millie's spices, too."

"No one thinks to bring spices to an emergency shelter," Ma said.

"I did!" Icky pointed out. "How else were we going to flavor the food?"

"We should be thankful we had any food at all!" she pointed out. "And never in a shelter would we expect hot meals—which is what you men gave us."

"Everyone made the best of a bad situation," he agreed. "And one bad situation that needs to be rectified if we're staying here even one more hour is this coffee. This tastes like sludge. Who's in charge of cleaning the urn?"

Icky left to get the job done, complaining all the way.

"We aren't stuck in a used car shop," he groused. "Coffee is the one thing we still have plenty of, so it better be good."

"The next question is what we'll find when we get home," Pa Haut said, changing the subject, 'though he'd like a fresh cup of coffee, too. Sleeping on the cold floor had taken a toll on his bones, and he was ready to get back into his own bed. Ma nodded in agreement. She wanted to get started cleaning up whatever mess lay ahead of them.

"Gordon and Richard took a walk to see what downtown looks like," Icky said as he returned with fresh cups of coffee for everyone. "They can let us know if the roads are passible."

"What's the latest news on the radio?" Ma asked.

Icky turned on the Philco, and tuned to the local station:

> Water continues to rise downstream as the Allegheny River rushes from the high plateau region in Potter County, Pennsylvania. Flooding is expected to crest at over twenty feet in the lowest areas of the flat grades near Olean, New York. . . .

"Twenty feet!" Icky said. "Where are the lowest areas?"

"Around here? Streets run downhill from State and Union," Pa said. He knew the grades from pedaling across town to work at Socony every day.

The radio announcer continued:

> . . . The Coast Guard and Red Cross have been working together to evacuate entire villages in both states. Washed out bridges are reportedly making that effort more difficult. In towns up-stream, demolished buildings show the devastation wrought by the worst flooding seen in this area in decades. Thus far, sixteen lives have been lost.

"Oh, my dear Lord!" Ma Haut exclaimed. "Those poor souls!"

"Thank God that we're here," said Pa Haut, "and that we're all together so we know everyone is safe."

"Everyone, except Henry," said Ma Haut, not wanting to leave out her youngest son when referring to God's grace.

"That's different," said Pa Haut. "We can't think about that now."

"I always think about that, Pa," she told him directly. "Always."

THE WOMEN PROPPED OPEN the Club's front door to air out the community room, and welcome in a breeze.

"I thought that old sun abandoned us!" said one of them.

"It's good to see everything bright again," said another. "But it all still feels dank."

"Smells like a bog," agreed the first.

"It'll be like that for a while—at least until the flooding recedes."

"How's it look up at State and Union?" one of them asked Gordon and Richard as they tromped inside.

"You should see it," Gordon said. "The roads are full of debris."

"Looks like the river had a temper tantrum," Richard added. "What a mess!"

"Hey, Ick!" Gordon called toward the kitchen. "We're going back to see how deep the flooding is down West State. If we get as far as Seventh Street, do you want us to check your house?"

"That would be great!" Icky said. "Thanks! The doors are unlocked."

"Yep, ours, too, although I don't think we'll get as far as Thirteenth Street."

"Don't take any chances," Icky said. "We'll save leftovers for your lunch."

WHEN GORDON AND RICHARD returned, their pantlegs were soaked past their knees.

"We got to your house, but you're not going to like the news," Gordon reported.

"How bad?"

"Water is over your front porch," he admitted. "We waded up the steps to look in, and saw it up couple of inches into your living room.

"Isn't that about right?" he asked as he turned to Richard.

"About right," he agreed. "Over the tops of our shoes."

"So we went in, and put the refrigerator and a few pieces of furniture up on pans we took out of Millie's cupboard. I think we saved some of it."

"Thanks," Icky said, "but don't give Millie that much detail yet. She's worked hard getting the rooms painted. No sense getting her worked up about the mess 'til we have to."

"Right," Gordon agreed. "But the point is that there's no going home yet. In fact, most folks will need to spend at least one more night here. I'm going to go tell Marg. She'll want to do some hand laundry."

"I'll survey the remaining food to see what we can throw together for dinner," Icky said.

TWO DAYS LATER, THE floodwaters receded enough that Icky could walk down to Seventh Street, and inspect the damages at his house for himself.

"We can't move back in until it's all cleaned up," he told Millie when he returned. "We can stay with your dad, or we can go to my parents' home. Both have offered to take us in."

"Actually, Marg's mother out at Cuba Lake is going to take Mary Lou and Patty," Millie told him. "She's got room, and they can pretend they're on vacation."

"Good plan. Thank her for us," he said, relieved.

"Done," she agreed. "So, I think you and I should bunk in with your parents for a few days. That way, we can help them get their place cleaned up."

"First, though, I'm going to try to start the car. I want to get it going while Gord is still here, so he can diagnose what's wrong if it doesn't turn over."

Icky held the key on Start while he pumped the accelerator to drive some fuel into the engine. It rumbled roughly as a gray fog coughed out of the exhaust pipe. Apparently, the car didn't like chugging gas.

"You know you're flooding that engine," Gordon said.

"Flooded just like the town," Icky responded. "You going to your dad's house?"

"I am. I want to get a look at it to be sure it's safe. Marg and Patty are going to her mother's cottage. So is Mary Lou, I hear."

"Yes, thanks for inviting her," Icky said.

"Doing what we can. And I bet my Pa could use an extra hand."

"He seemed to enjoy this storm a lot more than most people," Icky ventured an observation about his father-in-law and someone who appeared to be a new lady friend.

"I noticed a crooked smile on his face, too," Gordon said. "It was almost like seeing a teenaged Bull in the Woods."

"How'd he ever get the moniker, 'Bull in the Woods'?"

"Don't know. Probably his easy-going nature," Gordon speculated sarcastically.

"Spot on," Icky said. "I won't repeat that."

"My sister . . . correction: your wife . . . takes after him, too," Gord added.

"And I definitely won't repeat that!" Icky emphasized.

"Abso-damned-lutely not!" Gord said, laughing. "Not if you want peace under your roof."

"Good to spend the time together," Icky said, shaking Gordon's hand. "Thanks for all your help in the kitchen."

"You know what they say: We were cooking with gas!" Gordon concurred.

❖ ❖ ❖

"How MUCH LONGER WILL it take to finish cleaning up our house so we can move back?" Millie asked Icky.

"I know you're chopping at the bit," he answered, "but a musty smell is still lurking somewhere. It's not safe until we figure out where it's coming from."

"Where was that smell located at Gord and Marg's house?"

"Everywhere!" Icky said. "Worse than ours, for sure! The floodwaters were deeper down at Thirteenth Street."

"Maybe that's why the bank sold the place to them at such a good price," Millie suggested. "The expense of cleaning up the property and making repairs was probably going to be more than the rent they'd bring in."

"Could be. Anyway, we got it fixed enough for them to move back in," Icky said.

"They were lucky you knew what to do!" Millie pointed out.

"The disinfectants used at the bakery turned out to be a good start," Icky said. "The smell finally lifted."

"Thanks for helping," she said. "Gord wouldn't have known what to do."

"Well, it pays to begin a career at the bottom," Icky smiled, recalling his first job as a laborer at Bolles. He'd had to steam and sanitize everything back in those days.

"I hope our house is next on your list," Millie said.

"We'll probably finish by the end of October—or, maybe into November, if it's anything like Gord and Marg's situation. Then you can get back in there with your paint brush, and make it look the way you want it again."

23

Hand to Hand

"WE GOT A LETTER from Henry," Ma Haut said, handing the mail over for Icky to read. "He sent it ten days ago, just before he shipped out to some island called Bougainville."

"It's part of Papau New Guinea," Pa said. "Way out in the Solomon Sea. We looked it up at the library."

"What's the deal with fighting for a South Seas island?" Icky said.

"It's got an airfield," Pa answered. "The Japs are using it to stage offensives, and the Allies need to take it away from them."

"The newspaper reports a lot of fighting there," Ma said. "Last week they wrote about one called the Battle of Piva Forks."

She poured coffee, adding, "It's never good when a campaign gets a name."

"I think I saw that article," Icky said. "It involved units from the 3d Marines group."

"That's Henry's group," Pa said.

"I thought so," Icky said, "but I didn't want to speculate."

"*Ja*," Ma understood. "A 'bitter and bloody battle' against the Japanese, the report said, with 'close, hand-to-hand combat.'" The brutal language was branded onto her heart.

"You look your enemy in the eyes with that sort of fighting," Pa interjected. "The U.S. lost over a thousand men in that one."

He paused, finally conjecturing an impossible supposition: "Henry could have been there."

"Don't think that," Ma said.

"Can't be ignored," Pa said. He'd been on the front line in his own day. He knew what his son was going through.

"Well, there's no need to imagine the worse," Icky suggested.

"Whether he was there or some other battle, it's all the same," Ma asserted, refusing to allow her voice to quiver. "He's fighting in some far-off jungle. A mother doesn't have to like that."

Pa patted her hand.

She patted his back.

There was nothing else to say or do. Except pray.

"WHAT TIME DO YOU want us to arrive tomorrow?" Millie asked. She telephoned her in-laws early on Wednesday to finalize their plans for Thanksgiving Day dinner.

"We'll sit down at two o'clock," Ma Haut said. She was preparing a traditional American turkey dinner. She'd have preferred a *Masthühnchen*, as a chicken bred to be fattened up for more meat was less gamey. Even *Der Kapaun* would be better, she thought with nostalgia, but it was not to be. She would do in this country what was traditional here.

"Come an hour early so we can visit a bit before the meal," she added.

"Are you sure we can't bring anything?" Millie asked again. She was happy to contribute to the dinner.

"Just bring yourselves," Ma said. She always liked to prepare the Thanksgiving meal herself. And this year, she needed to be busy.

But later that day, Ma Haut telephoned back, her voice tight and restrained.

"I need you to come over here," she told Icky. "We got a special delivery letter about Henry. He's . . . he's been hurt."

"We'll be right there," Icky said obediently, planning to take Millie, too. But as he hung up the phone, he realized the possibilities that a special delivery letter might hold, and decided that this was no time for a child's questions or distractions.

"I don't think Mary Lou should come," he told Millie.

"No, no. We'll stay here," she agreed.

"I'll be back as soon as I can."

He arrived at his parents' home within five minutes, The Reverend Garber right behind him.

"Good to see you, Icky, but I'm sorry about these circumstances," The Reverend said.

"Thanks," Icky acknowledged as they walked toward the back porch. "How bad is it? Do you know anything?"

"No, I don't," The Reverend said. "They called me just a couple of minutes ago."

"Me, too," Icky said.

He opened the door into the kitchen, and invited their minister in.

"Hello, Mr. and Mrs. Haut," he said, taking Ma's hand, and then Pa's. Even after so many years as their pastor, The Reverend Garber wisely respected the German custom of addressing his adult parishioners by only their last names. First names were reserved for family and a few close personal friends. "I'm so sorry to hear that Henry's been hurt."

"Thank you for coming, Reverend," Pa Haut said, pointing to his chair at the head of the kitchen table. "Sit here. Make yourself comfortable."

"Thank you," The Reverend Garber said. "How are you doing, Mrs. Haut? This is quite a shock, isn't it?"

"We will manage, of course," Ma said. "And we're grateful to the Lord that it's not one of those hand-delivered telegrams."

"Here it is," Pa said, handing the correspondence to Icky.

The letter came in an official-looking envelope with a Marine Corps logo emblazing the upper left corner, and an impression of the American flag across the back flap. Ma had slit it open cleanly with a sharp knife.

"Read it for yourself," Pa continued.

Icky removed a thin crisp sheet of onionskin paper. But before he could read a word, Ma interrupted.

"He was at that Piva Forks battle," she said. "And then they sent him to some place called 'Hellzapoppin Ridge'. What kind of name is 'Hellzapoppin'?"

Icky could see that she immediately regretted the interruption, so he gently prepared to read aloud, saying, "Let's see, Ma":

> Your son, Henry Haut, demonstrated extreme valor and courage in the face of the enemy, . . . some of the toughest fighting of the campaign occurred at Hellzapoppin Ridge. He was engaged in a frontal assault to dislodge the enemy. . . .

"The enemy there would be the Japanese, right?" Icky paused, not to confirm, but to give his parents a moment to breathe, deeply, slowly.

"*Ja,*" Ma said, holding back her emotions.

"This week's newspaper story said that the other enemies in this part of the war are the jungle and the swamps," Pa recalled. "The Marines waded in, foot by foot, clawing and hacking through underbrush."

"I believe I read that article," The Reverend Garber nodded thoughtfully over his tented fingertips. "The men who took on that mission must be courageous beyond our experience here."

"*Ja*," Ma Haut said again. "That would be Henry."

Icky continued to read aloud:

> The 21st Marines reached the crest of the ridge on the sixth day of fighting. Japanese troops were finally cut off from their supply sources.

"That would be so they can't wage war in some of the other South Sea islands," Pa repeated.

"So, where is Henry?" asked the minister. "Do they say?"

"He's in military hospital somewhere," Pa said. "They're going to patch him up, and ship him back to the United States."

"It doesn't say anything about what happened to him," Ma complained. "We don't know anything except that Henry's been hurt!"

"You're right, Ma," Icky said. "It doesn't say anything about that. We're going to have to wait until . . . well, until we hear more."

"Waiting is one of the most difficult things we are called to do," The Reverend Garber said. "Just as God is patient with us, at times like this we need to be patient, as well."

Ma breathed in, but stiffly held her breath this time. She didn't want to be patient. She wanted to know what had happened to her second son, her youngest child. And she wanted to know when he would be home, in Olean, not just on American soil. She wanted to see his face, and look into his eyes.

"Patience," Pa noticed, and defended her, "is very difficult for us now."

"Then, let's pray together about that, shall we?" The Reverend Garber offered.

They folded their hands, and bowed their heads.

"Heavenly Lord," The Reverend Garber began, "who suffered with the people of Israel in their captivity and remained steadfast as they endured the trials of their enemies: we are gathered here to pray for Henry, a dear son and brother in this family, and a member of our church. We ask that you shine the light of your presence on him as he heals from injuries suffered in this war. We ask, too, that you bring all of us news of his condition, that it might ease our hearts. In these coming days, we pray that you would teach us patience and fortitude. Establish our hearts in you, that your strength may sustain us. Comfort us in knowledge of your kingdom, and fill us with hope in the victory of your son, Jesus Christ, in whose name we pray, Amen."

"Amen," they repeated together.

The Reverend Garber stood, preparing to leave.

"If you receive any other news, I trust you will call me," he said. "I've known Henry since he was in catechism classes. He's a good fellow, and I'd appreciate hearing about his situation as soon as you know anything."

"Thank you, Reverend," Pa said as he walked the minister to the back door. "That we will do."

Icky stayed with his mother and father, the three of them sitting quietly at the kitchen table with the letter from the Marine Corps centered among them.

God made no words for times like this, he thought to himself.

The sun fell into the western horizon, the direction of the South Pacific, the place where Henry was just one more Marine, Ma thought to herself. Her worry had a compass of its own as she imagined all the injured boys lined up just like the day they were inducted. Only this time, instead of standing in straight rows, they're lying on hard cots, waiting for help.

Ma suddenly realized how dark the room had become.

"Make on with the light, Pa," she said. "And you, Icky, go home to Millie and Mary Lou. Tomorrow is still Thanksgiving Day, and I have work for the dinner to do."

"Oh, Ma, are you sure you still want to do that?" Icky asked.

"Of course," she assured him. "Henry is injured, but he's alive. We can be thankful for that. And busy I need to be."

"If you're sure," he allowed. "But don't wear yourself out. And remember that you can change your mind anytime if you want to."

"I won't," she asserted.

"Be sure to tell Millie about this," Pa said as he prepared to shut the door, "and tell her we'll see her tomorrow."

"YOUR MOTHER JUST RANG," Millie said the following week as Icky came in the door from work. "They got another letter today, this one from Henry."

"Then his right arm and hand function well enough for him to write," he surmised. "And he can think and see well enough to compose a letter."

"Probably, unless one of those Red Cross workers took dictation for him," she cautioned. "Anyway, your mother wants us all to come over this time."

"Let me change out of these sweaty clothes first," Icky said. The bakery was busy all day, and working near the ovens was like being in a sauna. "Give me about ten minutes, and then we'll go."

On the drive over to Pa and Ma Haut's home, Millie apologized for suggesting that Icky not get ahead of himself with presumptions regarding

Henry's injuries. "I should have known this was on your mind, and I didn't mean to say we shouldn't have hope," she said. "I'm sorry if I was negative."

"Didn't take it that way," he said honestly.

The three of them climbed the back steps into the kitchen, and Millie reminded Mary Lou to be on her best behavior. "Play quietly, so Grandpa and Grandma can see what a polite girl their first-born granddaughter is."

Mary Lou put her index finger over her lips, and nodded obediently.

Ma opened the back door and ushered everyone in quickly before hanging their coats on hooks behind the door.

"It's really cold outside!" Icky said.

"What do you expect for winter!" Ma pointed out. "Sit down here, and warm your toes." She'd heated some bricks in the oven, and then wrapped them in quilted rolls under the table to take the chill off the dead space. "Pa will be right in, and then we can show you the letter."

"How are you doing, Ma?" Icky asked, hoping her answer would offer some indication of its content.

"Good to know what's what," she said, refusing to give anything away. She poured cups of steaming coffee as Pa came in, and laid the letter in the middle of the table.

"Henry wrote it himself," he said.

"*Ja, Ja*," Ma said, and immediately wished she hadn't repeated herself, as she knew it revealed how her heart was touched on seeing their names written in Henry's own hand. "We knew it right away," she added with a no-nonsense tone in her voice.

"You can see for yourself," Pa said, nodding at the envelope.

Icky braced himself for whatever news it might contain, and gently picked up the letter. It wasn't very long.

"Shrapnel," he said when he came to that paragraph, "but the doctors think that when he heals, he will walk again." He stopped, and looked around the table.

"Keep reading," Pa instructed.

Icky nodded, going slower. What else could it say?

"He will be transported back to the United States before the end of the month—maybe before Christmas—but he'll still be in recovery, so he won't be in Olean for the holiday."

Icky looked up at his parents.

"Keep reading," Pa said again.

"'When I woke from surgery,'" Icky read aloud, "'I found a Purple Heart pinned to my hospital gown.'"

"Henry got a Purple Heart?" Icky repeated, both proud of his kid brother, and concerned for the extent of his injuries. How badly must he be hurt to receive a Purple Heart?

"Go on," Pa said. "Just one more thing now."

Icky turned the letter over to finish it. "It says that Major General Alan Turnage presented the award right there in the hospital.

"So, the General himself was there?" he asked. "And he recognized Henry's service right then? Is that what it means?"

"We were hoping you knew," Ma said.

"That's what it says," Icky answered, handing the letter over to Millie, so she could read it, too.

"What exactly is shrapnel?" she asked.

"When a bomb explodes, it sends off metal scraps that impale anyone in its range," Pa answered, recalling stories from the Great War. "Or the flying metal could come from a mine."

Ma shivered. She tried not to imagine the circumstances of how Henry was hurt. No, even though she wanted to know, she also didn't.

"I'm going to take the United States citizenship exam," she suddenly proclaimed.

"What?" Icky said.

"I'm going to study like Pa did, and I'm going to become an American citizen," she repeated.

"When did you decide this?" Pa asked.

"Right now," she answered. "If my son fights for this country, and earns a Purple Heart, then I want him to come home to a mother who's a citizen. Just like the rest of you!"

All eyes were on Ma.

Finally, Pa broke the silence. "You never said you were thinking about this."

"I mean it!" she insisted. "I'm doing it!"

"Yea, Ma!" Icky cheered her on with a smile. "Henry will be so proud."

"We're proud of him," she said defiantly. "So, I got to do this, and that's all there is to it."

24

Settling In

As World War II ended, over fifteen million servicemen sought employment in the U.S., and married the sweethearts who'd been waiting in the wings for them. The nation emerged as one of the globe's major economic players, and with that, demand increased for housing. Realtors shifted their sales approaches to cater to a seller's market.

"What would you think about renting out your upstairs unit to Millie and me?" Icky asked Gordon.

"Why would you want to move back up there?"

"We got that musty smell out of our house, but the structure just isn't as solid as it was before the flood," Icky explained. "It needs an owner who can give it more attention than we can right now."

"So, you're thinking of selling it?"

"Done already," Icky said. "We put it on the market last week, and it was snatched up in a couple of days."

"That quick!"

"We couldn't believe it either, but guys are coming home from the war, and getting married. They want places where they can start out."

"How's Henry doing, now that he's back?" Gordon asked. Everyone had been focused on his return—wanting to celebrate it, and at the same time, not wanting to make him relive experiences on the battlefield.

"He seems to be adjusting," Icky said. "Ma's decision to take the citizenship exam meant as much to him as it did to her. He's helping her study."

"Glad to hear it," Gordon said. "So, about this move: when do you want to be in?"

"The buyers want to take possession immediately, so if it's available, how about next weekend?"

"Well, sure, yes, of course!" Gordon agreed. "If Millie is okay with it."

"She's already packing," Icky confirmed. "She knows we have to go someplace. We thought it might be my parents' house, but this would be so much better."

"Seems to me that Marg and I helped you move from the upstairs unit to our downstairs unit a few years ago," Gordon remembered. "Now you'll be moving up again."

"And you were taking the upper. Remember? Millie asked if you would mind being close to a fussy toddler."

"Right! Marg and I were newlyweds!"

"I don't think Mary Lou will remember living here, but she'll like being near Patty," Icky said.

"And Marg will be glad, too!" Gordon said. "The last couple upstairs kept the radio on loud all the time, and threw parties every weekend. She finally had to ask them to find somewhere else to live. She'll be really happy to rent it out to you."

"Why is the Allegheny River spelled differently than Allegany, the town?" Mary Lou asked, looking up from the newspaper Aunt Marg and Uncle Gord passed upstairs when they finished with it. She'd always liked to read the funnies, of course. But her fourth grade teacher said students could earn extra credit by reporting on interesting stories.

"The river flows from here to Pittsburgh. The people who settled Pittsburgh came from France. Since they named the river, they got to decide how it's spelled.

"But our nearby town of Allegany was settled by people from England," Millie continued. "so they got to decide how the town name is spelled. "Okay?"

"Okay."

"Why do you ask?" her mother pressed.

"It looks bizarre with two spellings," Mary Lou answered. A moment later, she asked another question.

"Where's Akron?"

"Akron? It's in Ohio, near Cleveland," Millie answered. "It's about a three-hour drive away, maybe more."

"Oh," said Mary Lou, making a face. "It must be a despicable place."

Millie paused, and looked straight at her daughter.

"'Bizarre'? 'Despicable'?" she repeated. "Have you swallowed a dictionary?"

"Huh?"

"Where are you getting these words?" Millie asked.

"Reading," she answered easily.

"All right. Then why do you say Akron is 'despicable'?" She wasn't sure Mary Lou knew what it meant.

"Not Akron; Cleveland is despicable, because Grandma Haut's sister lives there. Right?"

"She does," Millie said slowly, waiting for an explanation.

"Everybody hates when she visits, because she's so mean. Daddy said she never gets a cold because even the germs don't like her."

"Mary Lou, I don't think you ought to repeat that."

"Well, . . . " Mary Lou stopped for a moment. Should she tell what else she overheard? That Grandma Haut's sister also lives with a man she isn't married to. Children aren't supposed to know some things, so if she defended herself, her mother would realize she was listening in, and then the grownups would make sure she wasn't privy to any other forbidden family tales.

She'd keep quiet.

"Why are you reading these stories in the first place?" Millie insisted.

"I just like certain ones," she diverted, "like this story about women drivers. In Akron, they don't get speeding tickets because they cry, so the policeman feels sorry for them. Or, if they're pretty, he doesn't give them a ticket."

"Let me see that," Millie said.

The article seemed to want readers to question why fewer women are ticketed for traffic violations than men, and in so doing, suggested that it's not because they're better drivers. Rather, it's because police officers don't enforce laws fairly.

"That officer admits to not having the guts to give tickets to women, and then talks behind their backs," Millie instructed her daughter. "What a bunch of hooey!"

"So, are women good drivers?" Mary Lou asked. "Even Grandma Eva?"

She remembered hearing about a little trip the newlyweds took right after they said their vows. Eva wanted Ed—or Grandpa Huff—to meet her relatives in Baltimore. She had a car, but didn't drive any longer because she couldn't see well enough. Pa could see, but he didn't know how to drive. So, they teamed up, and she took the wheel while he navigated.

"Grandma Eva needs new glasses," Millie said guardedly for young ears. "Other than that, she's probably a fine driver.

"Besides," she added, "Grandpa Huff is happier than he's been in a long, long time. And that's more important. Right?"

"Abso-damned-lutely!"

"Mary Lou!"

"That's what Uncle Gord says." She would defend herself this time.

"Living above Uncle Gord is giving you some bad habits," Millie criticized.

"Patty said it, too."

"When!" she demanded.

"When Aunt Marg was on the phone, and Wilda and I were keeping an eye on her."

"Did Aunt Marg hear?"

"Uh-huh," she admitted.

"What did she say?"

"She told her not to," Mary Lou admitted again.

"Then why are you repeating it now?"

"I wanted to try it. See what it was like."

"One try is enough," Millie warned. "Two tries is soap."

"WHEN ARE WE GOING to Grandpa Huff and Grandma Eva's house for Christmas?" Mary Lou asked.

"Christmas morning," Millie answered. "Uncle Gord and Aunt Marg are going, too."

"And Patty," Mary Lou added.

"Especially Patty! She's six, so Christmas is a big deal for her."

The holiday was a big deal for Mary Lou, too, but she wouldn't admit it. After all, she was almost ten years old, and that meant two digits! Some sort of privilege ought to accompany that coming of age; at least, that's what her friends and she wanted to believe.

A couple of days later, everyone piled into Icky's car, with Mary Lou in the front seat between her parents, and Patty in the back between hers.

"What about presents?" Mary Lou asked, noticing the tight quarters.

"Maybe there will be some if you were good, and Santa brought you any," her mother answered.

Mary Lou was about to protest that she knew where presents come from, but Patty was in the back seat. She still believes in Santa, she reminded herself.

Still, how would everything be brought home? The car didn't seem to have room for hauling back as much loot as she hoped for. And there would be Patty's gifts, too.

They arrived before Mary Lou could ask about return transport without seeming greedy. As they got out of the car, she automatically took Patty's hand to help her wade through the deep snow and up the front steps, while their parents unloaded the breakfast treats from the trunk.

"Merry Christmas!" Grandpa Huff and Grandma Eva greeted them.

"Welcome to our new house!" she added. They'd just moved to a new place out by Hinsdale Highway.

"Merry Christmas to you!" the guests cheered in return, adding, "Oh, how nicely you've decorated!" And, "Look at the tree!"

Mary Lou peeled off her coat, and helped Patty tug hers off, too. The six-year-old's eyes were fixed on the Fraser fir, covered top to bottom in tinsel and decorations. Its bubbling candle lights seemed to have her mesmerized.

"It's just perfect!" Marg said. She considered herself the unofficial authority on decorating since Bradner's put out the nicest holiday window displays in town. "We have a couple of small gifts to include."

"Let's take this food to the kitchen," Grandma Eva said to Gordon. "Thank you for bringing it. It smells wonderful!"

"Icky and Millie made it," Gordon said. "They're the bakers, you know."

"Yes! And I can hardly wait!" Eva smiled amiably.

"Me, too!" Mary Lou agreed. She was right behind the adults, eager to get them going, because after eating, it would be time to open presents. She'd mind her p's and q's, just as she had been doing, minute-by-minute, day-by-day—for weeks! And weeks!

As the grownups poured second cups of coffee all around, Mary Lou sensed that they were going to drag out their breakfast conversation. She slid off her chair and slipped out to the living room to sit with Patty, who was hovering near the tree again. Under the guise of keeping an eye on her little cousin, she'd at least be able to scrutinize all the boxes. If she weren't too obvious, she might get a peek at the names on the gift tags, too, although what she really wanted to do was dig through the stack and give each box a good shake, like she did at home when no one was looking. She'd even lifted the tape and slipped off the paper from a couple of boxes to see what was in them, but she was very, very careful so no one knew she'd been snooping. She was sure she got away with it.

But peeking now wasn't possible, not with the grownups going in and out of the living room every so often, and saying how wonderful it was to be together at Christmas, especially with little ones around. They meant Patty, of course, as Mary Lou was halfway to being a grownup. She didn't mind. As long as they didn't dawdle into third cups of coffee.

Finally, she heard someone suggest, "Should we open presents?"

"Maybe one or two," said another. "We don't want to rush."

"Sometimes it's more fun to anticipate what's in the boxes," said another, intentionally loud enough to make a point about not sneaking peeks into wrapped gifts.

"Let's play a guessing game," suggested one more grownup who knew the girls were listening. "Maybe we can figure out what is in . . . oh! But look! Some of the boxes have been moved around!"

Mary Lou was sitting on the floor near Patty, and near the tree, too, by default. She wore her most innocent expression.

"There's plenty of seats," Grandma Eva said, providing a cover story for anyone who might need it. Pa and she had arranged the chairs in a circle to be sure everyone would have a good place to participate in gift-giving festivities.

"Pa, how about if you play Santa, and hand out presents," Millie suggested.

"I can do that," he agreed, picking one up. "Let's start with these two since they have Santa pictures on them. This tag says . . . Patty! And this one says . . . Mary Lou!"

"Thank you," they each said, accepting their packages.

"Can we open them now?" Mary Lou asked tentatively.

The hopeful looks on their faces couldn't be mistaken.

"Of course!" the adults chorused. The girls had been so patient, so willing to put up with delays which everyone knew had to be torment for them. The fact was, though, that watching them was the moment the grownups had been waiting for, too.

Mary Lou read the tag, thanked Grandma Eva and Grandpa Huff, ripped off the paper, dropped it onto the floor, and turned the box around so she could lift the lid. It looked like . . . "It's a new sweater," she announced politely. "And blue is my favorite color."

Patty did the same thing, saying, "Pink!" when she opened her sweater box.

Mary Lou got up and gave each of them a hug and kiss, accompanied by another "thank you very much."

But she really wanted to sigh. She'd been hoping for toys. Certainly, one of the other boxes had to be paper dolls or furniture for her doll house. Her campaigning had been somewhat indirect this year as she was learning the fine art of suggesting gifts—a skill all girls need to learn—without coming right out and asking. But certainly, her parents couldn't have missed her clues:

corners of Sears catalog pages folded, and pictures circled in store flyers. Piles of advertisements suffered her perusal. She'd even discussed her choices with Wilda, making sure Mommy was in earshot at least a couple of times.

Oh, the anguish!

The cruelty of not knowing!

If waiting wasn't mistreatment of children—extended even into Christmas morning!—then, what was?

And worse: the gifts she'd sneaked a peek at after they were wrapped could have been the ones taken to church for its community collection. She didn't know about that when she pulled back the tape. Bitter agony!

Grandpa Huff handed out the next presents, first for Marg and Millie, and then for Gordon and Icky. Each of the women carefully removed wrapping paper, folded it, and set it aside so that they could use it again. The men clawed their packages open, crushed the giftwrap into balls, and tossed them across the room into a wastepaper basket. Patty watched the whole proceeding; she seemed to be trying to figure out how to play this game.

"Here's another one for Patty!" Grandpa Huff said next.

"Yea!" she squealed, shredding the giftwrap as her daddy had done, and smiling widely as she announced, "A dolly!"

"This is just what you were like," Icky said to Mary Lou. "But now you're getting more grownup presents."

Grownup presents were clothes and tools.

She smiled weakly to hide a worried response. Did this mean she wasn't getting her wish?

Icky nodded to Grandpa Huff, who reached way behind the tree to pull out a box hidden beneath a pile of other packages. Millie had to hide it off premises once she saw how the gifts were being investigated by her daughter at home.

"I believe this one might have your name on it," he said, handing it to Mary Lou.

The box was about the right size, and the weight suggested it could be what she'd been wishing for, too. But it was wrapped in brown shipping paper.

She pulled the ugly stuff off, hesitantly at first, until she saw bright red wrapping paper and a ribbon underneath.

"Grandpa," she said, "I know you did that."

"What?" he said as if he hadn't.

"I bet it's . . . " But she didn't dare finish the sentence, and jinx the possibility that her wish might be fulfilled after all.

"It is!" she shrieked, holding up the one gift she wanted more than anything else.

"It's doll house furniture!" she continued with glee. "There's a plastic bathtub with seahorses on the front! And a pedestal sink, and a little toilet! All the faucet parts move! See?"

She opened a little interior box. "Oh! A hamper, wringer washing machine, and ironing board!" Mary Lou added, holding up pieces for everyone's approval.

"And Grandma Eva crocheted that little bathroom rug, and made towels to match," Grandpa Huff pointed out.

"Oh, that's wonderful!" Millie acknowledged. "Mary Lou, look! They're blue!"

Mary Lou didn't miss a beat, immediately getting up to give hugs to her grandparents. "I love blue!" she said.

When all the packages were opened, the living room straightened, the leftover food stored, and the dishes done, Grandpa Huff and Icky and Gordon packed as many gifts as they could manage into the trunk of the car.

"What about the rest of the presents?" Mary Lou asked.

"Santa will move them later," Icky said.

"Really?" She looked at him skeptically. She wanted an answer: When would her gifts arrive home?

"Well, the *really* real answer is that we'll load the rest of the boxes when we come back to pick up Grandpa Huff and Grandma Eva for dinner," Icky clarified. "I wouldn't forget any of your precious stash."

"Good!" she affirmed. "Because I know what I got."

"And I know you'll take inventory," he answered.

"Mary Lou, it's for you," Millie said as she handed the telephone receiver to her daughter. "It's Grandma Haut."

"For me?" she asked as she crossed the room. Grandma Haut never called unless she meant business, and that meant Daddy or Mommy.

"Speak quietly," Millie cautioned her. "Daddy's asleep in his easy chair."

She nodded and took the phone.

"Hello?" she whispered into the handset. . . . "He did? . . . We can come get it now. . . . Oh, later will be okay then. . . . I love you, too. . . . Bye."

"What was that about?" Millie asked.

"Grandma Haut says she found a present that Santa left for me, but that I didn't open yet!" she answered.

"Oh! I wonder what that could be," her mother answered quietly. As if she didn't know.

"She said that I can get it when I go for my sleepover tomorrow."

"That's a good plan."

"Or we could call her back, and say we'll pick it up now," Mary Lou suggested.

"We could, but tomorrow will be soon enough. You have so many other new things to enjoy now, right?"

"Yes," Mary Lou allowed. But wondering what this extra gift might be was going to torture her again! And since she knew Grandma Haut would never give out any clues, she hadn't asked.

"How come Grandma Haut always wears heavy black shoes, and pins her hair back like she does?" Mary Lou asked.

"Keep your voice down," Millie said, reminding her again that Daddy might hear. "The shoes are called orthopedic. They're sturdy, and good for Grandma's feet. And as for her hair, she wears it in a bun because she's proper, and that's what proper ladies want to look like."

"Oh," Mary Lou said. She just thought Grandma Haut was fussy. And she was sure she'd never put those shoes on her own feet.

"Why does her skin look like waxed paper: the kind she flattens out and saves to use a second time?"

Millie sighed. How to answer innocent questions about age: that was the catch, as she didn't need her response to be repeated.

"Grandma Haut likes to save everything she can, especially things that are soft and still have value in them," she said.

"But her skin?" Mary Lou insisted.

"Is soft, too," she allowed. "That's one more thing that makes grandmothers special."

"But . . . ,"

"And like Wilda and you," she returned to the surprise gift, "she can keep secrets."

Mary Lou remembered how the two girls trusted one another with their thoughts and dreams, such as what they wanted for Christmas. For now, though, she wished Grandpa Haut had been the one to tell her about the unexpected gift. He was someone she could count on for a hint or two. He might even have let her come over right away.

But he hadn't been the one to call. She'd have to wait.

"I'M ALL PACKED!" MARY Lou told her parents after lunch the next day.

"It's only two o'clock," Millie said. "They aren't expecting you until dinner."

"I know. I just thought we could go over early."

"Four o'clock will be soon enough," her mother insisted.

Millie and Icky exchanged knowing glances. They were looking forward to Mary Lou's sleepover as much as she was. Maybe more, in fact, as they were celebrating their wedding anniversary that evening with a candlelight dinner reservation at Lucia's Italian. No children allowed.

But it would be a long, long time before they'd be able to say that again. Mark was born nine months later.

25

Caught in a Wringer

DURING THE DECADE OF the Great Depression when Mary Lou was born, the U.S. birth rate hovered at just seventeen percent; it was only slightly higher at twenty-one percent during World War II. But in 1947, the year Mark was born, the number of babies brought into the New World rose to nearly twenty-six percent, the highest ever recorded. Millie and Icky's son was part of a baby boom, and their boy was riding the highest curve of that wave.

His personality matched. From the moment he could focus his eyes, he was curious about everything going on around him: every footstep crossing the floorboards of their apartment, every smell wafting into his room from the kitchen, every light cracking through a doorway when his parents checked on him. He stared at bright colors dancing in the mobile over his crib, and screamed with delight whenever people came near: anything that moved fascinated him. Even when he was sleeping, Millie could see that something was going on with the boy.

"His eyelids never rest," she told Icky. "And he kicks at his blanket constantly. I can't keep him covered."

"As soon as he's out of the crib, he'll take off, too," Icky said.

"Augh! Don't tell me that! I don't like the idea of chasing him around a second-floor apartment. I can just see him slip past me through an open door and topple down those stairs."

"You said that when Mary Lou was taking her first steps, too," he reminded her. "This kid seems more likely to crawl and climb before he walks."

"Which means he'll come crashing onto these wooden floors and hit his head," she worried.

"Boys just need to explore," Icky diverted.

"That's how it was with my brothers," she agreed as she considered Mark's baby-steps stage.

"We'll figure it out," he assured her.

"Sometimes I wish we would have kept the house on Seventh Street. It . . . it . . . it had a yard!" she said, punctuating her remark with a sneeze.

"*Gesundheit!*" Icky blessed her health. "Fret about managing his high energy when the time comes."

"You're right," she agreed. "And thank you. Besides, I'm so much busier now, I hardly have time to think about tomorrow's problems."

"Busier with what?" he asked. After all, the apartment was smaller than their house, so Millie didn't have as much to clean. And Mary Lou was ten, so she took care of herself. How much busier could she possibly be?

"With di . . . di . . . dia!pers!" she sneezed repeatedly. "Excuse me. Lots and lots of diapers."

"*Gesundheit* again," Icky said. "Are you coming down with something?"

"I don't know," Millie said. "I'm a little tired, so maybe something's going on, but it's probably nothing. Besides, with two kids, I don't have time to deal with more than a few snee . . . snee . . . sneezes!"

Two days later, Millie was down for the count for the first time since they'd been married. While Icky wasn't practiced on how to take over laundry, housekeeping, and childcare duties, he thought he could step in. How difficult could it be? Besides, he had no choice, because he needed a set of baker's whites for work the next day.

"Mark needs diapers, too," Millie told him. As long as he was lugging out the wringer washer, he might just as well run those through. That's how she'd organize the work anyway.

Icky decided to wash the diapers first, thinking that that job would be easiest: they were flat. And weren't they already half-clean from soaking in the pail overnight?

It was full, of course, so he tilted the bucket gently over the edge of the toilet to empty the bleach and water, while holding back the dirty diapers. Both of his hands were occupied, so he got a full dose of the smell.

Ugh! Chemical and stink, one nasty combination, he thought as all the muscles around his nose tightened in disgust. He was glad to leave the bathroom, even for a minute or two, as he dragged the wringer washer from the back hall landing. He set it up next to the kitchen sink, and turned on the tap. Since the water heater was in the basement, a few minutes passed before hot water reached the second floor. While the spigot ran open, he retrieved the drained pail of diapers from the bathroom.

He filled a two-gallon bucket, and poured it into the laundry tub. The bottom was barely covered, so he added a second. And a third. And a fourth.

That ought to do, he decided.

"How much water?" he yelled to Millie, just to confirm. She was wrapped in a blanket, and curled up in a corner of the sofa where she could keep an eye on Mark.

"Five buckets for diapers," she yelled back. He decided four was probably enough.

"Where's the laundry soap?" he yelled next.

"It's new: Tide. On the shelf in the hallway. Orange box with blue letters," she yelled back, sniffling through her answer.

He read the side of the package: oceans of suds . . . washday miracle . . . cleaner than soap.

"What's this Tide stuff?" he asked, carrying the box into the living room. "I've never seen this before."

"Laundry detergent. It's supposed to be better than lye."

"Better how?"

"Suds up better, and rinses easier," she repeated the advertisement.

"Okay," he said, checking the ingredients list. "Maybe we ought to look at detergent products for the bakery." He remembered working as a laborer when he was a teenager. Keeping the locker room clean was one of his jobs.

"You'll see when you do your baker's whites," she agreed. "Add some of that 20 Mule Team Borax to the laundry tub, too."

"Where is it?"

"Same cupboard where you found the Tide, but on the bottom shelf."

And what was this 20 Mule Team stuff? He read the label: sodium borate . . . boosts cleaning . . . also can be used as hand soap. Okay. Sounds safe enough for a baby's bottom.

After the diapers swirled around in the soapy water for a few minutes, Icky hooked up a hose from the sink to the bottom of the tub so he could drain it. Then he got the bucket again, and turned on the spigot so he could add rinse water—but this time, he had to boil some first. He'd emptied the water heater with the wash load. Or maybe Gord and Marg were pulling water off the heater from their apartment downstairs.

"What a hassle," he said, wishing he'd offered to do some other chore for Millie.

After the diapers swished around in the rinse water and looked clean, he hooked up the drain hose a second time to empty the tub of rinse water.

The final step was wringing excess water from soppy diapers.

He brought in the seventeen-gallon galvanized aluminum tub from the landing, and positioned it beneath the wringer. Then, one by one, he inserted each of the diapers between the rollers, and turned the crank to pull them through.

He looked at the clock on the wall. Two hours! Just to wash baby diapers!

He tried speeding up the wringer process by inserting two diapers at a time, but that only made turning the rollers more difficult. Plus, the second diaper got caught, going round and round instead of falling out on the other side.

"How are you doing?" Millie called.

"This kid uses too many diapers!" he answered loudly.

"What?" Millie said.

"Nothing," he answered. "I got it." And under his breath added, "we're going to stretch the kid's four-hour feedings to six hours! We'd save a third of the work!"

He toted the heavy laundry basket down the back stairs—he'd do the second load when he returned—and hung the diapers on the clothes line. The winds were brisk, and he wondered how long it would take the laundry to dry in the cold. He recalled snippets of how Millie and her mother dried Mary Lou's diapers on the back porch when the weather turned to snow. Then they laid them over wooden racks near the radiator indoors. Of course, since he was working nights and sleeping through the morning, he never saw the whole process, but he remembered hearing something about it.

When Millie and he moved into their first apartment—which happened to be this same one, in fact—she'd argued that she'd be carrying laundry up and down these same back stairs every other day.

Winter is on its way now, he realized, and the snow is going to be as high as our thighs. Millie's not going to be able to hang diapers on the line in the yard. Maybe she hung them on the upstairs porch the last time. If not, our living room is going to become a drying arena for Mark's white flags: all this work just so the kid can dirty them again the next day! And this would go on for . . . months, at least. He thought back to when Mary Lou was potty-trained. She had to learn to walk first, so she had to be at least a year old.

No, it couldn't be!

When he got back upstairs with the empty laundry basket, he asked Millie, "When was Mary Lou potty-trained?"

"At twenty-seven months, I think," she answered. "It's in her baby book. Why?"

"So, this kid is going to be in diapers for two more years?" he asked.

"At least," she answered. "Boys take longer."

The next weekend, Icky went to Sears, Roebuck & Co. and bought a Kenmore automatic top-loading clothes washer, and had it delivered in two days.

"Let's see how it works," he directed when the installer finally hooked it up.

He loaded a drained pail of Mark's diapers into the machine, and added detergent and borax to the bowl at the top of the agitator, as recommended by the manufacturer. Then, he and the installer looked at one another with a kind of manly anticipation that guys exhibit when they're about to power up a new machine.

"Press the Start button," the installer instructed Icky.

Immediately, the motor snapped to attention, hummed obediently for a few seconds and then . . . water started flowing—at first sputtering as the line expelled air, but finally in a steady stream into the blue enamel porcelain tub. The motor jammed through more clicks, and then chugged into its wash cycle.

"It's completely automatic!" Millie said gleefully.

"Happy?" Icky asked.

"You have no idea!" she smiled at him.

"After last week, I think I do," he admitted. "I'm sorry that I didn't see what you've been going through."

"Well, that's over now," she said, "and this is going to make doing house chores so much easier."

While the machine finished running through the rinse cycle, Icky and the installer carried the old wringer washer down the back stairs, and loaded it onto the back of his truck so it could be taken to a used appliance dealer. When they returned upstairs, the dirty rinse water was rushing out of the new machine, and the spin cycle started.

"No more wringer!" Icky announced. He hated running clothes through those rollers. "That was the worst . . . " but he was interrupted by the new machine rocking left and right, then shuddering, and lurching forward inch-by-inch as the drum slammed into the inner walls: "Bam! Bam! Bam!"

The installer calmly stepped forward, stopped the machine by lifting its lid, and showed Icky how to reposition the load.

Just at that moment, Gordon showed up at their kitchen door. Marg was right behind him, the heels of her shoes angrily stamping up each stair step.

"It just gets off balance sometimes," the installer continued to explain, "which is why they made it easy to stop the spin cycle by just opening the lid. All you need to do is move the clothes around so they're equally distributed, and then, when you lower the lid again, the machine runs smoothly and finishes the spin cycle," he said.

"What was that noise?" Gordon asked, alarm in his voice.

"New washer!" Icky showed them, proudly. "The load got off-balance, but it's easy to correct."

The machine made a finger-snapping sound as if to confirm its adjustment as the spin cycle started up again.

"Well, that's it," the installer said, heading toward the door. "It'll shut off when the load is done spinning. Hope you enjoy it!"

"Thanks!" Icky said, waving him down the back stairs. Turning to Gordon and Marg, he said, "We just got it! Works like a charm, too."

"He said it will even turn off automatically!" Millie noticed.

"It's not going to make that noise every time you run it, is it?" Gordon asked.

"I don't know. Probably not, but as you saw, it's no big deal. If the load gets off-kilter, Millie will just open the lid, and . . . "

"You should have heard it downstairs!" Marg interrupted. "All the glasses were clinking against each other in our cupboards!"

"We probably should have talked about this before you brought an automatic clothes washer in," Gordon continued her thought.

"What do you mean?" Icky said, ready to stand his ground. As far as he was concerned, Millie and he could do whatever they wanted in their own apartment.

"I don't need our things chipped!" Marg raised her voice.

"Did anything break?" Icky asked immediately.

"No, not yet, but eventually, something will," she insisted.

"Well, if it does, then we can deal with it," Icky countered. And as far as he was concerned, that was the end of the discussion.

"You and I can talk more about this later," Gordon insisted, ushering Marg out the door. He knew better than to continue a dispute when she was upset.

"You wouldn't have walked away from a problem with any other tenant!" she accused when they shut the door on their own unit downstairs.

"They're not tenants; they're family. My little sister!" he corrected, intending to bring the crisis down to a boil.

But the moment he said it, a look of decisive contempt flashed across Marg's face, and told him that this problem was far from being solved.

HELPING MILLIE WHILE SHE recuperated from her short bout with a cold or the flu—whatever it was; it lasted only a couple of days—alerted Icky to the reality that his career needed a boost to support their growing family. Before Mark was born, Millie and he were eight years from being just a couple again. Now, with a son, they were essentially starting all over. And a toddler with as much raw energy as this one would need wide open spaces to run in, and maybe even a college education one day. Men coming home from the war were receiving tuition support and a living stipend from the G.I. Bill, and that meant a competitive job market was on the horizon. Suddenly, life was more complicated.

"C'mon Haut, ante up."

The men's poker game met at Icky and Millie's apartment that month. Millie had prepared a sandwich spread for the six guys, and took the children to visit her dad and Eva for the evening, so the men could puff on their cigars without bothering everyone.

"Maybe I've reached the zenith of my career," Icky said after he played his hand. He'd been distracted over the preceding few days by the possibility that he might have reached the uppermost rung of the ladder with regard to his earning potential.

"What's wrong with that?" said one of the guys. "You made it to the top, and you're still not even forty!"

"Yeah, relax and enjoy it," said another, blowing cigar smoke backward over his shoulder. And redirecting Icky's attention back to the card game, he said, "You're up."

Icky looked at his hand: a royal flush. At least the cards were in his favor.

"I'll call—and I raise you another nickel," he said.

"Good bluff," said the first, pushing the pot toward Icky. "You worry too much."

Icky lifted his chin and wobbled his head side-to-side in response as he smiled at his win, and stacked his coins. Maybe he was worrying too much. But wasn't there something he could do to advance his career? If he could convince the boss to branch out—that is, show him how bakeries in larger cities were moving forward—then he might be able to develop recipes. That certainly could offer opportunities.

Mr. Bolles would be returning the following week from one of his big game hunting trips. He'd purchased a 300 Weatherby Magnum, and wanted to bring home an elk head from Montana this time. Icky hoped he got one, for if the boss was in a good mood, maybe he'd listen to a few ideas.

❖ ❖ ❖

AFTER ICKY GAVE MR. Bolles a run-down on the bakery's performance while he was gone, he said, "I've been reading in the trades about culinary schools in Chicago, and . . . "

"Chicago?" Mr. Bolles interrupted with a frown. "I just drove through there! Awful place! Too much traffic! Full of Mafia!"

But Icky didn't want the boss to skewer his proposal with distractions. He wanted a few weeks off to study baking in a culinary school, and then time to conduct research on products and methods he might be able to introduce at Bolles Bakery.

"Some of the courses are only six weeks long," he persisted. "What I learn would be useful for an expansion. We could add new breads or maybe other bakery products, like cookies. That's what bakeries in other . . . "

"Bolles Bakery is doing fine as it is," the boss objected. The way he saw it, new products meant shifting from the core business, which would mean purchasing new equipment, developing new processes, and adding more employees—all of which would increase production costs.

And for what? Risk, that's what!

After all, people were buying his bread. Bakeries across the nation were paying royalties on his bun slicer patent, too. All in all, his business was making good money. He saw no reason to change.

Besides, the suggestion came from a baker, not a businessman.

"You just keep doing what you're paid to do," he told Icky. "I'll tell you if and when we need to divert resources into products that no one needs."

"But, Sir, . . . " Icky wanted to continue.

"Back to work!" Mr. Bolles ordered as he stomped off.

Icky wasn't dissuaded, though. Market predictions on specialty breads and new pastry lines made sense. A commercial market for cookies was building, too—and with a population explosion, more kids means more cookies. Why not buy them from Bolles?

He needed data. Then he could approach him again, this time with numbers. A new product line would have to be profitable right off the bat for Mr. Bolles to venture out, and that meant providing data so he could run his own income projections.

He'd work on it at home. But first, he needed to purchase an old stand mixer, as beating the dough by hand was unrealistic if he wanted to formulate a recipe that would work in a commercial environment. He'd keep it on the back stairs landing, where the old wringer washer used to be stored.

And that, he thought to himself, is how I'll advance my career.

26

Unintended Consequences

ICKY'S BRAIN KEPT STIRRING up cookie formulas, turning the bedroom ceiling into an imaginary chalkboard. Combinations of ingredients appeared, some for light, crunchy biscuits; some for chewy bars, and some for large, soft cookies. After about an hour, he decided that since he wasn't sleeping, he might as well be baking.

He went to the kitchen, shut the swinging door that separated it from the rest of the apartment, and pulled out flour, sugar, baking powder, baking soda, butter, eggs, and vanilla. The smell of cookies woke Millie at dawn.

"How long have you been up?" she asked as she padded into the kitchen, her pink suede slippers whispering quietly against the wood floors.

"A while," he said. "Try this." He handed her a cookie from the first batch.

"Mm-hmm, good!" she said. "Got any coffee?"

"On the stove," he nodded. The pot still had enough for one cup in it. "What about this?" he handed her a sample from the last batch.

"Chewier," she said. Over the years, she'd learned that, for Icky, evaluating baking wasn't personal, other than personal preference. He appreciated her opinion. "I like both."

"Me, too," he said. "More like Ma's cookies."

"What made you bake cookies in the middle of the night?" she asked.

"Just wanted to," he answered.

But before she could pursue his scant answer any further, she heard Mark hurl himself out of bed, ready for a bright, new day. The toddler peeked into the kitchen to see what adventure was at hand.

Millie handed him a small piece of cookie. He was cutting teeth, and drooled uncontrollably before taking off, running in circles, hands up, and arms extended in both directions.

"Come on, let's get you dressed," she said, guiding him back to the bedroom. "Daddy doesn't need any help right now."

She left Icky with his project, but as she did, she said over her shoulder, "How do you always know how to do this!"

He'd been up half the night, running tests, that's how. The truth was that he'd made four batches, each at increasingly higher temperatures. He'd adjusted ingredient percentages, and changed the timing on each run. He wanted to find the point at which the dough spread out, and record the amount of time needed for cookies to brown. He also wanted to define specific characteristics—in addition to taste, of course—that made them really good. Were they too soft, crisp, or chewy? Did they break easily? What about crumbs? When did they begin to look toasty on top? What about the bottom side: Was it shiny? Which ones smelled irresistible?

When Millie returned to the kitchen, she noticed a note pad with numbers written on it, and a small mound of broken cookies in the middle of the table. Icky was sniffing them.

"Now what?" she quizzed him.

"I'm inspecting," he answered, his eyes closed so he could focus on his sense of smell.

"Inspecting for what? Did you forget what ingredients you used?" she challenged. He better not! He'd used a lot of flour in his little experiment, and that meant her food budget was being compromised.

"Icky!" she insisted.

"Okay," he finally responded. "I'm not mixing and baking the same thing over and over right now," he said. "I'm making changes as I go. I want to get this right."

"Right for what?"

"Maybe a new product line at Bolles," Icky revealed. "I need to test it here first, so I know what I'm talking about."

"Can we have these then?" Mary Lou asked as she came into the kitchen. "Cookies would be a great breakfast!"

"Here, take this and go," Millie said. "Keep an eye on your brother."

Icky took Millie's rolling pin, and crushed a couple of the broken cookies.

"Now what?" she asked, as fascinated by his method as she was unhappy to see cookies ruined for no apparent reason.

"I don't know," he answered. "I just want to see how they break down."

The first batch had large, soft crumb, almost as large as bread crumbs. The crumb from the last batch, which baked at a higher temperature and less time, was powdery.

"So, what does that mean?"

"I don't know," he repeated. "I used processed flour instead of whole wheat, so maybe that's why they're dryer. Or maybe it was the amount of moisture. I'll need to . . . "

"I see broke cookies," Mary Lou interrupted again, Mark at her heels. "Kid sized." She snatched a broken piece of cookie for her brother, and then grabbed a couple of halves for herself.

"That's enough for you two," Millie told her. "Go on, now."

They retreated.

"You were saying?" Millie asked.

"It's just that I don't always know. Which ones taste better?"

They tried bites of cookie from each batch again.

"The first ones are softer," she said. "I guess I like them better."

"I do, too," he agreed. "But they take longer to bake. More time, more cost."

"Better cookies, better sales," she countered. "And they won't break as easily during shipping."

Hmm. Millie made good points. He'd remember them if the boss argued about how long his ovens had to be on, or brought up packaging costs. Assuming, of course, that Mr. Bolles likes the cookies in the first place.

"Seems to me that the next step is to sell a few," she continued. "If you're going to use all of my flour, you better get some money back for my household budget."

Icky smiled at her.

"You think they're good enough to sell?"

"Of course," she said. "That's obvious."

"Where?"

"How about Richardson's Grocery? We shop there. And everyone knows you bake for a living."

"I could give Max a couple to taste," he offered. "Maybe then he'd be interested."

"I would," she said. "No doubt."

Icky wrapped the remaining cookies into six-count paper packages tied with brown string. He attached tags that said "home-baked: 15 cents," and put all of them into a cardboard box. He'd offer Max three cents for each package that Richardson's sold: twenty percent was a nice profit just for just putting out a sweet treat!

"I'll be back in an hour," he told Millie as he headed down the stairs. He'd ask Max to set the box next to the cash register where the cookies would be an impulse buy. That way, the clerks will see how fast the cookies are selling, too. Maybe they'll want more.

WHILE IT WAS CLEAR that Mr. Bolles wasn't going to give him time off to attend culinary school in Chicago, Icky's research at home did eventually net some good data, and he was eager to share it with the boss. His plan was to run a few trays of cookie dough through the ovens at Bolles. That way, he also could make his case for how easy it would be to work the new product line into the schedule.

The possibility that using company equipment might be a problem for Mr. Bolles never occurred to Icky—but it should have. The sweet scent of baking cookies wafted up to the boss's office, and sneaked under his door like poison gas. Mr. Bolles stormed down the stairs.

"What are you doing with my ovens—making lunch?" he commenced his tirade before he even arrived at the bottom of the stairs. "Not on my nickel!"

"Not lunch," Icky said, holding out the tray of product. "They're cookies! I . . . "

"You do that again," the boss warned over curled lips, "and you'll be looking for work somewhere else!" In his book, using *his* equipment to bake something other than Bolles bread signaled an underlying tone of disrespect. He would not allow it!

But Icky didn't think he was stepping out of line at all. On the contrary, he was looking out for the bakery's future. And since he'd built up a good measure of loyalty capital with his boss, all he was doing was trading on years of good performance for a shot at innovation.

"Try one," Icky offered, genially. He could coax the boss with a sweet cookie, he just knew it.

"Look, Haut," Mr. Bolles snarled. "This is *my* bakery. That is not *my* product. I don't want it here."

"But these are good!" Icky insisted. "And they'll sell. I've already tested the market by selling a few at Richardson's Grocery. Max says they're gone in an hour."

"You're using my ovens to compete with me?" Mr. Bolles roared.

"No! . . .

"Enough!" the boss waved both arms at Icky. He didn't want any mutinous excuses. Leaning into his face, he ordered, "You decide: bread, or cookies! One, or the other!"

And with that, he grabbed the tray of warm cookies, and tossed the lot of them into the trash barrel. "Consider this is a warning!" he said, raising a fist and stomping toward his office.

"But Mr. Bolles, . . . "

Too late. He was already around the corner.

"People want bread, not cookies!" he railed up the stairs. Turning toward the bakery floor from the top step, he added, "Remember your history, and what happened to Marie Antoinette when she said 'let them eat cake!' It was followed by 'off with your head!'"

He slammed the door to his office.

Now what?

Icky had been formulating and testing a new product line for weeks and weeks, and after dozens of kitchen trials and market tests, he believed he'd finally created a cookie that could be scaled in the Bolles Bakery environment. He'd even computed data on how much a small run might earn in its first year, given, of course, adjustments along the way as they moved into production. He invested a lot of energy into preparing for a conversation with Mr. Bolles, not to mention his hopes for career advancement once the boss saw how the bakery's profits could be increased. Giving up didn't make sense. No, he'd persevere, and give his pitch one more try.

"What did you think of the cookies?" he asked one of the bakers who sampled one before Mr. Bolles showed up.

"They're good, but the boss sure didn't like the idea."

"He didn't even hear the idea!" Icky corrected.

The mixing bowl contained enough dough for another run. "I'm going to give this one more shot," he said.

"Are you sure you want to do that?"

"If he says no *after* he tastes one, then so be it," Icky said. He had no doubt, though, that a cookie product line would be good for business. No doubt at all.

Within minutes the smell of baked cookies stole up to the second floor again.

"YOU'RE HOME EARLY," MILLIE noticed as Icky trudged up the back stairs to their apartment. "How did it go? Did Mr. Bolles like the cookies?"

"He fired me," Icky said abruptly. The words vibrated as they passed his lips, as if a tuning fork was caught in his mouth.

"He *what?*" Millie exclaimed, mimicking Icky's attitude.

"You heard me." He didn't want to repeat it.

Millie straightened her shoulders to steady herself as she waited for Icky to continue. She had helped him evaluate cookies, right in her kitchen. And she was the one who suggested he test market them at Richardson's, too. Should she have realized how all this work might lead to his job loss? Cautioned him? She felt somehow complicit.

"I'll find a job somewhere else," he promised. "There aren't many bakeries around, at least not the quality of Bolles. The one down the road in Salamanca is good, but it's small—probably too small to hire another baker.

"Or maybe I ought to make a change. I could check openings at Olean Tile, or Hi-Q Aerovox. Maybe Clark."

"Maybe Mr. Bolles will cool down, and take you back," she suggested. He hadn't yet told her what led to the firing. "What happened?"

Icky leaned against the door frame, and crossed his arms.

"He threw the first tray of cookies into the trash without tasting any, and told me to forget it before even hearing my idea. I baked another batch, thinking that if he just tried one, he'd like them so much that I could show him numbers on profitability, and discuss how they could become a new product line.

"It was stupid," he admitted. "He told me not to use his ovens for cookies, and I did it a second time."

"Is there no way to turn this around?" she persisted. It seemed that getting back a job he'd held for nearly twenty years would be easier than finding a new one.

"No. No way," he said firmly. He'd made his decision.

She waited in the silence of his dismay, sensing his diminished spirit suspended midair.

"I'm sorry, Millie," he said in a low voice. "I didn't mean for this to happen."

"Of course not," she assured him. "After all you've done, all your unpaid weekends at Bolles, your nights at our kitchen table making drawings for a slicer *you designed* so *he* could file a patent, and . . . "

"I don't want to think about it," he said. Even as she defended him, he didn't want to suffer her anger.

"Sorry," she said.

"It's okay."

The room went silent again.

"What kind of work would you apply for?" She knew they had some savings, but the sooner he found another job, the better. They had two children now. Mark was only a little guy, but Mary Lou was old enough to feel insecure if something went wrong. They'd have to protect her from that.

"I don't know. I'll look around," he told her. "I'd take anything, except Socony-Vacuum." If I could help it, he admitted to himself.

"Oh, yes," Millie said, grasping the realization that Icky would have to tell his parents. "What do you think they'll say?"

"They'll be shocked, at first. But they'll take my side, our side," he said, dejectedly. After he took a deep breath, he continued, "At some point, Ma will say she didn't trust Mr. Bolles, and add that Roy didn't, either—because Ma always likes to have back-up for her opinions.

"And Pa will say that Mr. Bolles has lost his moral center," he added.

"So, you know already," she acknowledged, calmly. "Might as well get it done."

"Tomorrow," Icky decided, stiffening his neck again. "I've had enough today."

27

Coming to the Rescue

JOBS WERE TIGHT IN Olean, as all the men returning from the war were getting hiring preferences. And although Icky could point to two decades of service for one employer, his options were limited by the narrowness of his experience: he knew how to bake bread, and supervise a shift of employees, again, who bake bread. But, noted the personnel representatives, he had no heavy manufacturing experience.

Plus, he'd been fired. That didn't play well.

At the end of the day, he stopped by the Carpoletti's R.C. Cola distributorship, hoping to build on a personal connection. At least they'd be open to a conversation, he told himself.

"We pay by the job," one of them said, noting Icky's huge shoulders. Certainly, he was strong enough to load and unload heavy crates of soda pop and beer. "It's not as good as full-time, but it's all we got."

"It's something," Icky thanked them. "I can start now."

"Tomorrow, seven sharp," he suggested.

"I'm used to being at work at four in the morning," Icky said to confirm that he'd be on time.

"Good! We'll count on you for the first load then," they said.

On the way home, he stopped by his parents' house. Now that he had some sort of work, he'd tell them about Bolles. And while driving truck wasn't baking, it would help pay a few bills.

"So, he fired me," he finished the story, adding, "and as they say, there's no way to unscramble an omelet."

"*Zur Hölle mit . . . !*" Pa shuddered with principled anger under his breath. He rarely swore, arguing that if he reserved rebukes blasting some evil to Hell that his anger would be heard like a prayer. The very idea that Bolles could fire his son after years of service, often without pay: it was criminal!

Icky winced. Pa inhaled a deep breath then, for he saw how expelling his wrath had only intensified Icky's pain.

"Just because I never moved on from Socony doesn't mean that you got to stay in one place," Pa repaired his gaffe with the consolation he had intended.

"Thanks, Pa. This is going to be a tough time for us," Icky admitted.

"You'll find your way," Pa continued. "You're a hard worker, and something will come your way."

"We'll see," he said.

He wasn't so sure, though. Not yet, anyway.

THE HAUT FAMILY GATHERED at Immanuel Lutheran Church the following Sunday in celebration of Mary Lou's first communion and confirmation. The texts for the day were John 12:24, and I Corinthians 15, beginning with verse 35.

"What a wonderful day we have here today!" The Reverend Garber began his message. "The front pew is occupied by ten young people who have spent every Saturday morning for the last two years reading the Bible, and learning about the history of the Lutheran church. They've written essays expressing their faith, and completed an oral examination with the church council. Today is not the end of their faith journeys, however, but the beginning! As they affirm their baptisms, and accept their roles as members of this congregation, they become something new! And that, my friends, is the message of today's gospel and epistle lesson.

"In the book of John, Jesus says, 'Unless a grain of wheat falls into the earth and dies, it remains just a single grain; but if it dies, it bears much fruit.'

"So, let's consider that wheat grain," he continued. "It's full of potential, and has all the makings of something wonderful—just as these young people are full of potential with all the makings of something wonderful.

"Now, when the grains of wheat ripen, they are ground together into flour that becomes our bread. In Latin, the word for bread is *panem*, or simply *pan* in the proto-German and Scandinavian languages of our forebears. In English, the same word, *pan*, is found at the heart of words such as com*pany* and com*pan*ion," he emphasized the middle syllables. "These words refer, literally, to those who break bread with one another.

"I want to suggest that this sharing of bread together is the very essence of 'pan'—of bread—for it is in this coming together that we fortify one another's spirits. And in Holy Communion, we come together in the presence of the resurrected Christ: Who is the Bread of Life.

"Jesus points to the grain coming forth today, and says that it shares continuity with the grain from the last harvest. But also, he says there is discontinuity. Here, discontinuity does not mean disconnection. On the contrary, Jesus is saying that the plant which comes forth this season is indeed connected to last year's harvest. *But* it is *also* something new: a new creation.

"And that is what *we* are in this moment, here in this church. As we welcome ten young people into our congregation, we become a new creation: connected to who we were last week, but also, new together, in Christ."

Then The Reverend Garber spoke directly to the Confirmands: "All of you will join us for the first time in a few minutes as we come to this altar to break bread together in Holy Communion—for in this meal, we share a spiritual com*pan*ionship with one another."

Then he turned to the entire congregation, and invited everyone, "We ask God to bless our com*pan*ionship with our new members. Let them know that we welcome them, and that we seek their gifts—for they are a blessing to our congregation! I know! I've been working with them for the last two years, and I can see that they will bear much fruit.

"Let us now join together, knowing that in *Christ, the Bread of Life* our needs are heard! Know, too, that God is calling us to bring in the Lord's Kingdom, so *"Listen to your Bread!"* he said as he concluded his sermon declaring, "Amen."

The new communicants repeated "Amen" with the congregation to affirm the pastor's message, and the organ interlude began. But as the chords rose, it was the words, "Listen to your Bread" that resonated in Icky's ears. Wasn't that what Shots said when he instructed him on how to evaluate baked loaves?

Millie remembered Icky repeating that phrase to her, too, when he first became a baker. They looked at one another, aware that those same words were suddenly imbued with new meaning. The sermon was preached not only for Mary Lou, but also for them.

"We're somewhere between continuity and discontinuity," Icky whispered. "We have God's promise of life, and look for a new creation."

"I heard it that way, too," Millie agreed.

The void Icky had been feeling himself caught in was like the Saturday between Good Friday and Easter Sunday. He felt emptiness, because he didn't know what kind of future lay ahead, or how he would care for his family.

But he was not alone. No, any way he sliced it, he knew that the Spirit of God's promise, embodied in the Bread of Life, meant that their prayers were being heard. And he began to look forward to a new creation, whatever lay ahead.

OVER THE NEXT FEW weeks, as Icky delivered soda pop all over Cattaraugus County and the southern tier region of the state, he tried not to ruminate over his job loss. But if he was no longer a Bolles Bakery man, who was he? Was he still even a bread baker?

And what about his cookie idea? If the product was as good as he thought, he wondered whether or not he could scale the recipe just a little, and sell enough to bring in some additional income. Richardson's probably would take a few packages again, and he could ask other stores, too.

"It'll bring in a few bucks," he told his brother when they met for a beer at The Cabin.

"You're that tight on cash?" Henry asked.

"Getting there," Icky admitted. "Sledding's been tough."

They sat quietly on their bar stools for a while, gulping down the gravity of the situation Icky faced.

Finally, Henry asked the obvious question: "Ever think about doing something like what Roy and Herta did? Open your own bakery?"

"We've got two kids; they don't," Icky said. He thought that explained it.

But Henry wouldn't let him get away with an excuse instead of an answer.

"Sure, and that's the point. You got two kids who expect you to take care of them. And if you don't do this now, . . . " He left the sentence unfinished.

Icky wasn't used to being disagreed with. No, for years, he'd been the one giving orders at work. He'd become accustomed to taking the lead around the house, too, or at least Millie let him think so, most of the time anyway. Now, he wasn't so sure of himself.

He exhaled, his breath sizzling through his front teeth.

"I don't know," he finally said.

"Think about it," Henry insisted.

He did. Driving truck provided a lot of time to think, and Henry's suggestion kept stirring around in his mind. Start his own bakery? Now? Really?

Slowly, as the delivery truck ate up the miles of winding Allegheny Mountain roads, the possibility of starting his own bakery brought a crooked smile to his face.

He realized that hadn't smiled much lately, and it felt good. Then, he remembered how Roy had suggested the same thing years back. He hadn't taken his brother-in-law seriously at the time.

Okay, he argued with himself: that's two endorsements.

But operating my own bakery would be uncertain—as uncertain as . . . well, as not being sure from one week to the next whether or not Carpoletti might need an extra driver. To be honest, temporary income was as sure as a road full of pot holes.

He also had to admit that he was unexpectedly invigorated by the idea of running his own show, and he let himself imagine how he might start. What would it take?

Product: check.

Customers: check, if I'm right. Richardson's likes the cookies. And the baby boom suggests that lots of little cookie eaters are on the horizon.

Start-up money: . . . He left that one blank. For now. But a temporary lack of funds didn't have to be a permanent road block. He'd detour around that challenge for a while.

THE NEXT FRIDAY AFTER work, Icky met Henry for their weekly beer talk.

"I'm going to do it," he said after they downed their first swallows.

"Hey! I knew you would," Henry said.

"I haven't even told you what 'it' is," Icky pointed out.

"I know, though, for sure. You're starting a bakery," Henry said.

"Can't get anything over on you!"

"We shared a room for ten years. I know how you think."

Icky grinned. When the kid was just a little shaver he could be a pain in the butt sometimes, but it was usually good to have him around. Like Ma, he always seemed to be looking out for everyone.

"I've already got a line on a building for you," Henry continued.

"Yeah?"

"The government is unloading military surplus. Quonset huts built during World War II are on the list," he said. "*Stars and Stripes* says the government is unloading them now that the military is building brick and mortar quarters and offices."

"Are the huts any good?"

"I guess so. When I was in the service, they were used for barracks," he said. "The bakery and dining hall were in Quonset huts, too."

"Quonset hut bakeries?" repeated Icky.

"Sure. I did KP in one, just like all the other grunts," he confirmed, adding, "And you don't have to be ex-military to get in on these deals. Anybody can buy one. You just have to haul it off, once you pay for it."

Henry guessed that the contour of the building—sections of half-moon shaped corrugated steel—probably could be up-ended onto a trailer and towed.

"I could help you move it, if you like," he offered.

Icky considered the balance in the family savings account, and estimated that Millie and he might have enough money for one hut. And eight hundred square feet would be more than enough space for a start-up bakery. He wondered whether or not they all could live there, too.

"I might take you up on that," he said. "First, though, I've got to talk with Millie. She doesn't know about this yet, and I'm not going to be able to do it without her help."

Henry nodded. Finally, he said, "Call me if you two decide to take the leap."

28

The Shed

"MILLIE!" ICKY CALLED OUT as he marched up the stairs later that evening. She had just put the children into their beds, and was resting for a minute in her favorite old chair. He could see she was tired, so he would tread softly in discussing the possibility of starting a bakery together.

"Mark is getting around pretty good," he paced himself, inviting her to unload her day.

"Little boys don't stop," she said, but she was too exhausted to go into details. "He needs eyes on him every minute."

"He does," Icky agreed. His hands were positioned on each arm of his easy chair as if to steady himself. Springing this idea was not going to be easy, but he needed her support before he went ahead with the whole plan.

Or half plan, he had to admit. He hadn't worked all of it out yet.

"Look, Millie, I know you're tired, but I need to talk to you about something."

She nodded to let him know that she was listening, and leaned her head back.

"Could you live in a big shed for a while?"

He noticed that her eyes didn't move. And she didn't say anything.

She was waiting for him to explain.

When he didn't, she asked cautiously, "What do you call 'a big shed'?"

She'd known something had been going on with him in recent days. He'd been toying with that used stand mixer, taking it apart, and greasing the motor, so she thought he was devising a plan to supplement their sporadic income from Carpoletti. She hadn't thought they'd all need to move into a shed, though!

"Henry's got a line on a military Quonset hut we could buy," Icky ventured. "It's not large—only about eight hundred square feet. But if the four of us could camp out in it . . . I mean, if we use it for both a place to live and a place to work, the money we save from not paying rent ought to help us get a bakery going."

"Uh-huh," she said, unconvinced. "You want to open a bakery, and live in a shed."

"I'm serious about this, Millie," he said. He needed to find some long-term way to support their family.

She could see the determination in his eyes. She'd go along, at least in this conversation.

"Well, Marg is probably tired of hearing that automatic washing machine pound on the ceiling." She hadn't told him that her sister-in-law sought her out to reinforce how loud it was, for if Gordon wouldn't deal with the so-called problem tenants upstairs, she would. And, if the automatic machine was not going to be removed, Marg decided that the least Millie could do was time her laundry chore with the hours when Gordon and she were out.

No, Millie corrected; it wasn't just a suggestion: Marg had insisted on it. The ridiculousness of the mandate irritated her to the bone. Marg is getting as fancy-pants as her rich Bradner's clientele, she thought to herself.

And didn't Millie have enough to worry about, what with managing their budget on inconsistent income from Carpoletti? Besides, who can co-ordinate laundering diapers to the whim of someone's else's schedule! Marg ought to know better than to suggest such a thing; it wasn't that long since she had a toddler!

"I know it's been difficult," Icky said, "on top of caring for two kids."

You don't know the half of it, Millie sighed to herself, adding only, "Mark is going to be even more active as he gets to his second birthday."

"And I know you're worried about that, on this second floor," he continued. He'd let her ponder the possibility of solving that problem with his suggestion.

"Not to mention the noise his running makes on the ceiling downstairs," she concurred.

Mary Lou had been easy to rear. Always cooperative, she tippy-toed around the apartment so as to not disturb her aunt and uncle and little cousin below.

Not so with little boys, though, Millie realized. She remembered how active her three older brothers were: horsing around, and yelling, too. She admitted that she'd already begun anticipating the challenges that were coming.

"Where is this What-set shed?" she asked, emboldened by frustration and trying to be open.

"In Virginia. Henry and I would haul it in, and set it up in Ma and Pa's side yard, I hope," he said. He was still working out the logistics. "I bet they will give us use of the empty lot next to their house, and maybe we'd purchase the lot on the corner if we make a profit. It would be a start."

"We can afford this building?" she asked.

"Our savings are . . . well, they are enough," he told her bluntly. He could read her concerns now. He felt the same way.

"You think you can operate a business in a shed with all of us living there? With children under foot all of the time?" she put her last and largest concern onto the table.

"Yes!" he said. "Your kitchen will be the bakery, though."

"With that huge mixer?" It weighed at least one hundred fifty pounds and stood just over four feet tall. She was only a foot or so taller.

"Right in the middle, as I see it," he said, visualizing the space. "I'd build a counter for it. I'd need a commercial oven, too.

"Or rather," he corrected himself, "*we'd* need a commercial oven. I'd need your help to get the bakery operating."

"With a new oven?"

"Probably a used one. I'd try to find a non-rotational Haller Oven that still has some life in it." She could hear renewed strength in his voice then. It was the first time he'd seemed himself in weeks. And even if he hadn't worked out the details, it was clear that he'd put some thought into this.

"Well, then, I guess we should do it," she said. Hadn't they been making decisions in the presence of uncertainty for as long as they'd been married? The What-set shed might not be a traditional house, but her kitchen would be well equipped. She'd focus on that.

In no time, the ever-resourceful, soon-to-be entrepreneur disassembled the Quonset hut in Virginia, and with his brother's help, hoisted its parts onto a large trailer. By the end of the afternoon, they were ready to start the drive back to Olean.

"Two-lane roads all the way," Icky said. "But most of it is at night, so we won't block traffic."

"We should be able to make it," Henry agreed.

"Thank goodness, I've been driving truck for Carpoletti. I can handle a rig now," Icky said.

"Just take it one mile at a time," Henry added. Pacing himself was how he got through his military service, and he thought the same attitude would get them safely home. Ten hours later, they parked the truck in front of Ma and Pa's house.

"Wait 'til Millie sees this!" Icky said with happy anticipation as he turned off the truck engine.

"Really?" Henry answered. "You're gonna' let her first look at her new home be this gray metal shell, caked with road dirt and rust, and chained to a flatbed?"

Icky dropped back into the truck seat.

"You might want to re-think that one," Henry suggested, adding, "And I'm not even married."

"Right," Icky said. It was one thing for Army grunts to live in Quonset huts; moving his wife and kids into one would require some finesse, preceded by a major clean up. "Maybe we ought to get it unloaded and set up first."

The next day, Pa Haut, Henry, and Icky laid a foundation, and pounded down a wood floor, leaving a long space straight through the middle to run electrical and gas lines: enough to power a small bakery. Henry's boiler maker and blacksmith skills made fast work of connecting all the lines so they could install the equipment.

"How long do you expect to be living in this Quonset hut?" Ma asked. After all, Pa and she were going to be looking at the shed outside their kitchen window for the duration, and an army barracks wasn't the sort of view she'd ever expected.

"For as long as it takes," Icky said.

"And that is?" Pa asked. Ma and he would like to nail down some of the details.

"I don't know. I haven't done it yet," he answered. "Look, Pa, you always said 'a man's got to know where he's going,' and I do. I just don't know how we're going to get there yet."

"Fair enough," Ma said. Struggle has a way of revealing who a person really is, and if their son and daughter-in-law were ready to take on this bakery life, Pa and she would do their part.

Millie arrived with dinner in a basket and the children at the end of the day, just as the men were rolling pieces of the hut off the trailer.

"It's larger than I expected," she said, trying to say something positive about the gray corrugated metal shell that was to be their new home.

"Yeah?" Icky answered, hopefully. "It's not ready to occupy yet, and it looks rough, I know, but we'll be okay in it. I promise."

"A new adventure!" she acknowledged, disguising apprehension she would not share.

"And we couldn't do this without you," she thanked Pa Haut and Henry.

"Glad to help," Henry said. "And you know, I live right there," he pointed to Ma and Pa Haut's house, "so, if you two need anything else, just say so."

"Thanks," she answered, wondering what they'd gotten themselves into. Icky wasn't kidding: This is a shed. Secondhand. Discarded by the Army.

But she quickly reversed the direction of her concern. No one will be telling me when I can do the laundry, she reminded herself. And Mark will have a yard to play in.

She nodded at the thing. Home sweet home, home sweet home, home sweet home, she said with fresh resolve. She'd step into their uncertain future, and make the best of it.

IF MARK WAS ALWAYS running around, arms in the air, legs two steps ahead of the rest of his body—well, that sort of energy came from somewhere: It was Icky. But while the boy always took off before he had any idea of what lay ahead, his father always had a plan. Icky was sometimes the only one who knew what that plan was, of course, but Millie had learned to live with anticipation.

This time, though, she needed him to slow down enough to define what he expected of her. Exactly how had he envisioned the two of them working together?

"Cookie production is more complicated than bread," he explained, "because each cookie needs to be cut by hand. It'll be more labor intensive."

"More labor intensive for . . . ?"

"Well, you," he said. "I'll mix the dough, and you will cut it."

"I will?" she repeated.

"I've been thinking about how the operation should run," he continued. "With this much counter space," he stretched his arms across the work table he built next to the Haller oven, "we can prepare several batches of dough at a time, and keep the process going for hours.

"You'll stand here," he walked her to the end of the table, "and when I move a batch of dough over, you'll take a large hunk and flatten it with the palm of your hand. Then, you'll use this to roll it to about an eighth-inch thickness."

He held out a six-pound, eighteen-inch rolling pin from a box of baking tools he'd been collecting.

"This is as heavy as a newborn baby!" she said as her arms sank under its weight.

"And it's supposed to be. The weight presses down on the dough, and does some of the work for you. You won't tire as easily," he said.

"Glad to hear you're looking out for me," she said, perhaps a bit too wryly.

"We need to produce four thousand cookies a week to break even," he said seriously.

"Four thousand!" she repeated with a small sense of alarm. They hadn't discussed anything like production goals. No, she'd assumed that they'd simply bake as many cookies as they could, and whatever that turned out to be, well, that would be what they could sell. "Four thousand to break even?"

"At thirty-five cents a dozen, that's about a hundred twenty dollars a week, and that lets us cover the cost of the inventory: the flour, sugar, baking powder, all of it. And the utilities . . . "

"And the children's milk!" she pointed out, preparing to list some of the costs associated with running the household. "And . . .

"Milk to go with the cookies they steal," he sidetracked her argument before she could worry about priorities. "I've already accounted for losses due to stealing."

She smiled. He'd probably computed the entire budget.

"But, Icky," she interrupted. "Four thousand cookies a week is eight hundred a day! Divide by an eight-hour work day, and that's one hundred cookies every hour, non-stop!"

"Yes!" he said, pleased she caught on to his plan. "Like I said, I'll do the measuring and mixing."

"Which means I'm supposed to roll out and cut more than eight dozen cookies each hour—*and* keep an eye on Mary Lou and Mark at the same time?" Millie interrupted.

"We'll begin before they're awake," he said, sharing the schedule they'd need to follow. "Mary Lou gets herself ready for school, and she's out the door until mid-afternoon. Ma is right next door, and she can watch Mark each morning. We can get most of the baking done by noon, or so."

"I don't know," Millie said, hesitantly. She didn't want to impose on her mother-in-law. "He's a handful."

"She's had boys before," Icky pointed out. "Two of them, in fact, ten years apart, and at the same time. And three girls then, too. That ought to equal one Mark."

"She says so?" Millie asked. "You asked her?"

"And she says she's up to it," Icky assured her.

"Okay, for now," she allowed. But she wanted to make an allowance for her mother-in-law to back out of this chore. She was sure that one Mark was more work for a grandmother than two of her own boys when she was a young mother. She'd ask Ma Haut about this herself, and open the possibility for her to change her mind.

Focusing then on the job Icky expected her to do, Millie asked, "How long before we're up to full capacity, whatever that is?"

"As soon as we can," Icky said. "Like I said, if we start at four in the morning, product should be baked by noon. We'll package as we go along, and after lunch, I'll make deliveries, and get more orders."

Millie stood still, shaking her head.

"Can we sell this much?"

"The stores said they'd take whatever we bake," Icky said. "And they keep running out, so I hope so."

"This is . . . huge," she said. "I don't know how we're going to do it ourselves."

"We just will. And we will grow it into a business," he assured her. "Together."

She sensed the compulsion and contagion in his voice, and prayed to catch a small dose of it. After all, he believed the two of them could make this venture work. And for now, she was going to have to believe in it, too.

29

Rest-Less

WHEN A MAN WORKS for someone else, his job is defined by his employer.

When a man is self-employed, his job is defined by what needs to be done: he's in charge of all of it, from top dog to bottom of the pack.

Icky didn't mind. His hands were back in the dough—not just as a way to make ends meet, but as a career. Because, he reminded himself, I am a baker!

Each morning, at four o'clock, he turned on the oven: his own Haller oven now, to three hundred ninety degrees, the exact right temperature for the soft, hand-cut German cookies Millie and he would build their futures on.

While he measured and mixed dough, Millie showered and dressed. Then, as soon as she came into the kitchen to make coffee and start rolling and cutting out cookies, he showered and dressed. In no time, they worked into an easy rhythm.

Halfway through the morning, Mark happily rolled himself out of his bed. He was a bundle of impatience circling the door until Millie opened it so he could run next door to Grandma and Grandpa Haut's house with Buko, the family boxer, at his heels.

Grandma always kept an eye out for the boy and his dog to come charging across the lawn. Just as the morning's warmth shrugged off the last wisps of fog, she sat them down on the back porch with a big slice of freshly baked *Roggenbrot*, for in European fashion, Mark was fed the same meal that Grandpa and Grandma ate—never mind advice from cereal company executives who said every bite needs to be chewed thirty-two times. Nonsense, Grandma asserted. She wasn't going to count chews or waste her food budget on packaged foods. No, she'd turn out her own bread, fresh every couple of days. Rye flour's natural gum made the loaf dense, and kept a man feeling full all the way to lunch.

Even a little man like Mark. He got his *Roggenbrot* slathered with butter, downed with a half cup of strong coffee, which he preferred cooled with a heavy dousing of armored heifer. He wouldn't give up his time at the center of his grandmother's world for anything, especially since she let him share the last corner of his rye bread with Buko.

The boxer was just large enough to be a good sparring partner for the boy's wrestling contests. One morning as the two of them were having it out in the front yard, a neighbor spotted their match, and called out for help.

"The dog! The dog!" she shrieked.

"Oh, no!" Millie stopped packaging cookies, and ran to the door. Seeing her son and his dog rolling on the lawn, she joined Ma Haut, who was already calming the woman.

"It's just Buko," Millie heard her mother-in-law say. "He's trying to wear Mark out. It'll never happen, but every day we keep hoping the dog slows down the boy."

Ma Haut nodded at Millie so she could return to the bakery, and smiled indulgently at Mark as she ushered him back to the porch: another boy-sized calamity under control.

As the day approached noon and the last tray of cookies baked, Icky showered again so he'd be presentable when he made deliveries. Millie used that time to wrap the last few cooled cookies into twelve-count packages, and then packed them into labelled boxes so Icky could organize his delivery route. Grandma watched the truck being loaded from her window so that when it was full, Mark could run home for his peanut butter sandwich with Daddy before his afternoon nap. The schedule ran with the precision of a German cuckoo clock.

Since their mornings were occupied with watching their grandson, Pa and Ma Haut moved their weekly grocery shopping to the afternoon. As they entered the store, Ma removed her list from her purse. Items were written in the order that they were shelved so they could complete the job without forgetting anything they needed for the next week. As Ma filled her basket, Pa and she exchanged glances with mothers wheeling children up and down aisles in newfangled grocery carts outfitted with child seats.

"Now they treat the grocery shopping as if the experience is intended for the child's entertainment," Pa noted on the drive home.

"Shopping for the groceries is supposed to be a chore!" Ma agreed. "Turning it into a carnival ride: this is not necessary!"

"Did you see the packages with cartoon characters?" Pa added.

"Ja, and the boxes they place on shelves that face the children—who beg their mothers to go off the food budget!" she said with disbelief in her voice. "In our day, we did not cater to a little nipper's whimpering demands!"

Pa nodded in agreement. Times were easier when they could just take a list to the grocer or butcher, let him fill it from his larder, and wait for the delivery man to show up with their order at the back door later in the day.

They were quiet for a couple of minutes as they made their way through traffic.

"Did you see the people buying Icky's cookies?" Ma asked quietly.

"I did," Pa answered matter-of-factly. "The store still offers them near the cash register on the way out. I saw the mother with the two children put a package into her cart. People in the next line took some, too."

"Do you think we should tell Icky what we see?" Ma said.

"He probably knows," Pa said thoughtfully. "Every day he's there, making his deliveries."

"Ja, you're right," Ma agreed.

"Still, he should ask for some of that good shelf space," Pa insisted. "If they can line up the cartoon boxes, they can offer his cookies."

Ma nodded. They wouldn't butt in. But they would be ready to offer a suggestion if the topic came up.

MARK NEVER HAD TO wonder about whether or not cookies would be on his mother's grocery list. But his inquisitive nature wandered into other areas, and more often than not, landed him in a bucket of trouble, especially on Saturdays when his parents were trying to catch up on all the housework that didn't get done during the week.

"You can keep an eye on Mark for just a minute, can't you?" Millie asked Icky. She needed to bring sheets in from the clothesline.

Childcare was not a task that Mr. Bolles would be expected to assume as he ran his bakery, but yes, Icky would see that the boy behaved for a few minutes.

"You sit right here," he said, positioning the little guy on a chair at the corner of the counter. "Daddy has to work."

Icky was formulating a recipe for a new cookie. As he marched around the kitchen to retrieve ingredients, he didn't want to trip over the five-gallon pail of molasses sitting on the floor, so he moved it next to the chair where Mark was perched, and gave his son a little pat on his back.

As Icky turned on the mixer, Mark decided to run his own taste test. He edged himself over to the side of his chair, just far enough to dip a bare toe into the sweet, sticky molasses. Then, he wiped his toe with his finger, and gave it a little lick.

Yum!

He'd like more!

He leaned over, and reached his hand into the goo.

Even better! He giggled, and looked up at his daddy . . . who was still busy.

No one told him to stop, so he scooted all the way over, reached wa-a-ay down and, losing his balance, drove his whole arm unexpectedly into the bucket. The sound of the metal container scraping against the wooden floor was just loud enough to alert Icky. He turned as some of the molasses whooshed onto the floor.

"Mark! What did I tell you!" Icky shouted, punctuating each word as he grabbed the kid before he went in any further—and in the same moment, settled the pail before it went over completely. Mark was wedged across the rim as Millie came in the door. She'd heard Icky yelling.

"Oh! Oh, no!" she called out as she dropped the laundry basket and grabbed Mark out of the brown syrup, which by then had coated him from his chin to his belly.

Where to put him?

What to do with him?

She held the dripping kid straight out, turning first in one direction, and then in another, drizzling a thin stream of molasses in a large circle around the two of them. Of course, Mark loved spinning around, and reached out to Millie's face, marking her cheek with a molasses handprint.

"Stop that!" she commanded as she directed her distress at the boy and pulled her head back. Then, looking at Icky, she added, "*You* were going to watch him while I got the laundry off the line!"

"I told him to sit in the chair!" Icky protested. "And I'm working!"

"And I'm not?" she responded with exasperation. She tromped off to the bathroom, set Mark into the tub—clothes and all—and without hesitating, turned on the faucet full force.

"No kicking!" she ordered.

But the flaxen-haired little angel was oblivious of the trouble his exploration into the molasses pail had caused. He didn't even have the decency to stop smiling, ear to ear.

As the bath water warmed, Millie peeled the boy's clothes off while Icky stood in the doorway. Mark let out a delighted shriek—just for the pure joy of the moment—and in doing so, broke the tension he caused between his parents.

"I'll help you with that," Icky conceded, biting his lips in an effort to balance the loss of the precious molasses with the pricelessness of their precocious son.

"No, you . . . just go do your work," Millie answered wearily. She knew Icky was focused on his new recipe. "I'll deal with this . . . mess!"

"I won't get much done now," he told her. "I'll have to call for more molasses before I can mix the next batch." He certainly couldn't use the stuff Mark had taken a plunge into!

"Go on, then, make that call," she said. "I got him."

As Icky went out, Mary Lou peeked in the door and saw her mother purse her mouth at her brother, a look that was both vexed and loving. "Your sister never would have done this!" she admonished him just before he threw his sticky arms around her neck and hugged her.

"Boys!" his sister whispered under her breath.

BUKO'S WEEKEND ROUTINE INCLUDED a visit to his favorite neighbor, Rags, a cute black cocker spaniel owned by the Thompson sisters, Ruth and Ellie. On Sundays mornings, when the Hauts went to church and Buko was deprived of the measly bite of rye bread that Mark usually shared with him, the dog made a habit of slipping over to Rags's house and chowing down a dog-sized portion of brunch pancakes with syrup. Rags didn't mind sharing, and the sisters liked giving their pet some play time.

That weekend, however, the Thompson sisters decided to attend an early worship service, so they weren't home when Buko arrived. Not to be put off, he followed their scent to The Basilica of St. Mary of the Angels Roman Catholic Church, and arrived just as the sermon was beginning.

The sisters saw him slink down the center aisle, and take a place obediently at the end of their pew.

"I thought you were a Lutheran," one of them whispered to the dog.

After the last hymn, Buko followed them home, ready for communion pancakes with Rags. Then the sisters walked him home to Millie and Icky. When they arrived, Sousa marches were blasting loudly on the hi-fi. Icky played them every Sunday afternoon, and encouraged Mary Lou to enjoy the spirit of their heroic imagination.

"Why do you like them?" she asked, not impressed with her father's choice in music. She'd much rather listen to the sweet lyrics and feel-good tunes of singers like Eddie Fisher and Bobby Darin.

"But Sousa's beat is orderly," her father explained. "You can go at your work at a steady pace while you listen. And it's relaxing."

"Relaxing? You're marching around! That's not relaxing!" she insisted.

"Yes, it is, if you're trying to order your thoughts at the same time," he explained. "Pacing and thinking go with Sousa marches!"

"Okay," she allowed. The answer made sense if a person liked to pace. Her father seemed to be thinking about work all the time anyway.

The *Semper Fidelis* march performed by the Marine Corps band was blasting away when the doorbell rang. Icky turned the volume down on the hi-fi.

"We have Buko for you," said Ellie, who then launched into the story of how the dog slipped into their church that morning.

"No one minded at all," Ruth added. "But we thought you'd find it amusing."

"Besides, with all the Catholics in this neighborhood, you were bound to hear about it eventually. We just wanted a chance to laugh with you about it first," Ellie smiled broadly. "He's a good dog."

"Yes, he is," Icky agreed. "But he's got to learn to stay closer to home. Thanks for telling us."

"And thanks for bringing him home, too," Millie said.

After the door was closed, she turned to Buko. "Couldn't we have just one day of rest? Just one?"

30

You Eat, You Work

DESPITE ALL OF THE distractions, Icky and Millie baked their break-even four thousand cookies each week. And as orders increased and the bottom line on their bakery sweetened, Icky allowed himself to hope that their business might grow one day from a Quonset hut kitchen to a free-standing operation. An expansion would require hiring an employee or two—and that would mean formalizing their standards. They'd need to define product consistency, establish quality controls, and eventually, formulate their own flour blend.

Icky developed flour blends for Bolles Bakery. Their rustic loaves called for unbleached wheat flour with twelve to fourteen percent protein. The crust had a good chew to it.

But the cookies that Millie and he were baking were soft and less dense. "So," he explained to her, "our recipe needs a soft red winter wheat flour."

"What's so special about red winter wheat?" she asked.

"The protein content is only eight to ten percent."

"And . . . ?" she encouraged.

"And protein suggests the flour's binding power, its strength. Recipes that call for high protein flour are looking for a firmer texture than we want," he explained. "And like I said, red winter wheat is lower in protein."

"How do you know all this?" she asked.

"If we're going to grow, we're going to blend our own flour," he said. "We'll begin with the wheat that comes closest to the texture we want, and we'll adjust from there."

"The grocery store carries Swans Down cake flour," she noted, "but I've never seen cookie flour on the shelves."

"You're probably right," he said. "When Ma makes cookies for the church bake sale, she always blends her own: a two-to-one ratio of wheat flour to cake flour."

"Really?" Millie said. "Is that how you knew about flour blends?"

"I read about blends in trade magazines when I was at Bolles. Those articles talked about improving efficiency in commercial settings.

"But I probably understood what they were saying from watching Ma do it," he concluded.

"Because it's the German way to be efficient," Millie assumed.

"Ma probably blends because she can't find the flour she was accustomed to using back in Germany—and you're right; it's the German way," he smiled and shoved her shoulder gently, just as his mother would have done, if she were in the room.

Millie gave his shoulder a little shove back, and grinned in return.

"Are you going to offer some of your cookie flour blend to Ma when you get it worked out?" Millie asked then.

"If she wants it. But my guess is that she's happy with what's she's making up herself."

"You're probably right," Millie allowed. "But . . . we could offer it anyway."

"Go ahead," he said. *You* give my mother a suggestion on how to cook, he thought to himself. "As for me, I want to keep being invited over for her pork roast on Sunday."

Millie paused to consider his remark. Ma Haut set the family's quality standard when it came to anything that came out of a kitchen.

"Okay, so maybe that wouldn't be the best way to thank her for watching Mark," she allowed.

"How did your deliveries go today?" she changed the topic.

"Everything is still selling out. Richardson's says the sugar cookies disappear first. Maybe that one should be our signature product," he wondered.

"But, we need to be sure," she interrupted. She cut eight hundred cookies every day, and she didn't want to find out that they banked their reputation on the wrong one. Doing market research was one more task in a schedule that barely had enough hours in it already, though.

Before Icky and Millie could come up with alternatives, one pulled up on her bicycle after a few hours at the community pool.

"Mary Lou, it's time for you to earn your keep," Icky said as she came in the door.

"What?" she answered flatly with a teenager's lack of interest. She was tired and hungry from an afternoon of tanning in the hot summer sun, and didn't need a chore thrown at her before she grabbed something to eat.

"You got the bike you wanted," her dad reminded her as he pointed toward the door where it was parked. Pa Haut originally built it for her Aunt Alma some twenty years earlier, so it had some miles on it. But it had been reconditioned, and was good and sturdy: sure to serve her well in the enterprise Icky had in mind. "Take some of these cookies, and sell them to the neighbors."

"Sell?" Mary Lou repeated with a bored sigh.

"Yes, sell," Icky ordered. "You've sold things around here for school, so you know how to do it. This time, instead of magazine subscriptions, you'll sell cookies."

She understood the task. She could do it.

But would she?

"What's my pay?" she asked as if the job were being offered, not assigned, and therefore, allowed her the upper hand to decide for herself whether or not to accept.

"Food: you want to eat, you got to work," Icky answered automatically.

"Really?" Mary Lou answered, doubtfully. "I should get paid."

Apparently, he didn't realize with whom he was dealing.

Icky looked at his wife, expecting support.

"I'm not saying anything," she told him. She'd seen women's roles evolve during the war; it might be good for their daughter to learn to stand on her own two feet.

Besides, over the preceding couple of months, Daddy's first-born blonde sweetheart had been perfecting the personality of cinnamon red hots, practiced on her mother, of course. This time Icky could handle the debate, Millie decided, allowing for the possibility of a fiery exchange between the family's two spiciest personalities.

Icky crossed his arms in front of his chest, breathed heavily through his nose, and then said, "I'll give you . . . five cents for every package you sell."

"Ten cents!" Mary Lou countered.

"Seven cents, and not a penny more!" he snapped back, ending the negotiation.

She paused, considering. Ultimately, he could demand that she sell; she was still a kid, and he could boss her around. On the other hand, she was hungry for the freedom that came from coins in her pocket. Countering again probably would be a recipe for disaster.

She agreed to his deal.

Icky put ten twelve-count cookie packages into Mary Lou's bike basket, and pointed her down the streets he wanted her to work.

"Now get going!" he ordered, handing her one cookie to munch on.

She was right about reaching the upper limit in their negotiations. At a price of thirty-five cents a dozen, Mary Lou's sales effort could not eat up more than twenty percent of the bakery's profits. But, Icky realized, she was getting the same mark-up as the local grocery stores, so it was a fair wage. Besides, the stores were only providing counter space; she was going door-to-door.

When her bike basket was empty, Mary Lou pedaled home, smiling like a chipmunk with a mouthful of stolen peanuts as she computed her hefty earnings: ten packages at seven cents each for one hour's work. Not bad!

She carefully emptied a pocketful of dimes, nickels, and pennies onto the kitchen counter next to the stand mixer. But before she shoved the stack over to her father, she counted out her seventy-cent commission.

"Here's your part," she said, pushing the larger pile of coins across to him.

"My part?" he said.

"Really!" exclaimed her mother, dumbfounded by Mary Lou's escalating self-confidence.

"Uh-huh," she answered matter-of-factly. "That's what we said."

Millie looked at her husband with wide, knowing eyes. "That daughter of yours is one tough cookie, that's for sure."

"You think she gets this attitude from me?" Icky said.

Millie nodded. "Entirely."

Icky turned then, and looked straight at Mary Lou. If his daughter was going to divide her pay from the family profits, instead of waiting for earnings to be dispensed, then she should expect to regularly serve the institution that was putting food into her mouth and a roof over her head.

"All right," he said firmly, "Tomorrow, you will sell twice as many packages, even if you have to double back to refill your bike basket. I want you to understand that you're being paid for results, not blocks traveled or time required. Got it?"

She looked straight back at him, and crossed her arms, just as he had.

"I'll do it," she asserted. "And I'll sell even more than twice as much."

"Not so fast," he continued. "You also will keep records on which varieties of cookie each house buys, so when you load up, you carry the ones they like best."

She did, every day for the rest of the summer.

Neighbors were happy to buy the homemade cookies from the fledgling bakery down the street, and in no time, Mary Lou developed a tasty little sales territory. Mrs. Miller on Fifteenth Street would take sugar cookies on Mondays to pack in the lunch pail for her son, David. Mrs. Walsh would take sugar cookies on Monday, and molasses cookies on Thursday. Mrs. Cornell would take sugar on Tuesday, and molasses on Thursday; on Saturday, she'd also buy ginger cookies—she had two boys, Tommy and Topper, who ate a lot. Mary Lou knew all her customers' preferences and reported them back to her father—as she sifted out her pay, of course. This income was her ticket to go to the movies or join her friends at the roller skating rink. Finally, she didn't have to ask for money to participate; she had her own dough!

OVER THE FOLLOWING YEAR, Icky built relationships with all of the local grocery store managers, and could count on Richardson's Grocery, Loblaws Self-Service Supermarket, and A&P to take as many cookies as Millie and he could bake.

"You bring 'em all here," said Max at Richardson's. "The women, they love these little pastries."

The manager at Loblaws told Icky, "I can sell all you got today. We like being a test store for you!"

That, Icky suddenly realized, was a problem. If his customers saw his bakery as a small start-up instead of an ongoing enterprise that had a future in the business community, they'd continue to give him only day-to-day orders. Somehow, he needed to transform that image: help them see that he planned to grow with them.

"Loblaws is more than a test site," he told the manager.

"How's that?" he asked.

"Sales are good, right?" Icky pointed out as he moved the conversation to the retail side of the food business. "You're making a profit on this product line?"

"Oh, yeah, sure!" manager reported. "Customers ask for these cookies now. And they aren't happy when we run out either!"

"That's what I mean!" Icky said enthusiastically. "We're your partner in serving that customer. Just tell me how many more you want!"

The store manager nodded. He didn't say anything, though.

Still, Icky thought that maybe he'd repositioned the bakery's image, if only a little.

. When he made his delivery to Loblaws the next day, the store manager was looking for him.

"You got a name for that bakery of yours?" he asked. "Because when customers ask for your cookies, they just call 'em 'the ones in the brown paper tied with string."

"We could put our name on them if you like," Icky offered. He derided himself as he drove to his next delivery. He hadn't bothered to name the business—and if he didn't position the cookies as commercial bakery product, then none of the store managers would, either.

"Loblaws says we need to label the packages. We need to give the bakery a name," he told Millie.

"Call it Haut's Cookie Shop," she said at once. "Everyone in the neighborhood knows you're baking them, so you might just as well put your own name on the package."

"Okay, . . . " he hesitated.

"And if you call it a 'shop', you'll retain that home-baked image," she added, anticipating his question. "How will we get this done, though? We don't have enough hours in the day as it is."

"I don't know," he said. "We'll think of something."

Before she washed the dinner dishes, Millie cut squares from the brown wrapping paper, and gave them to Mary Lou.

"Your new job," she said, "is . . . cookie label maker. Here's a sample to show you how they're supposed to look."

"How much?" Mary Lou asked, expectantly. After all, she'd been interrupted from reading a library book, and this was not just a chore; it was a bakery task.

"Uh-uh," Millie responded. "This may be a one-time deal. Let's see how you do first."

Mary Lou grimaced.

"But . . . ,"

"Talk to the boss," her mother said before the question was out of her daughter's mouth, "if you dare."

"But . . . ," Mary Lou started again.

"Unless you'd rather do the dishes? And don't forget to sweep the kitchen floor."

"I can make labels," Mary Lou decided, adding, "since it could be a one-time deal."

With one more detail managed, Millie cleaned the kitchen and sanitized it so Icky and she could get started bright and early the next morning. She definitely wouldn't have passed that chore to a thirteen-year-old.

Not yet, anyway.

"Didn't you say that you started working as a laborer when you were thirteen?" Millie asked Icky when he came in a few minutes later. He'd been busy counting inventory so he could pick up flour after making deliveries the next day.

"That's what Pa required," Icky answered. "Why?"

"Meet your new laborer," Millie transformed Mary Lou from daughter to employee. "Her title is 'cookie label maker' this evening."

"Oh!" Icky said, catching on to Millie's routine. He'd let her take the lead, though, as he walked into the middle of this debate.

"She preferred this opportunity to cleaning the kitchen," Millie explained.

Icky looked over the tags Mary Lou was making—and almost complimented her on them.

"What do you think?" he asked Millie instead.

"She seems to have a knack for it," Millie smiled.

Mary Lou smiled back at her parents.

"Handmade, like the cookies," she explained.

"Good idea," Icky acknowledged. "I guess we can delay your promotion to kitchen clean-up duty for a while."

Mary Lou focused on her labeling project, refusing to respond to the offer of a promotion. Or to acknowledge the earlier reference to her father's job as a laborer when he was her age. It was bad enough that she sometimes had to keep an eye on her brother—and she didn't get paid for that chore either.

"THE ONLY THING WE don't have enough of is hours in the day," Icky told his parents over Sunday dinner.

"This problem we may be able to solve for you," Ma said. "Roy and Herta: they are moving home!"

"What? When?" Icky asked, delighted with the news.

"As soon as they arrive," Pa answered.

"Is everything all right?" Millie asked. She knew Ma had been worried about political problems in Cuba. Every morning while she watched Mark, she studied the newspaper from front to back over a cup of coffee. It was always piping hot—so hot that steam hovered over it on brisk mornings. Pa said it would burn anyone else's lips, but Ma was made of stronger stuff. She could take it.

But she couldn't take relaxing while her children were in harm's way. Her attention was always grabbed by reports on political turmoil around the globe, especially if they covered Havana where Herta and Roy lived.

Adding to her concern, The Reverend Garber told the church women's group about the value of their contributions to the synod's mission work in the Caribbean islands. The money they raised through their bake sales and white elephant raffles was a great help to the missionaries, he said.

"Every small effort here means a large opportunity for someone in need there," he told them, "for their communities are lacking in many things that we take for granted."

When Ma asked about Cuba, he said, "Our missionaries may face difficulties at times, but still, they do the Lord's work."

With these two sources of international news, Ma was positive that Herta and Roy needed to head home. Letter after letter was a plea that they pay attention to what was going on around them. She enclosed clippings from The Olean Times Herald, too, to support her concerns.

"These tensions between dictator Fulgencio Batista and revolutionary Fidel Castro, they are not going to end well," she wrote. "The government is about to be overthrown, so we need you to pack your bags and come home now!"

"Not only that," Ma intimated in her letter, "Icky is running his own business now, and he could use your help." She didn't need anyone to tell her; she could see for herself how fatigued her son and daughter-in-law were becoming.

Roy and Herta knew Ma was right about the political situation, so despite their preference for sunny and warm climates, they agreed to move back. At least for a while.

"The timing is right for us," Icky said. "We sure could use their help."

Pa nodded, grateful that it all would work out. Crisis averted: Ma resolved a family problem again.

"But did you enjoy living in Cuba?" Millie asked her sister-in-law.

"Loved it," Herta said, the rhythmic intonation in her words revealing the influence that living in the Caribbean had on her. "Havana is a city with a personality, like Paris or New York City, not that I've been to either of them, but everyone sort-of knows from books and newspapers what they must be like."

"You mean the bright lights, the entertainment, the fashions?" Millie asked.

"Everything! It's all so vibrant. The meals taste bright—like, sometimes a little citrus is squeezed onto dishes just before serving. And dinner is always presented on beautifully painted pottery. You know," she intimated as if she were sharing a secret, "they say we eat with our eyes before we taste. Every detail is thought through to honor the time it takes to prepare a meal."

Millie compared Herta's story to the way she made dinner. She was too tired at the end of the day to trouble herself with finding a special serving dish. Her only goal was seeing that everybody's bellies were filled.

"*And* the smells!" Herta continued with enthusiasm. "Havana is intoxicating! The scent of tropical flowers, the brininess of the ocean, the warm Caribbean spices—not to mention a constant hint of Cuban cigars in the background. All day long, we were swimming in a wonderful blending of aromas!

"*And* at night, we baked. The yeasty smell of bread coming out of the oven mixed in with the sweetness of the pre-dawn dew. Ahhh," she breathed in a whiff of fresh memories.

"*And! And! And!*" Millie repeated, "You really loved it!"

"Yes, yes, I did, *and* . . . !" she laughed at herself, "*and* already I miss it."

"Well, we're grateful you're here. We missed you!"

"I know, and thanks for saying that. Ma's letters were filled with worry, and she wouldn't let it rest."

"Was she right? About the politics, I mean," Millie asked.

"Seems so," Herta admitted. "We were beginning to hear rumors about customers we knew who were shot for being on the wrong side of a political argument. Since we didn't grow up in Havana, we didn't always know who we could trust. In the end, even though they loved our breads, they didn't think of us as locals, not like families who went back generations."

"Well, the timing couldn't be better," Millie said. "We appreciate your help!"

31

A *Mittelstand*

ADDING ROY AND HERTA to the baking team was a blessing, because Icky and Millie were stretched to their limit. And it was a bane, because the four of them working together raised production levels higher than Icky thought was possible. He was exhausted—but, he told himself, the bakery was beginning to make a name for itself.

That's also what Tom Hubbell, the Pillsbury sales representative whom Icky knew from his many years at Bolles Bakery, said when he dropped in.

"What a surprise!" Icky said when Hubbell pulled up on Fourteenth Street. "What are you doing here?"

"Looking for a new account!" Tom answered. "How's it going?"

"How did you know I was here?" Icky asked.

"After my meeting with Mr. Bolles this morning, I stopped at Richardson's Grocery to check out our product on local store shelves," Hubbell said. "I spotted packages labeled Haut's Cookie Shop next to the check-out counter, so I asked the manager—you know, Max, right?—about them."

"What did he say?" Icky asked.

"Said they're selling out, so I helped that along and bought some. They're really good, Icky!"

"Thanks. I'm glad to hear it," Icky said. "And glad that Max said good things."

"He did," Hubbell confirmed.

"So, that's how you found us then," Icky ventured.

"Right. I told Max, 'I've got to find Icky and get his flour business!'" Hubbell answered. "So, here I am. What do you need?"

"I'm not sure Haut's Cookie Shop is large enough to be worth your while," Icky said. But in that moment, he realized that he'd used the bakery name—as if their venture was a sizeable commercial operation. It felt right. "I sure would like to see what you can do, though."

"Let's talk about it," Hubbell suggested. "How are you sourcing your flour now?"

"Local warehouse," Icky said. "I just pick it up as we need it." If he could get a good price, though, he'd talk to Millie. Maybe they could make room to stock what they used every week. Or maybe Pa could help figure that out.

"How large does our order have to be?" Icky asked after they discussed volume. "And what about delivery? Any chance you can waive that cost?"

"That's an easy yes," Hubbell said. "We're already trucking out to Bolles every week, so we'll just load your order at the back of the trailer, and drop it off on the way."

"You sure you can do that?" Icky asked, surprised by the possibility.

"Don't you think I know how many times you ran interference for us when you were with Bolles? Especially those nutrient additives: that was a tough negotiation," Hubbell reminded him.

"I just did my job," he said, recalling Mr. Bolles's rant that day. He wasn't aware that Hubbell understood how his question regarding the taste of the nutrients was actually just a diversion, for if there was no problem, the boss had no real reason not to switch to enriched flour.

"Well, let's just say I know we owe you, and we'd like to be your supplier, so shall we set up that door-to-door delivery? Starting next week?"

"That would be great," Icky said, grateful for the help.

"You let me know if you need anything else. In time, maybe you'll blend your own proprietary flour," Hubbell said.

"That won't be for a while," Icky told him, "but you're right. I've been thinking about it." He knew Pillsbury could help with that red winter wheat, but again, he didn't think his volume warranted a specialty order.

"Might be sooner than you think," Hubbell countered. "Trade publications say that the post-war American diet is changing. Citrus is flying off the shelves, milk sales are up twenty-five percent, and the demand for commercial baked goods is up forty percent. You've tapped into a real growth opportunity with this cookie business."

"Let's hope you're right," Icky said, offering a handshake as Hubbell left. For the moment, he was just relieved that Pillsbury could ease the chore of managing inventory. The time he'd save could be directed to searching out seasonal ingredients. He had in mind a holiday cookie: maybe a macaroon, or a dried fruit-filled bite of some sort.

EVERY TIME A PROBLEM was solved—this time by Hubbell—Icky was energized by the freedom he felt, even when he was exhausted.

"Millie," he whispered as he fell back on the pillow when the day was over, "this bakery is about to swallow me up."

"Swallow?"

"Not literally. More like airplanes. They swallow up passengers, shut the door, and take them off somewhere."

"Where is our plane going?"

"The ticket says, 'To: Take-Care-of-Your-Family,'" he made up a destination.

"You're doing that," she assured him.

"*We're* doing that," he acknowledged. "This wouldn't be happening without you."

"I wouldn't have it any other way," she allowed.

"Are you sure?" he asked with a yawn. "Like I said, the bakery can swallow us up."

"I'm a bit tired, that's all," she admitted. "Tonight, we're both tired."

"Mm, hmm," he said, shifting his weight in the bed.

"Do you really think we need a holiday cookie?" she asked gently. "It's a temporary line . . . "

"Got to take the lead," he answered, his voice trailing. "If we don't set the standard, someone else will. I'd rather have them flying in our tail wind, than try to catch . . . "

He was out for the night.

"G'night," she said, quietly, shutting her eyes.

THE NEXT MORNING WHEN Icky went to the kitchen, he turned on the oven just as he always did, and then mixed a large batch of dough. When he opened the door to shove in the first two trays, though, the oven was still cold.

"Crap!" he said under his breath, trying not to wake the children. He pulled off the oven dial to be sure it was moving correctly; it was.

Then he dragged the oven away from the wall; everything seemed to be connected.

"What is going on?" asked Millie as she came in to make the coffee.

"The oven," Icky answered. "It's kaput. Used up."

"What?" she challenged. "No! It can't be! It's a commercial oven!"

He shoved it back against the wall.

"See if you can fix it!" she insisted.

"We have two hundred pounds of dough to bake first," Icky said, focused on the immediate problem of filling customer orders. "I'll go next door to see if we can use Ma's oven."

Dawn was breaking as Roy arrived, and the two men carried tray after tray of cookies across the lawn and up the back porch steps to Ma's kitchen, passing one another as they exchanged baked goods for each next batch of raw dough. By noon, Icky was more tired than ever—and his job was only half done, as product still needed to be delivered.

"Roy, you head out to the stores today," he decided, handing him the delivery manifest. "I got to get this oven repaired, or figure out where we can buy another one."

Icky worked on the oven through lunch, while Millie handled an incident involving the police and Buko. No one knew how the dog did it, but it seemed that in his rounds of the neighborhood, he followed the scent of the Thompson sisters downtown, and wandered into the lobby of the First National Bank.

The bank was the tallest building in Olean: seven stories high, towering the corner of State and Union Streets. Once inside, the dog slipped past the lobby guard, ducked behind marble columns, kept his nose beneath the teller cages, and followed brass railings up the stairs. Way upstairs! Keeping his toenails pulled into his pads, he slid past private offices, bank employees, and even a few customers. The door to the top of the building must have been open, probably by one of the Olean Ground Observer Corps volunteers. Since the end of World War II, they performed naked-eye and binocular watches for enemy aircraft, and telephoned unusual sightings to Air Defense Command ground control interception centers. Buko, for his part, was more interested in reporting his observations to passers-by on the street below. Finally, one of them went into the bank lobby to ask if his money was being protected by a barking dog.

The manager immediately called the police and animal control, and rang up the maintenance department. Before anyone arrived, though, one of the secretaries took out her sack lunch, put a bite of her sandwich into a small box, took the elevator to the seventh floor, climbed up to the roof, and coaxed the guilty dog over. Once she had him back inside the building, she shut the roof access door, and urged the boxer back to the lobby with the rest of her sandwich.

A few minutes later, the police collared the friendly beast, and checked his harness for an owner's address. Then, one of them told Buko to get into the back of the squad car. The guilty offender jumped in, dropped his head onto the seat, and hunched over like the criminal he was. He must have sensed that he was on his way to the Big House—aka home—where Millie and Icky would hear all about how he failed his job interview as a watch dog.

"What next!" she said as she ushered Buko indoors, and apologized to the officer. "It won't happen again."

And to thank him for the inconvenience of transporting their dog across town, she offered him a package of cookies.

"Thanks!" he said. "Hey! My wife buys these. They're great!"

As the officer was about to leave, Mark tapped him on the leg. "Um, um, could I, um, could I be next to ride in the police car? Um, and see the bank roof, too. I know the way up there."

Anticipating her son's desire for a big adventure, Millie pointed a finger toward Mark's nose, and said, simply and firmly, "No!"

She'd had enough distractions for one day.

MILLIE TOOK A BREAK to pick vegetables from Ma Haut's garden for dinner, while Icky continued to work on the oven. As he jostled it to-and-fro, he smelled a hint of something like gas. Thinking that he may have caused a small leak in the line, he wondered if the fumes could be coming from somewhere below. If he could find it and repair the leak, they'd be back on track the following morning.

He reached for a small box of matches on the table just as casually as if he were about to take out a cigarette. He'd light just one, and pass it around . . .

And with that, a small explosion shook the house, lifting the floor-boards, and making the walls tremble!

"Mark!" Millie yelled as she ran toward the door of the Quonset hut. "Mark! Icky!"

Ma and Pa Haut heard the explosion, too, and they raced across the lawn just as Icky emerged with Mark in his arms, not a single blond hair on the boy's head disturbed.

"What have you been getting into?" Millie said as she took him from Icky.

"It wasn't Mark. It was me," Icky admitted. "I smelled a little gas leak, and lit a match to see if I could find it."

"What?" Millie exclaimed.

"No such thing as a 'little' gas leak!" Pa said with alarm, and Pa ought to know: he was an oil refinery fireman.

"I . . . I don't know what I was thinking," Icky allowed. He wouldn't blame that sort of thoughtlessness on being tired.

At that moment, big, red fire trucks came wailing around the corner, and stopped in front of the house. Three firemen in long, black coats jumped off and ran toward the house, one of them yelling, "We have a report of a gas explosion!"

The ear-splitting sirens and the loud strangers in long, black coats scared Mark, and he grabbed Millie tightly. She patted his back, and told him everything was okay. The firemen were friends who came to check out the big boom.

"Before you can go back in, we have to inspect the premises to make sure the building is safe," they told everyone.

Mommy and Daddy seemed happy with the strangers running into the house, so Mark tried to squirm down. "I want to go see the big boom again!"

"No!" the grownups said in unison.

It was awful to be told no twice in one afternoon: first when he wanted to go for a ride with the policeman, and now when he wanted to follow the firemen. He trudged to his grandparents' porch, and sat down on the step, pouting the whole time. Grandma Haut saw him off by himself, and went over to sit on the porch, too.

"Lots of activity is going on today," she said.

"Yep," Mark said, solemnly. But then, he added, "Nobody will let me do anything!"

"You met a policeman today. And you got to meet three firemen," Grandma pointed out. She would remind him of the day's blessings, but leave out the fact that no one was blown to smithereens when Icky lit the match.

"But I wanted to go for a ride in the police car!" he complained, squaring his small shoulders the way he'd seen his daddy do when he was explaining something to Grandma.

"Buko slinked out of the back seat when he got home," Grandma said. "You saw his head down and his sad tail, didn't you?"

"Yes, but . . . "

"He was embarrassed," Grandma explained. "When someone rides in the back seat of a police car, people know they've been bad, and they're in Dutch for it."

Mark's grandma waited for a few seconds to let him absorb what she was saying.

"You don't want people to look at you in the back of a police car, and say you were bad, do you?"

He considered the possibility. Every time he did something he wasn't supposed to do, he had to go indoors, and think about it; that's what Mommy and Daddy always said. He didn't like pondering bad behavior. Riding in a police car seemed like a lot more fun.

"I don't know," he sighed. Why did grownups have to complicate things?

"How about a cookie?" Grandma Haut asked, pushing herself up from the step.

"Okay," he agreed as he followed her.

After his snack, Grandma focused Mark on searching for worms in the garden.

"This is your spot, right here," she directed the curious invertebrate hunter.

As he got started, she asked if he could hear the wind blowing through the grass.

"It does that to remind you to shush," she shared one of the secrets of finding worms. "They won't come out if you talk."

Besides, she wanted to read her newspaper. With Roy and Icky traipsing through her kitchen all morning, she hadn't had time to study it.

"Okay," Mark whispered obediently. He had his very own spot to dig in! Grandma gave it to him!

Icky and Pa completed a temporary repair to the damage done by the gas explosion—good enough to last until the weekend when they'd finish the job. As they were dragging the oven out the door so it could be hauled off, Roy pulled in from the delivery run.

"Good timing," Icky greeted him while Pa walked back to his own house. Icky had in mind a plan to grab his brother-in-law as soon as he returned, so they could head out to buy another oven. "You're back quicker than I expected," he added.

Ignoring the energy in Roy's pace, he finished pushing the oven the rest of the way to the curb. As he returned, he said, "I'll drive," and motioned for Roy to take the passenger's seat. "I couldn't fix the Haller, so we're going to have to replace it. You go with me. We'll see what we can get quick.

We'll have to bring it back ourselves, and get it hooked up before tomorrow morning."

"Maybe you should look at this first," Roy said, pulling a paper from his pocket. It was a purchase order from Loblaws.

Icky glanced at it as he continued walking.

But before he got to the driver's door, he stopped short.

"How did this happen?" he said. Turning toward Roy, he continued, "Who did you meet with?"

"Nobody. It was already written when I got there," Roy told him. "They're ready to give Haut's Cookie Shop three feet of space on their shelves. Baked goods aisle. Eye level. With signage."

Icky stood still a moment. He hadn't stopped moving all day, and now, unexpectedly, his feet felt glued to the ground.

Then, buoyed by the news, he burst into a large smile and slapped Roy on his arm.

"This couldn't have come at a better time! What a day, Roy! Thank you!" he continued, sharing the credit with his brother-in-law.

"Nope. Nope. Nope," Roy disagreed. "This is your doing. All yours and Millie's."

Laughing out loud then, Icky bolted past Roy, and turned toward the house. He had to tell Millie! He was about to break into a run when she came out the door.

"Millie, look!" he exclaimed as he held up the paper.

But she was focused on Roy's return, and didn't pay attention.

"Hi, Roy. Thanks for making all the deliveries," she said, automatically. She felt emotionally drained from the loss of an expensive appliance, never mind that it had been used equipment when they bought it, and functioning on a schedule equal to ten. Then there was the incident with Buko and the police officer, followed by the gas explosion and the fire trucks . . . Her nerves were fried.

"Millie, wait a minute . . . ," Icky tried to interrupt.

"You two better get going if you're going to hook up another oven before the end of the day." She hoped the next one would last longer.

"Mill!-eee!" Icky repeated. With German precision, he separated the syllables so her name marched out of his mouth. "Look! Here!" he insisted, pushing the paper to her. "We've got our first real account."

Millie turned toward him then, and saw the purchase order. She studied it carefully. She had never seen one before.

"This is not only for *tomorrow*. This is for the *whole next year*!" he explained. "That's steady income: the kind we can count on!"

"All three varieties, every day?" she read. "Oh, no! Not now! Not with the oven broke! This couldn't come at a worse time!"

"It couldn't come at a better time!" he countered. "This lets us buy a *new* oven," he asserted with triumph in his voice. "New!"

"Well, we're going to need a really big one to handle all of this!" she lobbed back to him.

"Yes!" he agreed. "Bigger, and with better temperature controls. And we're going to need a production facility."

Her brow wrinkled.

"Millie," he continued, his arm circling her shoulder, "this is it: what we been working for! We got a business!"

"But . . . what do *you* think that means?" she asked. She'd become accustomed to their cozy home arrangement, unusual as it was. "The hut kitchen is working fine for us, just like it is. And when we're really busy, Mark can spend the day with Ma and Pa."

"He can still do that," Icky answered. "We still need their help."

"So, what are you saying?" she repeated her question.

"It's time to expand: buy the large commercial equipment we need in order to go after more long-term orders. Then, maybe we'll think about larger accounts!"

"What accounts?"

"Supermarket *chains*," he said. "A&P in New Jersey, Kroger in Cincinnati. Not today, of course, but soon, maybe soon. The market is changing, and Hubbell says the demand for store-bought bakery is expanding fastest. Forty percent, according to the trades. We're right where we need to be to grow with it!"

"Grow how?" she said, amazed by the sudden shift in the day's events. "We're Olean, small town, local . . . "

"Not local for long, Millie," he assured her.

"But . . . "

"We need to expand," he insisted.

"How much?" She couldn't imagine how bigger equipment would fit into their Quonset hut bakery / living quarters.

"A lot," Icky said, thinking out loud. "First, we need a commercial oven with rotating racks. But we can't operate that equipment in the space where Mark is running around."

"Oh, no!" she concurred. "That boy is into everything!"

"Where is he, by the way?" Icky asked, suddenly aware that Mark was not in sight.

"Don't worry. He's digging for worms in Ma's garden. Last I looked, he had dirt all over his face."

"What?" said Icky.

"Ma said that Pa would take him fishing, if he found enough worms."

"She won't be happy if he tears up her *Kleingarten*," Icky warned.

"It's okay. I saw her standing over his shoulder, aiming a stiff finger at the spot she was letting him dig in. It's over next to the *Gartenzswerge* gnome, where she pours out the coffee grounds."

Millie paused to look over her shoulder to be sure Mark was still there. He was, and Grandma was still watching over him. She told him to stay out of her patch of St. Peter's wort. The little plants were just coming into bloom, and she planned to take some to church for the altar on Sunday, as this variety was said to represent the keys of heaven. It was a sweet memory from her dear Germany, and she didn't want little feet clomping on them.

"He'll be busy for a while," Millie confirmed.

Returning to the purchase order and its implications, she asked Icky, "If the equipment isn't going to fit in the hut house, how can we possibly fill this order?"

"Maybe we just add on to the back of the hut for now. We can put on a temporary porch to house the larger equipment, so we can fill Loblaws's order for the next year," he suggested. "That oven will let us commit to filling shelf space in other stores, too."

"More stores?" she repeated.

"But what we really need is a larger building, because if I'm right, we're on the way to becoming a *Mittelstand!*" he continued.

"*Mittelstand?*" Millie repeated the word. It sounded like another one of those German terms she'd heard Icky and Pa Haut talk about.

"Small business. Maybe a medium-sized business. Not a major corporation like Socony, but in time, a few employees.

"Then we can take up Pa's offer to let us buy this lot, and ask him if he will sell the one on the corner to us, too," Icky said. It was the future he had been hoping for.

"Do we need all that?" Millie asked, surprised at his revelation.

"We do if you want to live in a house instead of the front part of a Quonset hut bakery!" he announced. Icky had been imagining next steps in the expansion of their business, and praying, too, for God's help in getting his family there.

"Are you okay with this?" he asked suddenly.

"Of course!" she agreed. She'd never dreamed that they'd be able to build a house. Well, she'd hoped for it, but imagined it in some distant future, maybe after the children finished school, maybe then.

"A separate building for the bakery and a house, Millie," he said. "In a year, maybe two."

"Really?" In the corner of her heart, she was lifted by the prospect of relieving Mary Lou from the nasty teasing she'd endured. Some of her classmates mocked her for living in a military barracks, and she didn't like her daughter feeling embarrassed over something she had no control over.

"We'd live on the main floor, and put offices in the basement," Icky continued. "We could make it a ranch, if you like."

"A ranch?" she repeated. "Icky, any kind of house—with real floors again, not just plywood set on pallets—would be fine with me!" And then she closed her eyes briefly to thank God for the Lord's amazing grace and incredible timing.

They went next door to show off the purchase order, and to ask Ma and Pa if the offer to sell the lot was still open.

Of course, they couldn't have been happier.

"In Germany, we say, "*Himmel und Hölle in Bewegung setzen,*" Pa Haut said.

"Which means . . . ?" Icky asked.

"It's 'to put heaven and hell in motion,'" he said. "Especially on a day like today, when so many things get in your way: still Millie and you persevere!"

Tsk-ing his tongue over the back of his front teeth, Pa insisted with a smile, "So many good expressions. You got to learn the German!"

Then he added, "And, of course, I sell you the lot."

THE END

Author's Note

THIS STORY IS BASED on the early career of Edward A. ("Icky") Haut, who apprenticed as a bread baker, and later, with his wife, Millie, founded Haut's Cookie Shops, a home-based bakery in Olean, New York. In the 1950s, the business was trademarked *Icky's Cookies*, and expanded to serve grocery chains throughout the northeast quadrant of the U.S. While pseudonyms were used where it seemed prudent and liberties were taken with regard to conversations and the actual timing of events, the narrative nonetheless represents the family's resilience and hope-filled spirit born out of their trust in God who always is with us in our struggles.

Biography

ANN HAUT BEGAN HER writing career at The Detroit News where she wrote a man-on-the-street [*sic*] column in the news department and feature articles in the Sunday magazine. She moved on to public relations and wrote speeches delivered by Fortune 500 presidents and vice presidents to audiences such as The New York Society of Security Analysts. She also contributed to a script delivered by George C. Scott on the NBC television special, *Happy Birthday, Bob* (Hope), and generated pre-game Super Bowl content that aired on the *Today* show.

Upon the completion of her PhD, she edited two volumes on the life-work and teachings of The Rev. Dr. Walter R. Bouman entitled *Jesus is Risen: Theology for the Church*. Dr. Bouman chaired her doctoral committee. When he learned he was dying of cancer and would never write his own theology, he asked her to take on that task. He was familiar with her writing and her work in ethics, and said that he trusted she would represent his arguments with integrity. (All proceeds from these volumes go directly to the Bouman Chair at Trinity Lutheran Seminary in Columbus, Ohio.)

For as far back as she can remember, Dr. Haut recalls being told that she was born with ink in her blood. Her grandfather was a typesetter for The Toledo Blade, and her father was a locally acclaimed columnist and reporter with The Detroit News; he covered The Detroit Tigers during the Denny McClain years, and finished his career writing award-winning obituaries honoring the lives of everyday people.

As a third-generation news enthusiast, Dr. Haut never questioned her calling to report the truth. However, she also felt drawn to teaching and became an associate professor of business communications and business ethics in The Boler School of Business at John Carroll University. The opportunity to work with wonderful students easily made teaching the happiest years of her working career. Indeed, many of them inspired the reflections on John 12:24 in *Listen to Your Bread*, for they enrich our creation today.

Dr. Haut left the university when she married Mark Haut, and they moved to North Carolina. She is now working on books set in his home town of Olean, New York.

Dr. Haut can be reached via her website at www.annhaut.com. Readers who enjoy *Listen to Your Bread* also are encouraged to write reviews on the Amazon website.